AROUND 1945

AROUND 1945

Literature, Citizenship, Rights

EDITED BY ALLAN HEPBURN

McGill-Queen's University Press
Montreal & Kingston | London | Chicago

ISBN 978-0-7735-4731-5 (cloth)
ISBN 978-0-7735-4732-2 (paper)
ISBN 978-0-7735-9902-4 (ePDF)
ISBN 978-0-7735-9903-1 (ePUB)

Legal deposit second quarter 2016
Bibliothèque nationale du Québec

Printed in Canada on acid-free paper that is 100% ancient forest free (100% post-consumer recycled), processed chlorine free

McGill-Queen's University Press acknowledges the support of the Canada Council for the Arts for our publishing program. We also acknowledge the financial support of the Government of Canada through the Canada Book Fund for our publishing activities.

LIBRARY AND ARCHIVES CANADA CATALOGUING IN PUBLICATION

Around 1945 : literature, citizenship, rights / edited by Allan Hepburn.

Includes bibliographical references and index.
Issued in print and electronic formats.
ISBN 978-0-7735-4731-5 (cloth). – ISBN 978-0-7735-4732-2 (paper). – ISBN 978-0-7735-9902-4 (pdf). – ISBN 978-0-7735-9903-1 (epub)

1. English fiction – 20th century – History and criticism.
2. Literature and society – Great Britain – History – 20th century.
3. Citizenship in literature. 4. Human rights in literature.
5. Law in literature. I. Hepburn, Allan, author, editor

PR478.S57A76 2016 823'.91409 C2016-900238-1
C2016-900239-X

Set in 10.5/13.5 Calluna with Gill Sans Nova
Book design & typesetting by Garet Markvoort, zijn digital

CONTENTS

PART TWO: VIOLATIONS

PART THREE: RIGHTS

ACKNOWLEDGMENTS

The essays in this collection derive from a two-day colloquium, entitled "Literature, Citizenship, Rights," held at McGill University on 21–22 August 2014. That event was made possible by generous support from a Fonds de Recherche du Québec Société et Culture (FRQSC) research grant dedicated to research on the novel. Other funds were provided by the James McGill Chair in Twentieth-Century Literature and a Social Sciences and Humanities Research Council grant. I owe particular thanks to Isabelle Daunais and Juan Ortiz-Apuy for, respectively, their financial and technical support.

Prior to the colloquium, I convened a summer-long reading course on literature and human rights with three graduate students: Mitchell Brown, Kevin Droz, and Carolyn Ownbey. In fourteen animated meetings, we discussed books by Hannah Arendt, Samuel Beckett, Diana Chang, J.M. Coetzee, Joseph Conrad, Graham Greene, Nadine Gordimer, Uzodinma Iweala, Arthur Koestler, Wyndham Lewis, Primo Levi, David Malouf, Caryl Phillips, Stephen Spender, and Ngũgĩ wa Thiong'o, not to mention a daunting repertory of theoretical texts. Conversation was never less than daring, and usually much more than thrilling. For their keen interventions, I owe Mitch, Kevin, and Carolyn an immense debt of gratitude. I owe special thanks to Carolyn Ownbey for help in preparing these essays for publication. Two anonymous reviewers gave helpful feedback; their comments have made this book better than it was. Lastly, I wish to thank Jonathan Crago at McGill-Queen's University Press for his interest in and support of this project.

ILLUSTRATIONS

AROUND 1945

Introduction

ALLAN HEPBURN

All citizens have rights, but not all people are citizens. From one state to another, citizenship does not confer a uniform set of civil or human rights on individuals. Through legislation, nation-states add and subtract rights for citizens and non-citizens as they see fit. Sometime around 1945, thinking about citizenship moved away from national expressions of rights towards the universal applicability of rights. Although aspirational, the declaration of universal rights detaches rights from the prerogatives of citizenship and the sovereignty of nation-states. At mid-century, writers and philosophers pondered the meaning of the human condition, namely the common denominator of humanity that united everyone in the world into a human family. If such a common denominator exists, rights can be understood as natural rather than arbitrary or legislated. Although everyone might appear to belong to the family of man, the Second World War and the threat of nuclear annihilation in the postwar years sorely tested such putative kinship structures. Either the human race could be made extinct in a nuclear war, or the assertion of universal rights could offer some hope for the continuation of the human species. Although mid-century discussions about citizenship and rights culminated in some ways in 1948 with the signing of the Universal Declaration of Human Rights (UDHR), the juridical, atomic, constitutional, global, and human consequences of 1945 are still being felt.[1]

The essays in *Around 1945: Literature, Citizenship, Rights* focus on citizenship and rights as they are articulated in cultural representations, mostly novels, though the perplexities of rights thread through other media as well. Literature provides one way of accessing the historical transformations of citizenship and rights that happened around 1945 because it imaginatively configures social relations among individuals. As sequences governed by causality and consequence, novels are a privileged genre for representing the dilemmas of citizenship and rights. In fiction, actions lead to punishment; behaviour determines outcomes. Rights are established, disputed, denied, or affirmed through narrative sequences. Characters in novels assert their dignity or inhumanity through the actions that they perform. Joseph Slaughter argues that the *Bildungsroman* is the human rights genre par excellence because it makes "the convoluted, esoteric, and improbable narrative grammar of citizen-subjectivation not only legible but ordinary" (252). Novels of development articulate how individuals exercise their freedom and what they learn from experience – or fail to learn, as the case may be. Pointing out the correlation between narrative fiction and human rights, Rachel Potter and Lyndsey Stonebridge emphasize the political dimension of narrative: "of all writing, the novel genre has been the best suited for imagining what it means to be a modern person – with or without entitlements – in ways that are socially and politically visible" (5). In the pursuit of liberty, characters may be punished for infringing on the state or the freedom of other characters or they may increase understanding of how rights are acquired through the dramatization of conflict.

If international law articulates "a fictional human rights personality that it aspires to bring to life" (Slaughter 60), the novel, in some respects, has already beaten jurisprudence to the punch. Through the instantiation of individuals in specific plots, literature traces the dynamic process by which individuals identify the limits and freedoms inherent in citizenship within a community. Martha Nussbaum claims that novels document "the interaction between general human aspirations and particular forms of social life that either enable or impede those aspirations" (7). Novels mediate competing human needs – the need to develop, the need to belong – and moral judgment. Literature interprets the relative freedom and equality of human beings. In this regard, the novel, which plots dilemmas and corrects injustices, is particularly suited to the representation of citizenship and rights claims, as, in their own ways, are poetry, drama, and visual culture.

Although literary critics tell a well-rehearsed tale about the correspondence between the decline of the British Empire and its symptomatic resonances in mid-century novels – a tale in which lateness, anguish, and post-imperial melancholy feature prominently – British literature is robustly committed to new configurations of citizenship and rights that emerged after the war. That is not to deny the importance of decolonization as an explanatory structure for mid-century British culture. But decolonization hardly tells the whole story of British writing from 1945 onward. William Golding's *Lord of the Flies* (1954) provides an allegory of colonialism gone awry, but it can also be interpreted in light of mid-century debates about statehood, authority, and leadership. Like his contemporaries, Golding proposes that human societies need rules to arbitrate disputes. He also proposes that one does not reach the political future through mayhem and militarism. In Golding's novel, the conflict between responsible Ralph and warmongering Jack offers alternative visions of statehood. Whereas Ralph wants to preserve equal rights for everyone, Jack usurps those rights to feed his own sense of "uniformed superiority" (22). Ralph wants to form citizens through consultation; Jack trains warriors and creates apparatchiks who do his bidding through fear. The personal interests of one individual do not translate into the best interests of the community, either in the present or in the future. Although a certain British triumphalism reigns at the end of *Lord of the Flies* when a naval officer restores order on the island by appearing at just the right moment, Golding's larger point touches on the necessity of diplomacy and common sense in political situations. No one likes Piggy, but at least he tries to "put first things first and act proper" (50). As *Lord of the Flies* indicates, novels reflect on human possibility, within or outside the law. In this sense, novels permit sustained engagement with justice in Britain and abroad, as it affects individuals and entire societies.

Like a particularly sensitive gauge or instrument, fiction registers changes in citizenship and rights through time. Novels record the impact of laws and legislation; they represent social injustices and their redress. Novels also promote changes to social structures by imagining alternative forms of citizenship. After the war, those alternative forms of citizenship were most often articulated in international terms. In *The Judicial Imagination*, Lyndsey Stonebridge argues that "the law was at its most audacious and creative in the immediate postwar period" (2). In particular, as Stonebridge points out, British writers expand the meaning of citizenship and rights by responding to the audacity shown in international law: the adjudication of war crimes and crimes against humanity at Nuremberg in 1945; the reframing of national frontiers and jurisdictions at the Paris Peace Conference in 1946; the drafting and passing of the UDHR in 1948; the ratification of the Genocide Convention in 1948; the ratification of the Geneva Convention governing the humanitarian treatment of prisoners of war and civilian non-combatants in 1950; the European Convention for the Protection of Human Rights and Fundamental Freedoms drafted in 1950 and brought into force in 1953; the UN Convention Relating to the Status of Refugees in 1951; and other agreements applicable to the global community.

The audacity of postwar legal thinking extends to constitutionality, and hence to the shifting definition of citizenship and rights. Constitutions typically enshrine principles of statehood. In the wake of the war, many countries felt an urgent need to establish legal grounds for governance as a counterweight to the lawlessness and thuggery of fascist regimes in Europe and military or colonial regimes elsewhere in the world. As the Third Reich collapsed, Austria hastily re-adopted its Constitution on 1 May 1945. France founded the Fourth Republic in 1946, the Third having been abrogated by the Nazi occupation. The Constitution of Japan, written in English and modelled closely on American rights and principles, was imposed by the US and other occupying forces in 1947. An independent country since 1947, India adopted a constitution in 1949. Basic Law was approved in Germany in 1949 with the consent of the Allied Forces. Although this rush to affirm constitutionality was necessitated by the return to peace, constitutions also determine limits for governance within nation-states. The concern about formulating international and constitutional law attests to an unease about the location of sovereignty. On the one hand, the UN understands sovereignty to reside, at least to some degree, with international authorities rather than separate nations. On the other hand, constitutions affirm the need to have a national framework of law for citizens' obligations, entitlements, and responsibilities.

Discourses of citizenship and human rights were transformed by the Second World War and the transition to peace in 1945. In their inquiry into the nature of rights, novelists and filmmakers frequently return to the war as to a conundrum that cannot be resolved. This observation may be especially true in Britain, where the consequences of the war continued long after 1945. Austerity measures that began during the war did not end until 1954. The nation, bankrupt because of wartime expenditures, reckoned with ongoing economic hardships even as the welfare state levied higher taxes to support social programs. The special relation between Britain and the United States, established during the war and continued as a Cold War necessity, influenced British foreign policy. British novelists assessed the revised role of their nation in the world. For instance, in *The Towers of Trebizond* (1956), Rose Macaulay explores the relation of Britain to the Middle East and the Soviet states, albeit in a comical manner. In mid-century writing, novelists register the after-effects of the Second World War, even as they represent shifts in global power brought about by decolonization and the Cold War.

Most but not all of the essays in this collection constellate around citizenship and rights in British literature and culture at mid-century while reaching back to Joseph Conrad's assessment of the human in *The Secret Agent* (1907) and ahead to Caryl Phillips's analysis of race and statehood in *Foreigners* (2007). Some essays address the intersection of British imperialism and the colonial assertion of rights. Others speak to the position of Europe vis-à-vis world politics, as exemplified by Samuel Beckett's monitoring of torture during the Franco-Algerian War and Muriel Spark's skepticism about humanitarian interventions in Haiti. Writers such as Graham Greene, Arthur Koestler, Doris Lessing, George Orwell, Angela Thirkell, Ngũgĩ wa Thiong'o, Sylvia Townsend Warner, and Evelyn Waugh imagine versions of citizenship that respond to totalitarianism and the Cold War. Han Suyin and Kazuo Ishiguro return to mid-century events – the Chinese Revolution, the bombing of Hiroshima – as resources for autobiography and fiction in which national belonging is, to say the least, tenuous. Not all postwar conceptions of citizenship begin with the premise of disenfranchisement. *The Family of Man* photography exhibition, launched by the Museum of Modern Art in New York in 1955, promoted a saccharine version of universal humanity. Around 1945, dread of renewed warfare mixed with cautious optimism about the capacities of humankind to make a better world for itself.

In *Postwar*, Tony Judt refers to the period between 1945 and 1989 as "an interim age: a post-war parenthesis, the unfinished business of a conflict that ended in 1945 but whose epilogue had lasted for another half century" (2). The essays in this collection circle "around" 1945 like electrons around a nucleus or satellites around a planet. As they orbit, they draw wider or narrower circumferences for understanding the mid-century debates about rights and the human person. As Janice Ho demonstrates in her analysis of *The Secret Agent*, Joseph Conrad anticipates discussions about what constitutes the human in the later twentieth century by calling attention to the status of aliens in Britain. *The Secret Agent* takes a definite stance on outsiders and marginal citizens within British society – internal exiles, whose rights are compromised by their ambiguous legal status. Indeed, Conrad's novels have an abiding pertinence to discussions of citizenship, race, rights, and terrorism. Other essays in this volume reflect on legislation, including constitutions and human rights law. Throughout this volume, 1945 should be understood as an organizing, even gravitational, point for questions about citizenship and rights, not as a year in which everything happened and everything was resolved.

Around 1945

The epochal change that happened in 1945 was felt as it occurred, which is not always true of epochal changes. Summing up the spiritual costs of the Second World War, the theologian Ronald Knox claims that "the world of 1945 seems a world that is safe for nobody, but with a slight margin in favour of the gangster" (79–80). If the atom bomb is not abandoned, Knox prophesies, then the world will have done "something wrong in 1945" (68). According to Knox, citizens of the atomic age risk annihilating each other with nuclear weapons unless they muster reason and self-restraint. For Knox as for others, nuclear weapons altered the sense of time. After the levelling of Hiroshima, one newspaper began dating "its issues by the fifth or sixth day, or whatever it might be, 'of the Atomic Age'" (16). The tempo of world events quickened, or so it was felt in 1945. World citizens lived in anticipation of a dire future; instead of looking forward with limitless hope, they counted down to doomsday.

No synopsis can do justice to a year so charged with events as was 1945. In February, Franklin D. Roosevelt, Winston Churchill, and Joseph Stalin met at Yalta, in Crimea, to discuss plans for the military occupation of postwar Germany and governance in Europe. Roosevelt, advocate of the "Four Freedoms" – freedom of speech, freedom of worship, freedom from want, freedom from fear – died on 12 April 1945. On 8 May, the war in Europe officially ended. In June, fifty countries met in San Francisco and signed the charter to form the United Nations. On 26 July, votes were counted in the first general election held in the United Kingdom since 1935; led by Clement Attlee, the Labour Party swept to power. The United States bombed Hiroshima on 6 August 1945 and Nagasaki three days later. The Allies proclaimed victory over Japan on 15 August. Abiding by provisions set forth in the UN charter, the International Court of Justice was established in October 1945. In November, delegates from thirty-seven countries signed the Constitution of the United Nations Education, Scientific, and Cultural Organization (UNESCO), which explicitly promotes "the intellectual and moral solidarity of mankind" (Preamble). On 20 November, the trial of twenty-two Nazi war criminals began in Nuremberg, Germany. A twenty-third defendant, Martin Bormann, was tried *in absentia*.

Amid these events, transformations in citizenship and human rights were set afoot. In Britain, many saw the spirit of wartime fraternity as a prelude to social transformations after the war. The Labour Party victory in Britain in 1945 crowned the wartime expectation of a revolution in social organization. In *Citizens in War – and After* (1945), a book about his experiences fighting fires and fraternizing with the working classes, Stephen Spender cautions readers that warfare can be avoided in the future by recognizing "the continuity of conflict" and facing it "in peace as resolutely as we do in war" (11). This sentiment resonates with the UNESCO Constitution, which declares that, "since wars begin in the minds of men, it is in the minds of men that the defences of peace must be constructed" (Preamble). During the war, people from every stratum of British society united in fighting the Nazi enemy; aristocrats, milkmen, and stockbrokers met on equal terms of citizenship. Spender fervently hopes the spirit of "neighbourliness" (104) and "community" (109) that prevailed during the war will carry into the postwar as a model for civic cooperation. For Spender, democratic citizenship is a dynamic exchange between the needs of the individual and the provisions of society: "In peace every single individual is responsible to society in order that he may maintain the utmost freedom of individuality; in war, he sacrifices individuality" (105). If freedom is to be preserved, responsibility does not end when war ends. In war and in peace, the community safeguards the freedom of the individual. Reciprocally, the individual owes a debt of responsibility to the community, even to the point of sacrifice.

Citizens in War – and After is triumphantly propagandistic in naming the virtues of civilians on the home front, especially volunteers in the Civil Defence Service. The book was endorsed by Herbert Morrison, Home Secretary and Minister of Home Security, and packaged by Adprint, best known for its nationalistic "Britain in Pictures" series published by Collins. *Citizens in War – and After* includes photographs of ordinary folks going about their business: donning gas masks, making toys, drinking tea. Yet "citizenship" is something of a misnomer for British participation in the war, insofar as civil liberties were put in abeyance under the Emergency Powers (Defence) Act for the sake of national security. First passed in 1939, this act was renewed each year for the duration of the war. Under the act, landowners were required to put their property at the disposal of the crown. The coalition government had the power to direct all supplies, services, and labour to the defence of the realm without having to consult parliament. While this legislation was meant to allow the efficient prosecution of the war, its mandate could have had the effect of alienating British subjects if measures had been applied wilfully. In the event, courts and trials were not suspended. Nor was industrial labour conscripted.

In Britain, volunteers and civilians fought as front-line combatants in "the People's War." According to the prevailing myth, the Blitz united Britons in a common cause. As Angus Calder states, "the people of Britain were protagonists in their own history in a fashion never known before" (17). Civilians fought the war in their houses, yards, streets, and cities. In this account of the home front, "the people" were the hardy folks who withstood bombardment in

Humphrey Jennings's *London Can Take It!* (1940) or the invisible populations in the photographs of bombed churches and monuments in *The Bombed Buildings of Britain* (1942; rev. 1947). Citizenship was not just a form of national pride, but also an emerging form of entitlement. If allegiances between citizen and state are not mutual, they mean nothing at all. Yet who exactly comprise the "people" remains something of a mystery.[2] In *Which People's War?* Sonya Rose demonstrates that American GIs, Jews, good-time girls, and aliens – a cluster of "villainous and contemptuous 'anti-citizens'" (92) – did not share a core understanding of national identity. As Rose comments about the place of British women in the war, "Fulfilling the obligations of citizenship by undertaking certain kinds of wartime service actually exposed young women to the charge of lacking the essential virtues of citizenship, particularly if they were away from home and family" (149).

Prior to the 1940s, Britons and colonials were "subjects" rather than "citizens." In contrast to a "subject," a "citizen" participates in his own governance. The citizen, either by birth or by naturalization, belongs to a state; while owing allegiance to the state, the citizen also holds certain rights and duties vis-à-vis the state. A subject, by contrast, may have obligations without having any rights. In *Politics*, Aristotle defines the citizen (*politês*) in terms of deliberative justice: the citizen is entitled to participate in assemblies, sit on juries, and attend councils. Legal constitutions (*politeia*) enshrine rights and obligations within the polity. Generally a democracy does not recognize a sovereign outside the group of citizens who, elected as representatives or directly engaged in deliberations affecting the polity, govern themselves. The British Empire, as a polity without a formal constitution, was organized around the sovereign, and subjects owed allegiance to that sovereign. In return, the subject benefited from the sovereign's protection, even in far-flung colonies. Yet within the empire, it was never clear, from either legal or social points of view, whether all subjects enjoyed the protection of the sovereign equally. In the colonies and dominions, British subjects enjoyed full entitlements and rights afforded by the law, whereas native populations were subject to limited entitlements and rights.[3]

In Britain, nationality and citizenship underwent incremental change, via legislation, through the early decades of the twentieth century. The Aliens Act 1905 sought to define the rights of resident non-nationals by emphasizing constraints rather than liberties. This law restricted immigration and created mechanisms for deporting people deemed undesirable, namely paupers and criminals. Further complicating the idea of citizenship in the UK and its colonies, the British Nationality and Status of Aliens Acts 1914 regulated the entitlements of British subjects throughout the colonies. Although British colonies and dominions might allow for citizenship, these citizens remained subsets of the category called "British subjects." Although a "Canadian citizen" might exist notionally – the term is used in the Canadian Immigration Act 1910 – that citizenship was understood to be a colonial instantiation of Britishness, not a separate identity.

When it passed the Canadian Citizenship Act in 1946, Canada challenged British authority over citizenship and immigration within the empire. The act, which came into effect on 1 January 1947, arrogated to Canada the power to grant citizenship, through birth or naturalization, to people living in its geographical territory. By laying claim to this power to decide who was and who was not a citizen, Canada exerted its national sovereignty over and against the British crown. It also made an attempt to clarify the status of citizens who might have been resident in Canada without being British subjects.

The Canadian law had immediate and significant repercussions. At a conference held in London in 1947, certain states within the British Commonwealth agreed to legislate their own citizenship. New Zealand passed a citizenship law in 1947, and Australia followed suit in 1948, as did other countries. As a result of these changes, Britain developed a new definition of citizenship in the British Nationality Act 1948. In this act, the term "citizen" appears for the first time in British law as a marker of identity and nationality. In effect, people in the dominions and colonies that had their own citizenship laws were no longer British subjects, except vestigially. In a bewildering locution, the act specifies that "the expression 'British subject' and the expression 'Commonwealth citizen' shall have the same meaning" (Article 1.2). Making British subjects synonymous with Commonwealth citizens is a bit of having one's cake and eating it too. The Commonwealth citizen has no particular legal protections from Britain. He or she is understood to be a citizen of a nation-state not directly administered by Britain, such as Canada or New Zealand. At the same time, as Ian Baucom notes, "some individuals who failed to qualify for citizenship under the particular rules laid down by individual commonwealth countries discovered themselves to be subjects of Britain but citizens of nowhere" (*Out of Place* 10). The British Nationality Act rendered Britishness more fictive than actual. The term "Commonwealth citizen" proffers this fictive identity – neither practically meaningful nor legally binding – as a vestige of British imperialism.

The value of a British passport was not lost on British subjects and Commonwealth citizens, even in fictional situations. In *The Light of Day* (1962), a spy thriller by Eric Ambler, Arthur Abdel Simpson, son of an Egyptian mother and British father, claims that he is "British to the core" (8). British or not, he carries an Egyptian passport. Citizenship is a fetish for Arthur, and with good reason: he is multiply dislocated. Despite his biological heritage, he lives in Greece on a visitor's permit. Caught up in a neo-Nazi scheme, he is coerced into driving a car from Athens to Istanbul. For this border-crossing trip, he travels on his Egyptian passport, which, as luck would have it, has expired:

> I had made up my mind to tell the Egyptians what they could do with their passport, and approach the British with a view to reclaiming my United Kingdom citizenship, to which, I want to make it clear, I am perfectly entitled. The thing was that, being so busy, I had just not bothered to fill in all the necessary forms. My Greek *permis de séjour* was in order, and that was all I normally needed in the way of papers. Frankly, I find all this paper regimentation we have to go through nowadays extremely boring. (41)

Brought in by Turkish police for questioning, Arthur protests that he is British even without a valid passport: "Under the provisions of the British Nationality Act of 1948 I remain British unless I have specifically renounced that nationality. I have never formally renounced it" (56). Despite this plea, the Turkish official who questions him pronounces him "stateless" (56) and therefore beyond international intercession from whatever quarter. Arthur insists on his Britishness to the end, although he does so only to ensure that he has an escape hatch should he find himself in difficulty: "You cannot take away a man's nationality by refusing to recognize his right to it. The 1948 Act is quite clear. The only way you can lose British nationality is by renouncing it" (218). Shaking his fist at his imagined persecutors – Turks, Egyptians, neo-Nazis, bureaucrats, police interrogators, whomever – Arthur threatens to take his case "to the United Nations. They caned the British after Suez; they can cane them again for me" (219).

"British to the core," Arthur raises the possibility that citizenship, hence identity, inheres in personhood and cannot be revoked, removed, or let slide, no matter how negligent a person may be when it comes to filling in the appropriate papers. Citizenship, understood by Arthur as a national prerogative, is an ineradicable aspect of identity. By insisting that his British citizenship cannot be annulled without a formal petition, Arthur implies that negligence in administrative matters is not his fault. The state has an obligation to all its citizens regardless of infractions and negligence. But Arthur misapprehends the implications of the British Nationality Act. The act confers an identity – British subject – without conferring rights. He further mistakes nationality for citizenship. His father's nationality is not enough as a proof of Arthur's citizenship; he has to assert his Britishness according to the criteria of "citizenship by birth or descent" as set forth in the act (Articles 4, 5). Indeed, he counters the claim that he is stateless with the claim that he has multiple citizenships and allegiances: Egyptian, British, Greek. Arthur appeals to a higher court, the United Nations, to arbitrate his alleged statelessness, but his case falls outside the jurisdiction of the UN. In the final analysis, citizenship is granted or denied only by nation-states.

The British Nationality Act 1948 demonstrates deep uncertainty about the relation of imperial subjects to national citizens. The situation, to say the least, was confusing for former colonies and Commonwealth countries. The act specifically responded to the definition of Irish citizens set forth in the Constitution of Ireland, ratified in 1937. Any members of the Irish Free State, as proclaimed on 6 December 1922, became citizens of Ireland in 1937 if they had resided in the country for seven years, or if they were born in Ireland, or if either of their parents was born in Ireland. In addition to outlining citizenship by birth in Ireland or by descent, the Irish Constitution defines citizens' obligations: "Fidelity to the nation and loyalty to the State are fundamental political duties of all citizens" (Article 9.2.3). At the same time, the constitution takes a genial, open-arms approach to Irishness as a heritage: "the Irish nation cherishes its special affinity with people of Irish ancestry living abroad who share its cultural identity and heritage" (Article 2). Although not quite citizens, such descendants have cultural claims on Ireland, or so the law implies. Prompted by these changes to citizenship in Ireland, the British Nationality Act 1948 provides an opportunity for Irish citizens to choose British citizenship: "Any citizen of Eire who immediately before the commencement of this Act was also a British subject shall not by reason of anything contained in section one of this Act be deemed to have ceased to be a British subject if at any time he gives notice in writing to the Secretary of State claiming to remain a British subject" (Article 2.1). To claim British citizenship, an Irish person had to serve the crown, hold a British passport, or reside in the UK, including its colonies and protectorates. From 1948 onwards, however, choice of citizenship was not an option. The British government did not officially recognize Irish sovereignty until the Ireland Act was passed in 1949.

The spectre of alienation haunts any definition of citizenship. The Constitution of Ireland defines citizenship through a series of negations: "a person born in the island of Ireland, which includes its islands and seas, who does not have, at the time of the birth of that person, at least one parent who is an Irish citizen or entitled to be an Irish citizen is not entitled to Irish citizenship or nationality, unless provided for by law" (Article 9.2.1). Numerous loopholes reside within such a definition, such as the eventual claim to Irish citizenship by at least one parent, which could therefore legitimate a claim by the child of that person.

If such a claim seems fanciful, one has only to recall the extreme measures that the prosecutors and defence lawyers undertook at the trial of William Joyce, also known as Lord Haw-Haw, who was born in Brooklyn, New York, to an Irish father who had become a naturalized American citizen. As a boy, William Joyce moved to Ireland with his family, then England as an adolescent, then Germany as an adult, where he became a German citizen in 1940. After broadcasting pro-Nazi, anti-British propaganda from Germany during the war, Joyce was charged with treason under British law. His lawyer claimed that he was not a British subject and therefore not guilty of treason; the prosecution argued that he held a valid British passport and therefore owed loyalty to the British king, even if he was a German citizen. The trial, as Rebecca West reports in *The Meaning of Treason* (1949), dwelt on the question of national jurisdiction. Sir Hartley Shawcross, who later led the prosecution at Nuremberg, argued that Joyce's British passport, even though he lied about his nationality to obtain it, entitled him to British diplomatic protection while he was living in Germany. Joyce renewed his passport in 1938 and 1939, each time for a year. He therefore did owe allegiance to the British sovereign when he made his anti-British broadcasts in 1939 and 1940. On these grounds, Joyce was convicted of high treason in September 1945. After losing on appeal, he was hanged on 3 January 1946.

As a legal entitlement, citizenship implies an allegiance between an individual and a state. Yet the UDHR, for which forty-eight countries voted in 1948 (eight countries abstained), avoids all mention of the terms "citizen" and "citizenship," in favour of the more elusive term, "nationality." The UDHR guarantees that "everyone has the right to a nationality" (Article 15.1). Yet "nationality" and "citizenship" are far from being synonymous: it is possible to have a nationality without having citizenship and vice versa. Moreover, the obligations of citizens in a particular country do not inevitably, or even necessarily, align with inalienable human rights. It is easy to conceive of national laws that run counter to human rights, as when a state bans citizens from assembling, or limits freedom of expression, or sequesters and tortures its citizens. Passive sentence constructions in the UDHR disguise who grants citizenship and how the rights and obligations of citizens are fulfilled: "No one shall be arbitrarily deprived of his nationality nor denied the right to change his nationality" (Article 15.2). In the declaration of such a principle, no agent in particular denies the right to nationality nor deprives anyone of that nationality. No state, it seems, is ultimately responsible for stateless people.

Citizenship and Statelessness

Stripped of their citizenship or born into statelessness, some people live outside jurisdictions that confer legal protections. Instead of being citizens of the world, such people are citizens of no specific place. A contradiction thus haunts human rights law. Although human rights are said to be universal and inalienable, sovereign states have typically guaranteed those rights by recognizing, in the first instance, citizens as the bearers of rights. From citizens' rights follow human rights. Not having citizenship means not having rights or, depending on the state, not having full rights. Stateless people can appeal to international bodies to uphold their human rights, but international bodies, whether courts of law or non-governmental organizations, have traditionally not been able to enforce rights for the stateless.

Statelessness demonstrates just how quickly the supposedly "universal" rights of man localize in specific populations. Tracing the origin of human rights to the eighteenth century, Lynn Hunt observes that the Enlightenment generated two versions of rights language: "a particularistic version (rights specific to a people or national tradition) and a universalistic one (rights of man in general)" (116). These two versions of rights discourse blur together. The American Declaration of Independence (1776) asserts the "Right of the People" to make and abolish governments, alongside the personal rights to "Life, Liberty, and the pursuit of Happiness." The term "citizen" is used once and then only to castigate King George III's navy for taking "fellow Citizens" captive on the high seas. The drafters of the Declaration of Independence favour instead such terms as "mankind" and "brethren" to refer to bearers of rights.

By contrast, the French Declaration of the Rights of Man and of the Citizen (1789) evokes the term "citizen" constantly, though the word blurs into similar nouns, such as "man" and "society." During the French Revolution, as Simon Schama notes, "subjects were told they had become Citizens; an aggregate of subjects held in place by injustice and intimidation had become a Nation" (859). Citizenship provided a guarantee of liberty, freedom, and security. As the Declaration of the Rights of Man and of the Citizen puts it, political association aims to preserve "the natural and imprescriptible rights of man" (Article 2). Although not written down or even capable of being written down, these imprescriptible rights are inherent to all men, even perhaps all humankind, though that was the subject of much debate among the French revolutionaries. As Hunt points out, the overlap of national and universal discourses of human rights had some benefit: "Human rights could only flourish when people learned to think of others as their equals, as like them in some fundamental fashion" (58).

Nonetheless, the ambiguity that surrounds the term "citizen" allows nation-states to disqualify categories of people – convicts, refugees, ethnic groups, races, non-citizens, un-citizens – from entitlements.

From 1939 to 1945, contradictions between citizenship and human rights accumulated to the point of crisis. Displaced by war, refugees and asylum seekers forced issues of citizenship and rights to the forefront of international concern. In *Refugees: Anarchy or Organization?* (1938), Dorothy Thompson, the American journalist and broadcaster who was expelled from Germany in 1934 for speaking out against the Nazi Party, argued that the refugee crisis could be appropriately addressed only if nations cooperated with each other. Thompson's book grew out of an article entitled "Refugees: A World Problem," published in *Foreign Affairs* (1938). While acknowledging that charity can temporarily alleviate misery, she rejects charity in both article and book because it does not address the root causes of statelessness: aggression, systematic discrimination, civil war, other kinds of belligerence. According to Thompson, refugees challenge both humanitarianism and democracy: "This chaotic migration has added prodigiously to world unrest, and not least in those countries which are trying to work out the problems of the modern state along democratic and constitutional lines" ("Refugees: A World Problem," 377). Thompson means that the state, as a concept, is being transformed by the mass movement of people across national borders. The modern state has to account for the influx and exodus of groups of people, whether internally displaced citizens or externally displaced refugees. In 1938, by Thompson's reckoning, there were four million refugees in the world, many but not all of whom were Jews who had been stripped of their citizenship and forced to flee from Germany and Austria.

When the Second World War ended, millions of people began to make their way home, wherever those homes may have been and in whatever condition they were left after the ravages of war. In Europe alone, ten million people zigzagged across the continent in search of family and shelter. The United Nations Relief and Rehabilitation Administration (UNRRA) set up camps for displaced people. In "We Refugees," Hannah Arendt points out that modern Europe invented "a new kind of human beings – the kind that are put in concentration camps by their foes and in internment camps by their friends"

(265). Throughout this essay, Arendt speaks in the first person plural in a gesture of solidarity and responsibility. Being Jewish positions Arendt as a stateless person, beyond any operative legal status. Acknowledging Jewishness means "that we expose ourselves to the fate of human beings who, unprotected by any specific law or political convention, are nothing but human beings" (273).

In *The Origins of Totalitarianism*, Arendt argues that the loss of citizens' rights does not inevitably entail a loss of human rights. The right to liberty or security might be suspended during war, but that suspension is not the same as rightlessness. "The calamity of the rightless," Arendt claims in the third person, "is not that they are deprived of life, liberty, and the pursuit of happiness, or of equality before the law and freedom of opinion – formulas which were designed to solve problems *within* given communities – but that they no longer belong to any community whatsoever" (295; original emphasis). Not only do the stateless lose their place in a community, they also lose their place in the world. Arendt insists that a man can lose all his human rights "without losing his essential quality as a man, his human dignity. Only the loss of a polity itself expels him from humanity" (297). In other words, the "right to have rights," as Arendt puts it (296), depends on the community or polity. Dignity, an ineffaceable human quality, might replace citizenship as the grounds for human rights.

The UDHR promises that "all human beings are born free and equal in dignity and rights. They are endowed with reason and conscience and should act towards one another in a spirit of brotherhood" (Article 1). Social relations, whether a community or "a spirit of brotherhood," are required for the unfolding of human rights. Outside community or society, the right to assemble, the right to speak freely, the right to be free of torture, the right not to be detained, the right to privacy, and so forth, have no meaning. Not without ambiguity, the UDHR codifies the interdependence of the individual and the community: "Everyone has duties to the community in which alone the free and full development of his personality is possible" (Article 29.1). Full development of personality, as against partial development or none at all, only occurs within the community. The article also implies – much depends on how one reads the tricky pronominal clause – that the fulfillment of duties to the community brings about the full development of personality. A person could live within a community and perform no duties towards it, which would leave human personality stunted or unrealized in its full capacities. In all events, the UDHR posits that integration into a community allows the human personality to flourish. By contrast, expulsion curtails development as well as the possibility of human rights.

Thinking about rights in terms of expulsion from the human community was persistent in 1945. In the summer of that year, Stephen Spender, sent to Germany with the Allied Control Commission to report on intellectual life after the fall of the Nazi regime, visited a displaced-persons' camp outside Bonn. In *European Witness* (1946), Spender despairs over the miseries that he observed in the camp: "The slave labourers, in their vast herds in Germany, look like human animals who have been put in a foreign zoo out of which they broke at the time of the Occupation, to be caged up again, though less completely, by the Liberating Forces" (77). Confronted by people who have been twice interned, once by the Nazis and again by the Allied occupiers, Spender realizes that his freedom sets him apart from them: "There was less social gulf between the King of England and myself than between these people and myself, because the fact that one is, comparatively speaking, a free agent gives one social equality with other people who are free agents. Inequality is lack of freedom, imprisonment, slavery, extreme poverty" (78). Without quite saying so, Spender insinuates that Britishness guarantees his freedom. Amid misery, Spender takes secret pride in his freedom based on citizenship. He talks to Polish refugees who think the British are "much too kind" to the Germans (33). He suspects the Poles may be right, but his British rectitude forbids himself from saying so outright.

As he gazes upon the ruins of Germany, Spender wonders about citizenship and national sovereignty. He reports that Germans in 1945 revile the French and the Russians, while assuming that "their fate and future was [*sic*] now cast together with that of Britain" (28). The Germans want to bolster their chances for recovery by aligning themselves with the most important imperial power in Europe. Spender worries that no lessons have been learned from the Second World War, even as smashed German cities smoulder and stink around him: "modern states are incapable, during what is called peace, of sacrificing national sovereignty in order to avert foreseen disasters" (67).

Although the conflict had not ended – the war against Japan was ongoing – he was already thinking about the next war, which would be fought, according to his German interlocutors, between Russian and Western powers. Thinking about the future, Spender hopes that responsible action will prevail, but ameliorative action will only happen if "a majority of the peoples of the world assumes complete and conscious responsibility for the future pattern of the world" (93).

To restore civil liberties and to integrate Europeans into one citizenry – these are Spender's immediate aspirations in 1945. A united Europe, he thinks, will mitigate the catastrophic tendencies of nation-states to protect their own interests and ignore appeals from refugees. Yielding to momentary doubt about such cheerful cooperation, Spender suspects that the Germans, hastily de-nazified in 1945, harbour "self-pity, cruelty, bitterness and potential fury" (205). He notes the sycophantic, self-congratulatory traits of Germans, among them an interpreter who bows and smirks "with the exaggerated respect shown by many members of the Master Race to their Occupiers" (42). Notwithstanding the hypocrisy that he sees around him, Spender advocates fraternization between Germans and other nations as the way forward politically. Forgiveness of evil Nazi deeds has to happen for an advance to be made in European political culture.

"There is no German problem. There is only a European problem," Pierre Bertaux told Spender during his travels in 1945 (120). From the premise that cooperation among European nations will bring about a better future, Spender thinks of beginning from "zero" in reconstructing ruined Europe (96). Reinventing Europe from zero might mean reinventing European citizenship. In order to reckon with the problem of statelessness, at least in Europe, Spender dreams of establishing a new, transnational citizenship. A European superstate would circumvent the limitations of sovereign nation-states; uniform European citizenship would allow for migration across the continent without penalty or loss of rights. Such a superstate would be, in Spender's estimation, a guarantor of citizens' rights and human rights at one and the same time.

Such migrations without passports were, even within Europe, some decades in the future. Meanwhile, the UN approached the problem of statelessness not through citizenship but through an internationally applicable protocol. The 1951 Convention Relating to the Status of

Refugees, generated by the UN High Commissioner for Refugees, expanded on the right to seek in other countries asylum from persecution as set forth in the UDHR Article 14. Echoing Roosevelt's advocacy of "freedom from fear," the 1951 Convention defined a refugee as a person who, "owing to well-founded fear of being persecuted for reasons of race, religion, nationality, membership of a particular social group or political opinion, is outside the country of his nationality and is unable or, owing to such fear, is unwilling to avail himself of the protection of that country" (Article 1.A.2). The convention articulates the principle that refugees shall not be expelled or returned to a country against their will because they fear for their lives or liberty. The Convention Relating to the Status of Refugees addresses perplexities caused by refugees in Europe during the Second World War by envisaging freedom of movement, freedom from fear of persecution, and freedom from penalty in the country of asylum. In recognition that refugees were not limited to the past or to Europe, a further UN protocol approved in 1967 removed all geographical restrictions from the definition of asylum seekers.

Literature, Citizenship, Rights

Beginning from the premise that culture, whether novelistic or visual, articulates the dilemmas of rights seekers and citizens, *Around 1945* is divided into three sections: "Citizens," "Violations," "Rights." The first cluster of essays addresses mid-century changes in citizenship. Marina MacKay analyzes the conceptual division between the nation at war and the state, with attention to the impingement of the state on individuals in novels published in or around 1945. MacKay considers despairing Tories in Evelyn Waugh's and Angela Thirkell's fiction, as well as the education of the citizen into the state in C.S. Lewis's *That Hideous Strength* (1945) and J.B. Priestley's *Three Men in New Suits* (1945). Reflecting on wartime youth and resistance to postwar realities in Rose Macaulay's novel *The World My Wilderness* (1950), Ian Whittington points out that Roosevelt's "Four Freedoms" directly influenced Macaulay. To Roosevelt's four freedoms, Macaulay added a fifth – the freedom of "getting about" – as an expression of youth, liberty, and transnational rights. In an opposite modality, Melanie Micir turns her attention to Sylvia Townsend Warner's *The*

Corner That Held Them (1948) – a historical novel about a medieval nunnery in which nothing happens – and women's work during the war. Warner, who lived for years with her partner, Valentine Ackland, imagines citizenship within a state that neglects those whom it chooses not to recognize, namely women and queer people. Emily Hyde identifies a universalist grammar of citizenship in the *Family of Man* exhibition, organized by Edward Steichen, photography curator at the Museum of Modern Art. This blockbuster exhibition, which attracted avid audiences in thirty-seven countries over seven years, promoted human rights through the medium of the photograph. Relentlessly middlebrow, *The Family of Man* was supposed to explain man to himself and to his fellow man. This group of four essays deals primarily with British citizenship and cultural shifts in the conception of citizenship through the media of fiction and photography.[4]

The second group of essays, "Violations," centres on bombs, torture, and reactions to violence. By focusing on texts about violations of human rights, these essays bring to light the interconnections among cognate terms: human beings, humanitarianism, and humanity. In *The Secret Agent*, a bomb carried by a feeble-minded lad explodes near the Greenwich Observatory. Janice Ho takes this novel as the starting point for an argument about the definition of "the human," with specific reference to the legal categorization of the "feeble-minded" in the early twentieth century and the consequent attribution of value to human life. In Muriel Spark's novel *The Girls of Slender Means* (1963) an unexploded bomb suddenly goes off in the garden of a women's club in London in July 1945. Using archival sources, I claim that Spark critiques humanitarian interventions in situations of violence, specifically United Nations attempts to provide better health and educational services in Haiti. Adam Piette interprets Samuel Beckett's *Comment c'est / How It Is* (1961/1964) alongside torture practised by the Gestapo in Paris during the Second World War, and the public debate about torture used by French soldiers on Algerians during the Franco-Algerian War. As Piette demonstrates, Beckett responded to Jean-Paul Sartre's, François Mauriac's, and Henri Alleg's essays on "*la question*" – interrogation under torture. Claire Seiler considers the so-called "humanitarian justification" of dropping atomic bombs on Hiroshima and Nagasaki in 1945. Seiler juxtaposes three novels – Shirley Hazzard's *The Great Fire* (2003), and Kazuo Ishiguro's *A Pale*

View of Hills (1982) and *An Artist of the Floating World* (1986) – with the American occupation of Japan after the war and trajectories of citizenship that emerge from the 1947 Japanese Constitution. Each of these four essays sets one sort of citizenship against another in a violent situation: British and Continental, cosmopolitan and Haitian, French and Algerian, American and Japanese.

The third section, "Rights," provides four fictional case studies of the relations between states and individuals. Theories of statehood typically attribute unity to states, even though such unity is more imagined than real. The state, everywhere invisible but nevertheless inferred, regulates citizenship. Mitchell Brown traces the discourse of refugees from Dorothy Thompson's book on the subject through Graham Greene's *The Third Man* (1949). Usually thought to be a writer restricted to a seedy world of gangsters and worn-out Catholics, Greene, as Brown documents, is fully attuned to the emergence of a postwar international human rights discourse mediated through the figure of the refugee. Nadine Attewell pursues the question of statehood through mixed-race identity in Han Suyin's novel *A Many-Splendoured Thing* (1952) as well as her multi-volume autobiography. As Attewell argues, Suyin presupposes that citizenship issues from family structures, which are complicated by children born of parents of different races and nationalities. Mixed-race citizens challenge the myth of homogeneity within the state. Peter Kalliney interprets the long process of decolonization – the ceding of statehood from an imperial power to independent states – in confessional literature, such as Doris Lessing's *The Golden Notebook* (1962) and Ngũgĩ wa Thiong'o's *A Grain of Wheat* (1967). The confession enacts a seesaw of truth: truth sometimes resides with the person confessing and sometimes with the state to whom the confession is addressed via the person to whom the confession is made. In the face of globalization, states adjust their laws to regulate immigration and citizenship. Lastly, Matthew Hart treats the question of the state in terms of race and freedom. In Caryl Phillips's *Foreigners* (2007), the state establishes the category of non-citizens who have certain rights of citizenship. In Phillips's novel, black Britons have citizenship, but they are nonetheless treated as foreigners within the state. In this regard, the state, figured as a unified realm of goals, ideals, policies, and programs, excludes some individuals in order to preserve its fictitious unity. Hart asks what it might mean for a narrative to function as a state or how a reader might incarnate the tactics and prejudices of a state. This third cluster of essays dwells on embodied individuals, whose, gender, race, or nationality renders them visible, and therefore oppositional, to the state.

NOTES

1 The title but not the content of this volume takes inspiration from an issue of *Critical Inquiry* devoted to the topic "Around 1948." In their introduction to that special issue, Leela Gandhi and Deborah L. Nelson note that "epochal changes" occurred after the Second World War: "In a relatively short span of time, from 1947 to 1949, a wide array of nation-states and other institutions would assume new forms" (286). Essayists contributing to the *Critical Inquiry* issue reconsider universalism in human rights, the aspirations behind the UDHR, and related topics.

2 Elizabeth Bowen, reviewing Calder's book, finds limitations: "The war on Britain was undergone by all types. Not only The People were people, so were others" (*Mulberry Tree* 182). She means that not everyone experienced the "mythical intensity" of bombardment that happened mostly to city dwellers (182). She also means that war allowed no time for thinking and scarcely any time for feeling. The people, as against The People, were numbed by the excess of events.

3 Baucom discusses systemic racism in the British Nationality Act 1948 (*Out of Place* 11–14). Nadine Attewell, in *Better Britons*, traces the longer history of Britishness and racism through the Commonwealth Immigrants Act 1969 and the Immigration Act 1971 (195–7 and passim).

4 Not everyone agrees that literature and human rights blend. According to Nick Mansfield, "It is unlikely that literature performed this function [of inviting participation of an imagined reflective citizenry] for the politics of national and international governmental institutions (as opposed to the politics of cultural and social identity and valuation) more than merely marginally, repeating and perhaps broadening awareness of some issues but not really pioneering ideas" (208). In order to redress the shortcomings of human rights discourse, such as its platitudes and loosely articulated aspirations, Mansfield proposes nothing less than "a radical reconsideration of subjectivity, sociality, politics, and history" (213).

PART ONE

CITIZENS

1

Citizenship and the English Novel in 1945

MARINA MACKAY

We are the masters at the moment – and not only at the moment, but for a very long time to come.
Sir Hartley Shawcross (2 April 1946)

Attorney General Sir Hartley Shawcross's intervention in a 1946 House of Commons debate on trades unions legislation may be the worst-remembered political pronouncement in postwar Britain. Contrary to popular belief, Shawcross's claim about the Labour government, on whose behalf he spoke, was almost certainly not the notorious, definitive, and triumphalist, "We are the masters *now*," but the more sober comment recorded in *Hansard* and quoted above. As the context of his comment makes clear, he was describing nothing more sinister than the Labour Party mandate to represent the interests of the trades unions against the Conservative Opposition.[1] Both the historical identity of the party and its electoral victory in 1945 confirmed that mandate. But Shawcross's original phrasing was unfortunate, and so was its starker abbreviation. His language of mastery seemed to proclaim that no longer – even according to the basic conventions of parliamentary rhetoric – did politicians "serve" the people who had elected them and whom they represented, but instead were their "masters." Such an unsettling reversal of relations between states and citizens suggests totalitarianism rather than representative democracy. Shawcross's ill-chosen words and their resonant, chilling redaction reveal in miniature a broader culture of power and fear in mid-century English culture, a period in which, as I shall show, the transformation of the British political climate generated a suspicion of the new "masters" prevalent enough in the literature of the period to warrant close attention.

"All the power to the supreme party ..."

On the one hand, the changes taking place in the British social order in 1945 were manifestly less dramatic than changes elsewhere; on the other hand, the magnitude of what was happening elsewhere may have contributed to the British atmosphere of tension, even, at times, of class hostility and paranoia. Around the globe, many had been forced to confront on a massive scale allegiances between the citizen and the state. In Asia, problems of citizenship were paramount. The drive towards decolonization advanced with the expulsion of the defeated Japanese from their conquered European colonies, such as British Malaya and Singapore, French Indochina, and the Dutch East Indies. The end of the war also gave the final momentum to the Indian independence movement. In continental Europe, 1945 is no less obviously a critical date for thinking about citizenship, given how many nation-states themselves had to be remade either because they had been occupied or because they had been among (or implicated by) the occupying regimes. During this time of reckoning with what had been done to those from whom the Nazis had stripped citizenship a decade earlier, the emergent Soviet bloc was placing new pressures on the concept of rights and national belonging. Although this chapter is chiefly concerned with relationships between the subject and the state in British fiction during the Labour government of 1945–51 – the government headed by Clement Attlee that was closely associated with the introduction of the modern welfare state in Britain – it is worth recalling these worldwide predicaments for two closely related reasons: first, the domestic problematics of citizenship in Britain in 1945 were self-evidently less dramatic than in many, indeed almost any, contemporary Old World instances; second and more importantly, one would not necessarily know that the problematics of citizenship were less dramatic if one were to judge by mid-century literary production, which routinely presents the transition through which the nation was proceeding in language more appropriate to the recent history of, for example, Britain's continental neighbours. Rhetoric of sudden and coercive regime change predominates: "We are the masters *now*."

Rhetorical inflation speaks to a subjective but not completely unfounded perception that Britain was undergoing a significant transition in 1945 when it made the switch from a world power at war to a peacetime welfare state. Symbolically and, of course, rather schematically, we might see the difference between these two versions of Britain – of war versus postwar, of nation-saving versus state-remaking – in the general election that year, which saw the war hero Winston Churchill driven out of office by the altogether different social vision of Attlee's Labour Party. What is good for war is not necessarily good for peace. The Labour landslide reflected a clear appetite for social change even as the wartime leader largely remained (and, for that matter, largely remains) a national hero. Nonetheless, many mid-century writers either saw that change as a catastrophe or pretended to. These writers all got great mileage in their fiction from a national transformation that they presented as both dismal and incomprehensible. The first assumption of this chapter is that 1945 is a significant date for thinking about citizens around the world in relation to their states. The second assumption is that notions of citizenship and the state find some of their most distinctive articulations in the novel. Of course in the British context, that is true from at least Sir Walter Scott onwards. What makes it especially true and characteristic of the British novel in the middle of the twentieth century is the novel's renewed engagement with social issues and forms at this time. In what was once typically misread as a relatively straightforward political and aesthetic repudiation of modernism and its signature concern with the inner life, the mid-century British novel is concerned with institutions, groups, and collective identities. As a result of residual structures of wartime feeling, the mid-century novel is interested not only in horizontal relationships among the members of a community, but also in vertical relationships between these people and authority.

Perhaps it is not surprising that after six years of war the vertical relationships between citizens and governmental authority recorded in postwar fiction should so often be marked by skepticism, hostility, and resistance, with citizens showing a deep reluctance to consent to the protraction of wartime state powers into the years of peace. The fears addressed in novels were widely prevalent in 1945, which produced admonitory texts arguing that state power tends towards its own aggrandizement, irrespective of the consent of those it purports to serve. Karl Popper makes this point forcefully in his proto–Cold War classic *The Open Society and Its Enemies* (1945), perhaps the most enduringly symptomatic publication of its year in its fearful sense of the perpetual vulnerability of liberal democracies. In his notorious "Gestapo speech" broadcast on 4 June 1945, Churchill brought anti-state discourse into British homes. In this controversial election speech, he smeared the opposition by associating it with the recently overthrown Nazi regime. Churchill proclaimed that "no Socialist system can be established without a political police":

> No Socialist government conducting the entire life and industry of the country could afford to allow free, sharp, or violently-worded expressions of public discontent. They would have to fall back on some form of Gestapo, no doubt very humanely directed in the first instance. And this would nip opinion in the bud; it would stop criticism as it reared its head, and it would gather all the power to the supreme party and the party leaders, rising like pinnacles above their vast bureaucracies of Civil servants, no longer civil and no longer servants. (632)

Churchill imagines a Labour government that resembles the regime just defeated ("some form of Gestapo"). As he goes on, this image aligns ever more closely with the mechanisms of a Soviet-style regime ("the supreme party and the party leaders ... vast bureaucracies of civil servants"). This is the language of totalitarian takeover that proves pervasive in the fiction of 1945 as it addresses the incipient welfare state. In view of this inflammatory rhetoric about enemies within the open society, it is hardly surprising that the period sees a flowering of dystopian fiction, although this was not the only generic language for articulating hostility to Britain's political transformations in 1945.

Still, this year produced one of the most famous dystopian novels of the century: George Orwell's *Animal Farm* (1945). In a sense, 1945 also produced Orwell's *Nineteen Eighty-Four* (1949). The state branding of consumer goods as Victory products – most memorably, Winston Smith's grimly medicinal Victory Gin – recalls the celebratory language of 1945. If some of the anti-state dystopias of 1945 have an iconic status, others are barely known, less obviously usable than Orwell for Cold War anti-Communists. Among the most interesting and revealing but also among the least known of mid-century dystopias is C.S. Lewis's *That Hideous Strength* (1945), set in an imagined period right after the war and in anticipation of a progressive government victory. Prefiguring Churchill's opportunistic and almost certainly disingenuous dystopian projections – disingenuous in that the opposition he slandered in his "Gestapo" broadcast included numerous politicians with whom he had worked for years in the wartime National Government – these progressive forces in Lewis's novel turn out to be unsurprisingly similar in their methods and effects as totalitarian regimes. *That Hideous Strength* is reactionary in fairly predictable ways: gender relations, class relations, academic careerism. Yet its attack on the anticipated postwar future is the most historically rooted, and definitely the most interesting, element of its conservatism.

The novel describes the co-optation of a semi-rural provincial university, thanks to its self-serving faculty and unprincipled administration, by a government institute that aims to extend into the postwar period the centralized planning of the wartime years on the grounds that "a nation which can spend so many millions a day on a war can surely afford a few millions a month on productive research in peacetime" (21). As the university cedes more and more ground to the institute, centralized planning slides rapidly into totalitarianism. Needless to say, this new regime is unqualifiedly evil. The novel ends with the university getting its comeuppance for its bad faith by being comprehensively obliterated. Aside from its evocation of totalitarianism to discredit progressive aspirations, the novel is particularly symptomatic of the mid-century in its characterization of these aspirations as somehow alien to the nation itself. Late in the novel, a passage schematizes two versions of "England." The novel distinguishes between the quasi-mystical Logres of Arthurian legend and an entity that is "merely Britain" (192). Lewis casts this as a difference between the good guys and bad. There is a difference, we are told, between John Milton and Oliver Cromwell, between Philip Sidney and Cecil Rhodes, between national tradition and brutal state power (367). On the one hand, there is the nation, which is good, and on the other hand, there is the state, which is irredeemably bad.

This effort to divide the nation and the state is a characteristic move in 1945 fiction. The nation is imagined as having strong affective power, whereas the state has none. The nation compels loyalty and inspires a sense of belonging, continuity, and affiliations both inherited and chosen; it is associated with the England of organic countryside where national myth and history germinate in the ground beneath your feet. This trope was a feature of propaganda during the Second World War. In *Put Out More Flags* (1942), Evelyn Waugh jokes about intellectuals at the Ministry of Information making films about, of all things, otter hunting. These films are "designed to impress neutral countries with the pastoral beauty of English life" (243), but that orientation towards a chthonic version of the nation was also essential to the novel. In a 1944 volume of her autobiography, G.B. Stern identifies "the Village-in-Wartime novel" as a pleasurable new genre: "I never grew tired of them ... I suppose I read about forty; they were usually extremely well written. If, misled by a title, I got hold of a volume that turned out after all not to be the Village-in-Wartime Book, I was genuinely disappointed" (55). Lest we think this new genre purely middlebrow or propagandistic, we should remember that Virginia Woolf – no middlebrow or propagandist, she – set her final novel *Between the Acts* (1941) in a highly traditional yet affectionately described English village. If the embrace in 1940s novels of a specific version of the nation bespeaks wartime loyalties, in postwar fiction, by contrast, the state elicits no such attachments. Instead, it impinges upon its citizens. The state cares primarily about expansion and consolidation; it is unowned and unaccountable. It is associated with the raw power of institutions built from scratch and imposed by force on the English landscape. These institutions turn "the heart of England into a cross between an abortive American hotel and a glorified gas works," as a character describes the totalitarian institute in *That Hideous Strength* (56). Lewis decries the systematic annihilation of traditional landscapes by those to whom these sites convey no meaning: "sixteenth-century almshouses, and a Norman church, and all that" (83), "old buildings and all that sort of thing" (87). The nation sustains and the state subsumes. In Lewis's theological dystopia, the difference between the two becomes the grounds for what is quite literally a battle between good and evil. In this conservative model, postwar state intervention and social planning of the kind anticipated from an early stage in the war can only ever be dangerous and damaging forces.

"The misfortunes of peace"

Conservative writers like Lewis would always be a likely source of anti-welfare-state rhetoric, not to say propaganda, but such sentiments also make themselves felt in writers of more complex political orientations. Indeed, among contemporary novelists working with the same rhetorical structures of a nurturing nation and an encroaching state is a writer we have good reason to believe would have been intensely hostile to Lewis's work: Henry Green, at one time Lewis's reluctant tutee at Oxford. Green held an exasperated belief that novels by religious writers make no sense to non-religious people. In this context Green specifically named Lewis's friend and major influence, Charles Williams, "who to me is meaningless" ("Unloving," 280).

Green's dystopian anti–welfare-state novel, *Concluding* (1948), is probably even less read than Lewis's. (Lewis at least retains a non-academic following.) *Concluding* is an extremely unusual production: a dystopian novel of extraordinary lyricism and romance set during "the high summer of the State" (64). A modernist day book, *Concluding* begins at dawn at a beautiful and ornate English stately home that has been taken over by an imagined socialist government. This uniquely unthreatening totalitarian administration has appropriated the country house as a training centre for hand-picked girls of eighteen years of age, more or less, who are to become civil servants for the current regime, a "privilege" and "a reward for preliminary work well done" (79). If they misbehave, they are threatened with "a job on the machines" (58). The reader deduces that in this socialist England of the future there are no prospects other than to be a state functionary or a factory worker. As in Lewis's novel, the scene is a pastoral England. It is perhaps even more English than Lewis's provincial landscape because it is lovely and unreal to the point of resembling never-never land. As far as the nation is concerned, then, we have a beautiful and very literary rendering of England; in contrast, the treatment of the state is wholly dystopic. To the extent that there is hope in this dystopia, it lies not with the proles, as it did for Winston Smith, but with the possibility that what constitutes England as a nation survives largely unmarked by the transformations of the British state. Unlike the bugged countryside of *Nineteen Eighty-Four*, Green's romantic pastoral landscape remains strangely unblighted, and his characters strangely free even in the face of the state's attempts at regimentation.

Concluding is an unusual political dystopia for all sorts of reasons. Among its odder features is a general aura of inconsequence every time the totalitarian projections from which it derives its setting and situation are addressed. The new order, which has been in power for many years when the novel opens, is characterized by anonymity and general irrelevance. The main character is an elderly scientist called Rock, who may or may not be honoured by the government "as one of the ornaments of the State" (39), as one character puts it. Obscure references to his protectors, "friends still in high places" (7), "the inner circles" (38), and "the powers that be" (38) never add up to a clear picture of who is in charge and what they are up to. Rock lives in a cottage on what was once a traditional country estate, a cottage gifted to him by the former landlord. For his part, the landlord has become "'the life tenant' ... which was their way of referring to the private owner of this estate, from whom the State had lifted everything" (13). Thus the novel manages to be both vague about the threat presented by the state and deeply bitter on behalf of those dispossessed upper classes "from whom the state had lifted everything."

This inflated sense of a totalitarian socialist takeover permeates the postwar fiction of Green's close friend Evelyn Waugh. "Then came the 1940s, first the war, after it the Cripps-Attlee terror," Waugh wrote darkly of the age of austerity. Cripps of "the Cripps-Attlee terror" was Sir Stafford Cripps, chancellor of the exchequer in the late 1940s, and therefore figurehead of the new government's redistributive economic policies ("Manners and Morals," 589). Elsewhere, Waugh wrote of his "bitter memories of the Attlee-Cripps regime when the kingdom seemed to be under enemy occupation" ("Aspirations of a Mugwump," 537). Sometimes he referred to this period simply as "the Occupation" ("The Scandinavian Capitals," 339). With its sense of a pseudo-totalitarian socialist state laid over a deeply traditional England, his satirical novella *Love among the Ruins: A Romance of the Near Future* (1953) picks up where his 1945 novel *Brideshead Revisited* leaves off. A stately home has been taken over, yet again, by the state – not by the army as in the case of Brideshead Castle, but by postwar social services. Mountjoy Castle is "the ancestral seat of a maimed V.C. of the Second World War" who has been packed off unwillingly to a state home for the disabled (*Love* 475). His beautiful house has become a prison, with the best rooms – in a rather characteristic Waugh joke – going to the murderers and the second-best going to the sex offenders.

Love among the Ruins shares its title with another work of anti-welfare-state fiction, Angela Thirkell's *Love among the Ruins* (1948). In Thirkell's novel, the good people of Barsetshire contemplate life in what the narrator calls "this horrible new world" (10), the "so-called peace" (19); by the end of the novel, these dismayed terms are rhetorically enhanced as "the Revolting New World" (158) and "the worse-than-war peace" (213). As if the sympathies of the County were in any way ambiguous, "Churchill" makes a silent cameo appearance at the combined Conservative Rally and County Pig Show, where one of Thirkell's forelock-tugging locals extemporizes a couplet in honour of the ousted leader: "Why we are downhearted I'll tell you exactly, / We chucked good old Winnie and now we've got Attlee" (428). Tory Thirkell insists on the unwelcome continuities between war and postwar. She characterizes the latter as more of the same but now quite a bit worse: "The war was long over, the raids organized by the Government on food, health, money, freedom, nerves, couldn't be avoided by getting under the kitchen table or into an air-raid shelter" (102). There are "the fortunes of war and the misfortunes of peace" (3). Among peacetime misfortunes is democratization. The County have to accept those people who would once have been shunned for the over-recent origins of their wealth, even as they fear not being able to keep up their own manor houses. In one such case, the house, recently released from its service as a wartime hospital, may be converted into "a sanatorium, or a lunatic asylum, or, even worse, a branch of a Government department" (6). Largely ignored by academics, and extremely popular in its time, Thirkell's work is an important corrective to our one-sided perception of how mid-century writers engaged the welfare state. In obvious contrast to the picaresque social mobility narratives of the mid-century, narratives associated most commonly with canonical 1950s novels such as *Lucky Jim* (1954) or *Room at the Top* (1957), what emerges in Thirkell's fiction in the 1940s is the social challenge presented to and resisted by those who had been the beneficiaries of the old order.

That Waugh and Thirkell hit on the same Robert Browning title, used satirically in both cases, is indicative of deeper similarities: both writers offer a conservative critique of an alien state superimposed on a traditionally conceived rural nation, a superimposition that results in shocking cultural diminution. Obviously there are differences. Thirkell's gentle social comedies of the rural gentry have a strongly escapist quality; she recalls those "lady novelists," alluded to in Graham Greene's *Ministry of Fear* (1943), who describe "tea on the lawn, evensong, croquet, the old ladies calling, the gentle, unmalicious gossip, the gardener trundling the wheelbarrow" (65). In comparison to Thirkell, Waugh's iteration of imposed statehood is fantastical in an exaggerated and self-conscious way. His *Love among the Ruins* opens with a pastoral scene at a stately home, "a rich, old fashioned Tennysonian night": "Strains of a string quartet floated out from the drawing room windows and were lost among the splash and murmur of the gardens. In the basin [of the fountain] the folded lilies had left a brooding sweetness over the water" (469). So far, so familiar from *Brideshead Revisited*. In another passage that recalls Charles Ryder's early meditations on the provenance of Brideshead Castle, we learn that "Mountjoy had been planned and planted in the years of which [the protagonist] knew nothing; generations of skilled and patient husband-men had weeded and dunged and pruned; generations of dilettanti had watered it with cascades and jets; generations of collectors ..." and so on (469–70). Like Brideshead, this centuries-old cultural project of the English country estate has come into its full flowering only at the moment when it is to be inherited symbolically by exactly the wrong people: the army in *Brideshead Revisited* and the peacetime government in *Love among the Ruins*. "All this had been planned and planted a century and a half ago so that, at about this date, it might be seen in its maturity" (16), Charles Ryder muses as he arrives at Brideshead with inglorious Hooper, illegitimate inheritor of a British past his modern education has left him unequipped to appreciate. The inheritor of Mountjoy – and its future destroyer – is Miles Plastic, a ward of the state and a compulsive arsonist. Despite the number of people he has murdered with his fire-starting habit, Miles has been recast as merely maladjusted by the high-minded liberal state. He is therefore the recipient of all possible resources for rehabilitation. As one character in *Love among the Ruins* explains, "In the New Britain which we are building, there are no criminals. There are only the victims of inadequate social services" (476). The mockery of modern carceral practices is a familiar motif in Waugh's fiction. In *Decline and Fall* (1928), for instance, the liberal prison governor, Sir Wilfred Lucas-Dockery, believes that "almost all crime is due to the repressed desire for aesthetic expression" (226). Sir Wilfred diagnoses a deranged murderer with "the frustrated creative urge," and, in pursuit of a cure, supplies him with the woodworking tools that he uses to chop off the prison chaplain's head (244). Similarly in the short story "Mr. Loveday's Little Outing" (1935), high-minded Angela makes it possible for a long-term patient in the County's secure asylum to have the single outing for which he longs; she does not realize that Mr Loveday craves a "little outing" in order to strangle another young woman. Aided by Angela, Mr Loveday repeats the crime for which he was institutionalized in the first place. Crack-brained Lucas-Dockery and naive Angela are the sentimental vanguard of the high-minded welfare regime travestied in *Love among the Ruins*.

Love among the Ruins is a compendium of everything that Waugh loathes, from liberal meliorism to the Auden generation. Miles Plastic works at a state-run euthanasia centre, which "had not been part of the original 1945 Health Service," the narrator explains with amusing topicality, but a vote-grabbing "Tory measure" (479). Implicitly, Conservative voters would sooner be put out of their misery than live in a country made by socialists. The clientele at the euthanasia centre goes beyond merely disenfranchised Tories. Characters based on W.H. Auden and Christopher Isherwood also report there to have themselves put down. As Parsnip and Pimpernell, they are recurrent minor characters in Waugh's fiction. In *Put Out More Flags* (1942), they take flight to America. In "Basil Seal Rides Again" (1963), they show up again in old age as distinguished creative writing professors:

"Dr. Parsnip, Professor of Dramatic Poetry at Minneapolis, and Dr. Pimpernell, Professor of Poetic Drama at St. Paul" (503). In *Love among the Ruins*, "old Parsnip" is a "veteran poet," "a poet of the '30s ... [he,] *New Writing*, the Left Book Club, they were all the rage" (496). In its fruition, socialism has turned out to be far too much for those among Waugh's generation who had embraced it before the war. Dr Beamish, for instance, is described as "a man whose character had been formed in the nervous '30s, now much embittered, like many of his contemporaries, by the fulfillment of his early hopes. He had signed manifestos in his hot youth, had raised his fist in Barcelona and had painted abstractedly for *Horizon*; he had stood beside Spender at great concourses of Youth" (480). The point about *Horizon* is unjust even by Waugh's standards, given that throughout its ten-year history *Horizon* had largely resisted political co-optation. Now Cyril Connolly's magazine and abstract painting – or painting "abstractedly," in Waugh's swipe – are being lumped in with fighting for the Spanish Republic. Yet Waugh is not interested in being especially discriminating in this case. All those harbingers and auguries of welfare-state England are cast as treasonous intellectuals; the brave new world, having taken on its own momentum, has left behind as fragments of the old world those who theorized and championed the coming social revolution, toward which the welfare state is merely a preliminary gesture.

The inclusion of the euthanasia centre in the context of the progressive regime recalls Waugh's remarks on socialist culture in Sweden, which he took to have supplied the model for the Labour Party platform in 1945. Waugh sums up Swedish socialism as "a low birth-rate and a high suicide-rate" ("The Scandinavian Capitals," 340). Waugh's gibe recalls a comment about Sweden made by George Orwell in 1949. Orwell claimed that he had "never been able to like these model countries with everything up to date and hygienic and an enormous suicide rate," as if one followed quite obviously from the other (450). It seems rather an unregenerate perspective for Orwell to take, but the idea of recidivism appears everywhere in mid-century fiction; Winston Smith in *Nineteen Eighty-Four* is one such recidivist. For that matter, backsliding is so pronounced in the novel that perhaps the only reliably programmed party members are the children who denounce their parents to the secret police: no one else proves to be as safely orthodox as the seven-year-old daughter of the slavishly conformist Parsons, who reports her father for the literally unconscious treason he commits when he talks in his sleep. If it seems a merely incidental detail of *Nineteen Eighty-Four* that children should be the perfect totalitarian subjects, Orwell's gesture is characteristic of how his generation came to think of the postwar British citizen.

Citizen Plastic

From a very early stage, onlookers noted the interest in children and childhood in the fiction of the late 1940s. Surveying the fiction of the immediate postwar in 1951, P.H. Newby suggested that one noticeable aspect of this body of work, particularly among younger writers, was its preoccupation with childhood. Childhood, Newby conjectured, offered something comparatively solid to fall back on amid the confusions of war (8–9). There may be another, political element to the interest that Newby identified in children's putative innocence. As David Kynaston describes in his history of austerity-era Britain, "a moral panic was brewing up nicely" about delinquent children (113). Orwell's nasty juvenile spies speak directly to the question of conditioning in the era of totalitarianism: they are, it turns out, not delinquent *enough*.

Children conditioned by violence are recurrent figures in postwar fiction. In Elizabeth Bowen's *The Heat of the Day* (1949), secretive children wear Nazi-looking armbands and perform military exercises. In Henry Green's *Caught* (1943), a child tortures birds and mice while pretending to be "a German policeman" (190); he imagines the birds as Polish people and the mice as Czechs. A juvenile gang in Graham Greene's short story "The Destructors" (1954) demolish a seventeenth-century house that has survived the Blitz, as if to complete what the violence in the background of their childhood has begun. Acculturation, in other words, is imagined as a hazardous affair. At best it is the grounds for a kind of black comedy, as when the evacuee Albert strangles a peacock in imitation of a London pub denizen who bites the heads off mice in order to pay his bar bill in Green's *Loving* (1945), or when six-year-old Penelope in *Nothing* (1950) proves so suggestible that upon seeing a war amputee for the first time she begins to carry one of her arms as if it were a stump. This interest in conditioning is neither new in nor unique to the 1940s. Experimental phenomena as various as Pavlov's salivating dogs and the Russian formalist idea of art as a means by which we are saved from habituated perception attest to the early twentieth-century interest in acculturation. In the postwar, however, writers anchor ideas of conditioning to forms of violence, both the physical violence of wartime and, instructively, the imagined psychological violence of peace. Writing in 1946 of "the grand climacteric of 1945," Evelyn Waugh claimed that the so-called "classless society" promised by the new administration would be brought about only by those methods made familiar by foreign totalitarianism. The new Britain "will not be the fruit of purely English measures," he wrote, recalling the period's standard characterization of state power as somehow a foreign imposition: "Judicial murder, mass deportations and the 'psychological conditioning' of young children will be the means" ("What to Do," 312–13).

This recurrent idea of a creepily imitative postwar child poses a conundrum about citizenship. From the passport point of view, one may be born a citizen; from the point of view of postwar writers, the welfare-state citizen is made rather than born. This in turn helps to explain the preoccupation with education and re-education across the fiction of the late 1940s, although re-education seldom works as comprehensively and effectively as on, to return to the most famous example, Winston Smith at the end of *Nineteen Eighty-Four*. Upon his release from prison in *Love among the Ruins*, Waugh's seemingly reclaimed arsonist Miles Plastic goes from being "Miles the Problem" to "Mr. Plastic the Citizen" thanks to a pile of papers that includes his all-important "Certificate of Human Personality" (478). What could be more malleable a material than plastic? In *That Hideous Strength*, likewise, the protagonists denounce the "humane, remedial treatment" (67) by which the totalitarian institute ameliorates the crime rate through some form of brainwashing rather than through punishment: "assaults on personal identity you call Remedial Treatment" (218). In *Love among the Ruins*, the brave new world is ushered in by "the conditioned personality." The story ends not at Mountjoy Castle, which Miles Plastic has burned to the ground in a brief moment of backsliding, but with a model of its replacement, "a familiar standard packing case, set on end":

> Miles gazed at the box.
>
> It fitted. It fell into place precisely in the void of his mind, satisfying all the needs for which his education had prepared him. The conditioned personality recognized its proper pre-ordained environment. (500)

In Waugh's short story "Scott-King's Modern Europe" (1947), the classics-master protagonist finds himself in Neutralia, a state strongly resembling fascist Spain under General Franco. He comes home to news of yet another fall in classics enrolments at his school. He is advised to take up teaching "economic history" rather than his own obsolescent subject in order to prepare his pupils better for the present age. Scott-King concludes, "I think it would be very wicked indeed to do anything to fit a boy for the modern world" (429).

By picking up on this cultural preoccupation with re-education, Angela Thirkell may have been more in tune with her times than she intended. *Miss Bunting* (1945), a novel about the end of the war, is topical not only because it schematizes the clash between Old and New worlds – cast as the difference between the New Town and Old Town in the Barsetshire town of Hallbury – but also because it is named for a highly traditional governess. The novel necessarily and explicitly dwells on the conditioning of the nation's youth. The elderly governess, Miss Bunting, intimately identified with the old order, dies at the end of the novel: "one of the remaining links with the old world of an ordered society had snapped. Nearly everything for which Miss Bunting had stood was disintegrating in the great upheaval of civilization" (310). Ventriloquizing a familiar Thirkell sentiment, one character forecasts the emergence of "a horrible new world ... with no room for us. We are nearly as dead as poor Miss Bunting" (310). In one way the novel is actually less pessimistic than these gloomy prognostications suggest. In what is admittedly an unusual moment of authentic emotional conflict in the Thirkell oeuvre, the heroine, Jane Gresham, who does not know whether or not her prisoner-of-war husband is still alive, begins to fall in love with the kind, wealthy ironmaster Sam Adams. Jane knows that he is "not a gentleman and never would be. And when she said gentleman, she meant what her father and friends would mean and all her own instincts knew" (291). Not only is Sam

Adams looked down upon by the County as the new man, but he is also linked, via a very familiar mid-century slur, with totalitarianism. Hearing him praised as "the kind of person who gets things done," Jane's father, the Admiral, retorts that "it was probably people saying things like that about Hitler that had got him where he was" (159–60). Yet the novel suggests less snobbish possibilities about what constitutes the gentlemanly. Even if this cross-cultural encounter is broken off upon the return from war of Jane's husband, the sense remains that even so unlikely a character as Sam Adams could be integrated into Jane's world eventually.

In line with *Miss Bunting*'s exploration of "conditioning," Thirkell's *Love among the Ruins* is full of jokes about "State control of young children" (94). Richard Tebben returns from Sweden, where he has fallen in love with Petrea Krogsbrog. He applauds Swedish nurseries as "models of efficiency and the children were growing up civically minded" (64). It comes as no surprise that Petrea is "frightfully keen on social work and child welfare" (67). Stuffed with Swedish socialism, Richard is insufferable: "Richard said he was a Communist, with the air of a Christian martyr demanding more and better lions" (97). Both *Love among the Ruins* and *Miss Bunting* ultimately reverse the conditioning that was in circulation in the anti-state fiction of 1945. Even Sam Adams's lumpish daughter Heather is "improved" by her encounter with the gentry: "though the world is full of sows' ears there are very few of them that can be made into silk purses, but here the transformation appeared to be almost complete" (*Miss Bunting* 252). Why have modern levelling down, Thirkell seems to ask, if you can have old-style levelling up of taste and of manners? On the other hand, Thirkell never bothers to ask why the taste and manners of the Tory gentry should represent such an improvement on other English ways of living.

Such strategies as Thirkell's for disrupting perceived attempts to condition citizens in the welfare state are prevalent throughout fiction of the period. Green's *Concluding* is vague on the details of its imaginary totalitarian program, yet the new regime plans to raise the age of consent from sixteen to eighteen. To be a young woman, thinks one character, is to be "like a child that could scarcely blow its own nose" (40). The state infantilizes girls the better to ensure its hold upon them; in having to do so, the state is already forced to act defensively by prolonging the girls' dependent condition. Eccentricity among the older generation survives and implicitly resists forms of standardization identified with the new socialist state. The scientist Rock continues to live with his pig Daisy, his cat Alice, and his female goose Ted, in an environment of obscure governmental Directives and Reports. (These nouns are capitalized throughout the novel.) In protest, Rock refuses to open his mail. He is also, tellingly, old and deaf: he literally cannot be interpellated by the state. Nor can the young be regimented. Miss Edge, the head of the institute, laments that "usually one has only to suggest what must not be done to find it carried into practice far quicker than any order" (64). This is an unremarkably headmistressy thing for her to say – at least until the reader recalls that this is supposed to be a totalitarian dystopia, in which all orders are unthinkingly obeyed by fully acculturated, fearful, docile subjects.

In short, mid-century writers produced a significant body of conservative fiction that refuses to recognize the modern state – "recognize" in the literal sense of registering its familiarity, and "recognize" also in the sense of acknowledging its legitimacy. This reaction against that alien-seeming state represents the point at which strains of modernist and anti-modernist conservatism intersect. At that point, Henry Green and Angela Thirkell, for all their vast differences of style and relative complexity, criticize the same things: homogenization, managerialism, centralization, and forms of instrumental and utilitarian reason that take no account of citizens' very real, if irrational and unexamined, attachments to older styles of being. The story of anti–welfare-state feeling does not necessarily end in 1951 with the re-election of the Conservatives, which many saw as the restoration of the natural party of government. If the Labour Party were no longer "the Masters," as Shawcross had so unluckily expressed it, many of the changes they wrought would survive for decades, as some, such as the castigated and cherished National Health Service, still do. The political discomfort recorded in late-1940s fiction also outlived its time.

The human being is not "a clockwork toy to be wound up by ... the Almighty State" (xiii), wrote Anthony Burgess in the retrospective introduction to his cult classic, *A Clockwork Orange* (1962). In its treatment of the state and its efforts at the re-education of citizens,

Burgess's ostensibly futuristic novel looks at least as much backward as forward insofar as it recalls the peculiar paranoia that the welfare state induced in right-wing figures at the time of its inception. The state infiltrates every cranny of the novel, in the form of "State Aid" or social security payments, the centralized medium of Statefilm, and the centralized food supply from "Statemarts." Above all, the "State Institute for Reclamation of Criminal Types" reforms citizens by torturing them. One of its reclaimed criminals, Alex, is a model success story much like Miles Plastic in Waugh's *Love among the Ruins*. Inevitably, Orwell casts his long shadow over any postwar British dystopia. Like the old prole who sings in *Nineteen Eighty-Four*, a homeless man in *A Clockwork Orange* sings a lament about a patriotic soldier returned from war. The song recalls the familiar sense that the national tradition is a thing of the past, merely a nostalgic fragment in the era of the overweening state: "Oh dear dear land I fought for thee / And brought thee peace and victory" (17).

As against the affectively powerful nation that no longer exists, the architects of the welfare state, who, it is implied, have made possible the dystopia the novel describes, are venerated in urban space. Streets include "Attlee Avenue" (12) and "Priestley Place," the latter incorporating "the big bronze statue of some [old] poet with an apey upper lip and a pipe stuck in a droopy old [mouth]" (22). Democratic socialist Priestley was, of course, the poet laureate of the incoming welfare state during the war. There is also Kingsley Avenue, presumably named for Kingsley Martin, editor of the socialist *New Statesman* in the years leading up to and institutionalizing the welfare state. Wilsonway commemorates Harold Wilson, president of the Board of Trade in the Attlee government and future prime minster. The Soviet dimension of the novel reinforces topicality. Art depicting the dignity of labour decorates Municipal Flatblock 18A, where Alex lives. In synthetic, Russified English, Burgess elaborates his version of "Ingsoc" – English socialism – in as polemical a way as Orwell did in the late 1940s.

The war could not help but bring into the foreground the demands of citizenship: after all, what the state can ask of you in wartime may literally be a life or death matter. But in Britain the events of the immediate postwar period also foregrounded the potentially exorbitant claims of the state on its citizens. Fiction casts those claims in ways that can be politically unsympathetic, to say the least. At worst, these largely forgotten protests can read like nothing more than outraged class privilege feeling itself under threat. Yet recalling these protests adds a necessary complexity to our understanding of mid-century British literature, a literature populated not only by angry young men but urbanely exasperated older men and women whose protests against a changing social order lent a great deal of energy to the period's fiction. This fiction can be exceptionally funny and penetratingly satirical in its hyperbolic dismay. At least some authors knew this at the time. Henry Green wrote to Rosamond Lehmann: "The truth is, these times are an absolute gift to the writer. Everything is breaking up." In Lehmann's words, this breaking up was perhaps "an incentive to look on the bright side" (*An Absolute Gift* 508).

NOTE

1 As Anthony Howard pithily puts it in the classic collection *Age of Austerity*, on the subject of Labour's failure to take advantage of its mandate, "No one, of course, ever said 'We are the masters *now*.' It might have been better if someone had. And it might even have been important had he really meant it" (20).

2

"A Rather Ungoverned Bringing Up": Postwar Resistance and Displacement in *The World My Wilderness*

IAN WHITTINGTON

Halfway through Rose Macaulay's novel *The World My Wilderness* (1950) seventeen-year-old Barbary Deniston is caught stealing eggs from a Highland hen by two Scottish farmers. The scene is broadly comic. Armed with a slingshot, she manages to hit one of the farmers before being yanked to her feet. As yolks leak from her pocket, the farmers question her about her identity and her origins, but she does not yield: "Barbary said nothing: one did not give information of that kind when caught; not a word, whatever they did to one; that was the first principle of the maquis. Not that most people were able to obey it to the end; it was known that the breaking point came sooner or later" (102). Barbary's reaction to capture marks her as out of place: only recently returned to Britain, she spent the Second World War living with her mother in the south of France. While there, she worked with the maquis, the bands of Resistance fighters who hid in the dense underbrush of the countryside. Barbary's first-hand knowledge of coercion was earned through her capture and beating by Nazis. She may also have been sexually assaulted. If the juxtaposition of farcical present and tragic past in this scene is unsettling, the unsteady relationship between those two registers serves only to amplify the absurd comedy of the theft. While Barbary's recent history of resistance, incarceration, and abuse has robbed her of a sense of political rights and responsibilities, the episode registers that dispossession as comic delinquency.

This scene in the Highlands is typical of a novel that, though regularly noted as one of Macaulay's strongest, has proven resistant to totalizing interpretations. The novel is most immediately noteworthy for Macaulay's ability to capture the wasted landscape of postwar London with a sinuous prose that sprawls like the ruinous city itself. Macaulay seemed to envision this reception when, in a 1952 letter to her friend and confessor the Reverend J.H.C. Johnson, she called the novel "a meditation on Ruin, physical and material" (*Letters to a Friend* 300). As she indicated in an earlier letter, Macaulay also aimed to convey the metaphorical meanings of material destruction: "*The World My Wilderness*," she wrote to Johnson in August 1950, "is about the ruins of the City, and the general wreckage of the world that they seem to stand for. And about a rather lost and strayed and derelict girl who made them her spiritual home" (*Letters to a Friend* 27).

In line with Macaulay's invocation of "the general wreckage of the world," recent critics have read Barbary's plight as the distillation of broader patterns of postwar crisis. Lyndsey Stonebridge notes that Macaulay invests her protagonist with the guilt of the age, forcing her to bear "the moral failings of the wartime generation" through her trauma-induced criminality (*Writing* 96). In this reading, Barbary's criminality is an expression of what Stonebridge calls "hope perverted," the desire of young people for a better moral universe in the wake of war. Ultimately, however, the novel can only gesture towards this better moral universe, without quite bringing it to fruition (*Writing* 98–9). Leo Mellor reads Macaulay's fascination with ruins as an explicit endorsement of the modernist yearning to establish order out of fragments; London's patches of wilderness become what he calls "zones of possibility" for Barbary and for the reader insofar as they offer models of regeneration and renewal born of chaos (Mellor 174). Beryl Pong has connected the ruins of the city to the question of Barbary's development as a protagonist on the cusp of adulthood. In Pong's assessment, the ruptured geography of the city and Macaulay's distorted take on the *Bildungsroman* represent twin symptoms of the imperilled futurity of the immediate postwar period (92–3).

While Pong's reading of the novel offers tantalizing claims about the tensions between Barbary's regressive personality and the *Bildungsroman* tradition, her commitment to spatial analysis leaves only so much room for considerations of a novelistic form and its relation to national belonging. This essay seeks to deepen and complicate the connections between *The World My Wilderness*, the *Bildungsroman* tradition, and the plight of children displaced by the war. The comic scene of a traumatized egg thief illuminates two related problems central to *The World My Wilderness*. On the one hand, the novel asks whether the adolescent traumatized by war can be successfully reintegrated into a peacetime society whose codes – juridical, cultural, familial, and sexual – have been all but effaced during her experience living under Nazi and Vichy rule. Simultaneously, *The World My Wilderness* asks through which genres, and in which registers, the novel as a literary form can express the wartime traumas that catalyze its plot. Although Macaulay's novel bears important traits associated with a modernist aesthetic – an aesthetic that is historically bound up with the psychic and social ruptures of war – it embeds those traits within a predominantly realist narrative of family tensions and adolescent development. This is a fiction of demobilization, both social and generic: its struggle to fit the traumatized child maquis into peacetime society is coterminous with its struggle to represent her damaged psyche within the genre of the realist novel of individual development. The severity of Barbary's wartime experiences – and, by extension, those of Europe – makes them difficult, if not impossible, to integrate within the frame of a popular, coming-of-age novel.

The vexed integration of Barbary, as representative figure for war-damaged youth, into the novel and into British society at large complements recent investigations into the relationship between rights, citizenship, and the novel. If, as Joseph Slaughter has argued, the European novel – and the *Bildungsroman* in particular – evolved in tandem with Enlightenment notions of the rights-bearing individual, and if both novel and rights suffered concomitant upheavals at mid-century, then Barbary's failure to adhere to the laws governing postwar British society indicates a kind of civic and characterological illegibility brought about by the breakdown of legal personhood in occupied France (Slaughter 4, 15). Stuck between nations, between narrative genres, and between war and its aftermath, Barbary embodies the difficulties inherent in the postwar rehabilitation of delinquent youth. Macaulay's tenuous embrace of the war-damaged child within a form unsuited to her containment foregrounds the limits of textually representing wartime trauma.

Familial Networks, International Politics

Macaulay's novel builds its allegory of national and individual development by insistently connecting micro-level interpersonal dynamics with the larger wartime and postwar socio-political landscape of Europe. Before the war, Helen left her English husband, a barrister by the name of Sir Gulliver Deniston. Shortly after her arrival on the Mediterranean coast, she met Maurice Michel. By the time of the German invasion, they had settled in Collioure with Barbary and Maurice's son by another marriage, Raoul. Over the course of the war, Maurice and Helen marry and have a son named Roland. Maurice and Helen thrive under Nazi-occupied France, because Maurice "collaborated mildly but prosperously from 1940 to 1945" (8). His collaboration is depicted as a casual acquiescence to the realities of the occupation: "Maurice ... had done business with the Germans, had them to his house, rendered them services, accepted their presence with a cheerful, contemptuous shrug. They had won, France had lost; it was the fortune of war; what would you have?" (28). Maurice never actively betrayed anyone during the occupation – "not so much as one Jew," says the local abbé (155) – and he even sheltered escaped Allied prisoners on their way from France to neutral Spain. Nevertheless, Maurice's cozy relationship with the forces of occupation marks him as a collaborator; he is killed during the brief and violent swirl of retribution that followed the German exodus from France. He becomes one of ten thousand French citizens executed extra-judicially in the wake of the Allied landings at Normandy, and before a judicial process for punishing collaborators took hold (Judt 42).

This history of familial relocation, collaboration, and compromise serves as backstory to the novel. In the narrative present of 1946, Barbary and Raoul live under the shadow of an unexpressed accusation: Helen suspects that they were directly or indirectly involved in Maurice's execution. Though only teenagers, they spent the war aiding the Resistance, engaged in what the narrator calls "well-meant, if somewhat jejune … activities in the juvenile fringes of the maquis" (8). In the words of Barbary's Uncle Angus, a psychologist, they had "a rather ungoverned bringing up," the habits of which she and Raoul have refused to abandon (120). When asked by her visiting eldest son, Richie, exactly what kind of trouble Barbary and Raoul engage in, Helen answers frankly: "Annoy the gendarmerie and the local authorities. Steal when they can; trespass on private property; sabotage motor cars; molest their fellow citizens" (12). Their continued acts of theft, sabotage, and petty criminality on behalf of the maquis become the pretext under which Helen sends the children away from her and away from France, a means of exiling them until their guilt can be assessed, or perhaps because it never will be. Both go to London: Barbary lives with her father in his well-appointed terrace house, while Raoul lives with his aunt and uncle. But it is in the ruins around the Church of St Giles Cripplegate that the bulk of the novel takes place. Alienated by cold and orderly London, Barbary and Raoul forge a life amid the rubble, stealing and consorting with army deserters and good-time girls who form what Barbary imagines to be a maquis of their own in the ruins. Barbary's continued intransigence puts her at odds with her law-and-order father, Sir Gulliver Deniston, K.C., a model of upright, if chilly, British common law and common sense. Barbary herself reflects that she and her father would never see eye to eye. "He stood for law and order and the police, she for the Resistance and the maquis, he for honesty and reputability, she for low life, the black market, deserters on the run, broken ruins, loot hidden in caves. All the wild, desperate squalor of the enfants du maquis years – would he even believe it if she told him? His clever, cultured, law-bound civilisation was too remote" (84). As this overview makes clear, *The World My Wilderness* maps the tensions of postwar political life onto a single extended family. Political disagreements between collaborator and saboteurs, as well as between the forces of postwar order and residual wartime anarchy, take the shape of familial struggles. In framing geopolitics as household contretemps, the novel domesticates the traumas of the Second World War and thereby makes them legible for a British reading public whose own experience of the war, though sometimes brutal, differed in important ways from life on the Continent.

Crossing Borders

This familial focus applies to the migration of characters as well. At multiple levels, *The World My Wilderness* maps the movement of people across geographic and national boundaries. Especially during the war, they slip in and out of state affiliations. Barbary's older brother, Richie, fights in the British armed forces, is captured by German soldiers, escapes across France, passes through Collioure on his way to neutral Spain, and returns to France as a victor following the landings at Normandy. Helen and Maurice's home serves as a node in the network by which individuals and information circulate during the war; it accommodates Vichy officials as easily as it does Richie. For her part, Helen attempts to drift apolitically through wartime and postwar turbulence in France; claiming no ideological affiliation, she prefers to immerse herself in gambling, reading, and forging medieval Provençal poetry. Just as her name suggests Hellenic affiliations, the narrative describes her in classical terms: she is like "the Milo Venus," her "neck a strong, rounded column" (17). Macaulay hints that even objects of classical beauty cannot escape politicization. "In a Greek-Iberian head-dress with great studded ear-wheels," the narrator tells us, "she would have been, almost, the Lady of Elche" (17). This seemingly casual reference to the Lady of Elche encodes geopolitical implications: discovered in 1897 outside of Elche, near Alicante, Spain, this fourth-century BCE stone bust is considered a national treasure in Spain, one that provides evidence of the connections between ancient Iberia and the eastern Mediterranean. Soon after its discovery, the statue was sold to a French collector and displayed at the Louvre until 1941. In a telling collision of ideology and aesthetics, the statue's "tragic exile" came to an end through negotiations between Franco's victorious Nationalist government and the recently appointed Vichy regime in France (Moffitt 27; Bazin 71). Macaulay's interest in classical scholarship and her friendship with the classicist Gilbert Murray make it likely that she was aware of the finer implications of politically enabled traffic in cultural objects (LeFanu 228). Like the Lady of Elche, Helen represents the illusion of disinterested aestheticism, which cannot help but be swept up in larger currents of geopolitical exchange across borders.

Throughout her works and her personal life, Macaulay displayed a fascination with mobility, travel, and border crossing. Rosamond Lehmann described her as "forever in transit" (qtd in LeFanu 3), perhaps the by-product of an ungoverned upbringing that combined travel and unsupervised outdoor play in Italy, Cornwall, Wales, and Cambridge (Mellor 172–3). This interest in travel and national borders flourished in Macaulay's novels of the 1920s. In *Crewe Train* (1926), protagonist Denham Dobie evokes the romance of border crossing as though it were a magic spell: "Not all the nagging *douanes* and impatient queues of passengers could spoil it. Say frontier, frontier, frontier, ten times, and the word unlike most words so treated, still retains a meaning. Love, hate, friendship, virtue, vice, God – these become as sounding brass and tinkling cymbals, but frontiers remain" (*Crewe Train* 35–6). For all the persistence of frontiers, Macaulay felt intellectually invested in the problems and possibilities of international governance. She wrote a lighthearted novel of intrigue set at the League of Nations, *Mystery at Geneva* (1922), which manages to convey a feminist yearning for "full participation and agency in the work of governance" while emulating the conventions of the romance novel (Hankins 4). Her interest in the League persisted as political and humanitarian crises proliferated in the 1930s. In a letter to her sister Jean in December of 1934, she recognized the difficulty, as well as the urgency, of British intervention in the affairs of other states:

> "Justice" is, of course, a fine slogan. But, in such an unjust world, a dangerous one. I mean, how are we to bring it about, except by force, and force is the thing to avoid. What is the good, e.g., of the League of Nations Union shouting for justice for German Jews, socialists, and Democrats, or for Italian Democrats, or Russian bourgeoisie, or for Hungarians in Jugo-Slavia (though this they are doing) when it can't enforce it? Of course the League itself is working half its time on all these European things, oppressed minorities, etc., but the drawback is that no one seems to care twopence about the oppressed of other nations except us, except when they are of their own political party. So we get called busybodies: as, indeed, we are, and always have been. [...] I *think* it's a good thing, on the whole, though it makes us unpopular. (*Letters to a Sister* 63)

Despite the failures of the League to intervene effectively in the crises of the 1930s – Spain, Abyssinia, Germany – Macaulay continued to believe that some form of international governance could take shape. In November of 1940, at the height of the Blitz of London and some six months before her own flat was levelled by bombs, Macaulay wrote to Jean, "Gilbert Murray says *all* the machinery for political and economic federation after the war is in the League" (*Letters to a Sister* 118).

The totality of the upheavals of the Second World War would test all structures of international cooperation and ultimately yield new approaches and new organizations for the management of war victims. Through characters like Richie and Helen, *The World My Wilderness* captures the national and geographic scattering of those who have been displaced by the war; yet Barbary most clearly bears the burden of displacement. She travels to England against her will; she would above all else have preferred to continue living, and wreaking mild havoc, in the south of France. In this enforced return to a nation she does not claim as her own, Barbary becomes a stand-in – admittedly, a privileged one – for the millions of individuals displaced by the war. If the Second World War was often characterized as a war of movement rather than entrenchment, the establishment of peace required a large-scale movement of its own in the form of the migration of millions of people. Tony Judt estimates that between 1939 and 1943, Hitler and Stalin had collectively "uprooted, transplanted, deported and dispersed some 30 million people" (23). Some of these dispersed people were refugees, meaning they were homeless, stateless, and in need of resettlement. Others were categorized as displaced persons, meaning that they had, at least nominally, a national home to which they might return. For some, the process of return was easier than for others; 3.2 million displaced persons had found their way home by 2 July 1945. Of the 1.2 million French citizens found in Germany at the surrender, all but 40,550 had been repatriated by 18 June (Wyman 19).

Though she might like to return to France, Barbary must make do in London. In the absence of the Resistance-harbouring wilds of Collioure, she and Raoul take up the wastelands of central London as a new kind of native territory: "They surveyed the gaping shells, the tall towers, the broken windows into which greenery sprawled, the haunted, brittle beauty, so forlorn and lost in the wild forsaken secrecy of this maquis: it was their spiritual home" (57). Barbary's description of ruined London as a maquis indicates a linguistic slippage inherent in the term; a maquis was originally a kind of dry scrubland, typical of Corsica and the Mediterranean coast of France. During the Second World War, as fighters of the French Resistance took to hiding out in the countryside, they took on the name of their own environment (*OED*). The wasteland camouflages its occupants; the locus of resistance becomes a name for the resistor herself. "It had familiarity," the narrator says of London's ruinous landscape, "as of a place long known; it had the clear, dark logic of a dream; it made a lunatic sense, as the unshattered streets and squares did not; it was the country that one's soul recognised and knew" (61). These quotations represent only two of the many and rapturous descriptions of blitz damage that appear regularly throughout the novel. Through these repeated invocations of bombsites as maquis, Macaulay draws connections among the ruins of London, Barbary's war-troubled mind, and the plight of Europe after the war.

Children, Rights, Trauma

Unable to shake off the lessons of the war, Barbary seizes on the ruins of London as her "spiritual home" and "the country [her] soul recognizes" as a means of coping with her forcible removal from France. She was not alone in finding an odd familiarity and consolation in the places and patterns of wartime behaviour. In the wake of the war, psychologists and social scientists were actively concerned about the effects the war and its attendant deprivations would have on the youth of Europe. For children affected by the conflict, reintegration to a peacetime order could be especially difficult. Dorothy Macardle, Irish novelist and popular historian, detailed the difficulties of this process in *Children of Europe: A Study of the Children of Liberated Countries* (1949). Even four years after the cessation of hostilities, Macardle notes, the effects of the conflict were still poorly understood. "In ten years more will be known. All we know at present is that there are thousands upon thousands of children in Europe in whom desolation and unendurable memories are hardening into cynicism or despair, and that all that is being done to help them is not a hundredth part of what is crying out to be done" (11). Macardle takes pains to emphasize that war had eroded the most basic structures of trust upon which children normally build their relations to figures of authority. France "had become a place in which men seized children and carried them off and put them to death" (Macardle 184). The inculcated fear of adults, both French Vichy forces and German occupiers, left children with a pervading skepticism and a pointed lack of optimism about the future. The literal and figurative destruction of their homes led children to stick together and to turn away from adults; authorities at displaced-persons camps in postwar Europe described child gangs forged in the concentration camps that would not tolerate being broken apart, despite an apparent absence of affection among members. One observer noted, "they will fight, even kill, to protect a child of their group" (qtd in Wyman 96).

As this postwar commitment to self-protection at all costs indicates, one of the more deeply rooted effects of the Nazi disregard for pre-war ethical and juridical norms was a proliferation of lawlessness in the occupied nations. The subjects of occupation took it upon themselves to challenge the legal abuses of Nazism through their own, smaller forms of resistance; black markets, shirking, and wastage became, in the context of totalitarian oversight, the junior siblings of sabotage and assassination. As Tony Judt has put it, "to live normally in occupied Europe meant breaking the law" (36–7). A resistance to authority became the self-imposed duty not simply of many adults but of many children, who played a variety of roles within the broader European resistance movements, from bearing messages and training other children to carrying out attacks themselves (Wyman 90). With delinquency a matter of pride and honour during the occupation, postwar governments had to overcome an entrenched resistance to law and order; British police resorted to large-scale roundups of undocumented individuals suspected of petty criminality, while in France, a special juvenile court system was organized in the wake of the war to deal with unruly child survivors (Kynaston 112; Macardle 193).

The continued problems of juvenile delinquency in both countries stemmed from the sense of disenfranchisement fostered in children during the war. To be without rights under a stable legal regime is to be less than a full and complete human person, a condition which has important repercussions for individuals both real and fictional.

Drawing on Hannah Arendt's *The Origins of Totalitarianism* and her shorter 1945 essay "Stateless Persons," Joseph Slaughter has elaborated on the connections among statelessness, rights, and fiction in the postwar period. Slaughter underlines the paradox inherent in the rise of human rights discourse after the war: the concept of universal human rights imagines a natural, intrinsic state of being in which humans will be unequivocally free, and yet under current geopolitical systems this universal vision can only be granted through the nation-state (Slaughter 12). The postwar drafting of the Universal Declaration of Human Rights (UDHR) in 1948 could only address the massive human rights abuses of the war through the available language of international, rather than supranational, governance. In claiming a role for itself as the administrator of those universal rights, the UN legitimizes the rights of the individual only to the extent that it solidifies the claim of the nation-state over those individuals. Though *The World My Wilderness* makes no reference to the UDHR – to do so would be anachronous, given the 1946 setting of the novel – Barbary is nonetheless bound by the condition of statelessness in which she spent her early teenage years. Deprived of basic rights under Vichy, she has no corollary sense of her responsibilities to those others with whom she shares the polity. Her theft of money, food, and material goods while in the UK is done without malice, but also without consideration for those from whom she is stealing.

Although the novel does not mention the UDHR specifically, it does mention an important document that preceded and contributed to it. In his 1941 State of the Union Address, US President Franklin D. Roosevelt outlined what he called the Four Freedoms, which he took to be foundational tenets on which modern democracies are built and towards which the wider world must aspire: freedom of speech, freedom of worship, freedom from want, and freedom from fear. These freedoms were hailed by many in the Allied countries as a crucial statement of the aims for which they were fighting; Norman Rockwell completed a series of paintings inspired by the Four Freedoms, the BBC commissioned a series of radio broadcasts dramatizing them for British listeners, and they were partially codified in the Atlantic Charter of 1941 (Borgwardt 8–12). The drafters of the UDHR, including Eleanor Roosevelt, integrated Franklin Roosevelt's terms into the preamble. The passage in question specifically recalls the origins of the declaration in the horrors of the war: "disregard and contempt for human rights have resulted in barbarous acts which have outraged the conscience of mankind, and the advent of a world in which human beings shall enjoy freedom of speech and belief and freedom from fear and want has been proclaimed as the highest aspiration of the common people" (UDHR "Preamble," 2). While the drive to build a global consensus on the rights of the individual superseded Roosevelt's more modest pronouncement, the freedoms he outlined in 1941 remained foundational to the mid-century discourse of rights. Their movement beyond strict political or civil rights – the right to vote, for example – towards social and economic security set the pattern for further expansions of human rights under international law (Johnson 20–3).

In *The World My Wilderness*, these four freedoms appear twice. In the first instance, Barbary and Raoul spend time with a trio of outlaws – two army deserters and a shopgirl turned shoplifter – in the ruins. Horace, the thuggish leader of the three, pronounces on the "Fascism" of the British police and armed forces: "Let's see, what are those four footling freedoms we used to hear about – freedom to eat, freedom to speak, freedom to get about – what's the other? Freedom from fear, that's it. Well, who's going to have freedom from fear with those bleeding M.P.s snooping round after him?" (80). Horace's mangling of Roosevelt's four freedoms seems to indict them as fantasies, or as corruptible in the hands and minds of those who would abuse such concepts for their own interests. But this passage accomplishes two things: the reference to the "freedom to get about" mirrors one of Rose Macaulay's own critiques of the limits to mobility during the Second World War. In an undated wartime essay preserved with the Rose Macaulay papers at Trinity College, Cambridge, entitled "The Fifth Freedom: Getting About," Macaulay bemoans the increasing controls all governments put on their citizens during warfare. "To governments," she writes, "it does not matter that people should be allowed to be happy and free and go unmolested about their business but it does matter what they are up to; they must be watched lest they prove to be the wrong people in the wrong place or at the wrong time ... There may come a time when we need passports and visas to go from one county of Great Britain to another" ("The Fifth Freedom," 4). She specifically links British restrictions on the movement of its citizens in wartime with German persecution of Jews and South African persecution of black subjects; while vastly different in their degree of persecution, such limits on movement represent differing applications of a similar desire for control. No published version of this essay has been traced, and it appears not to have been broadcast on the BBC, to which Macaulay made occasional contributions from the 1930s to the 1950s. Whether made public or not, this essay indicates that Macaulay was thinking about the emergent discourse of human rights and its connection to the nation-state, and that she saw liberty of movement within and across national frontiers as a key determinant of free citizenship.

The other effect of Horace's imperfect interpretation of Roosevelt is that it paves the way for a later remark by Barbary's Uncle Angus, whom Barbary and her father visit in Scotland. Having been alerted to her theft of eggs from his neighbours, he confronts her in hopes of determining the cause of her antisocial behaviour. "Naturally," he begins, "the owner of land on which one is purloining must be regarded as an enemy. But you know where such aggression might land you? In a police court" (106). The narrator takes over from Uncle Angus: "A flicker passed over Barbary's impassivity. Fear, he noted, observing her. She was frightened of the police. She possessed no one of the four freedoms. Least of all, freedom of speech" (106). In this encounter between adult and adolescent, Macaulay marks, while modifying, an emergent discourse of rights focused on the traumas suffered by the victims of war. Uncle Angus transforms the conventional understanding of "freedom of speech" from the freedom to participate in the expression of ideas in the public sphere to a more basic act of articulation. Any extension of the self into the world could be dangerous. To speak is to risk confession, betrayal, and punishment; it has little to do with the projection of a public persona. Still less does speech appear, for Barbary, to be a means of accessing and expressing her own memories.

The dislocations of war affect not only Barbary's status as a fictional psyche imagined to be accessible to herself, a simulated human, but also our ability as readers to access her as a fully rounded character. For all that Barbary serves as our paragon of childhood war trauma – indeed, because of that trauma – she remains a difficult character to read. Macaulay's rendering of the war-damaged adolescent involves relentless deflections of any attempt to plumb the exact nature of her experiences and her own understanding of them. Other characters view her as a mentally underdeveloped, unintelligible bearer of wartime traumas. Sir Gulliver's second wife, Pamela, says Barbary "hasn't the wits" for the gambling that has taken in her mother; the crooks hiding out in the ruins of London alongside Barbary and Raoul see them as "nuts. But harmless" (72). In Barbary's first appearance in the novel, she is presented as delayed, childlike, with "something defensive, puzzled, wary about her, like a watchful little animal or savage" (14). From time to time she appears about to revisit some aspect of her wartime experience, only to suppress the memory. When her Uncle Angus asks her to consider telling him about her wartime experiences as a means of breaking the cycle of delinquency, she balks at the return of repressed memories:

> She admired him; she felt what the patients in his consulting room no doubt felt, that to talk to him would bring a fatal ease, an end to concealment ... So she had felt before, years before (how many years? Two?) when keen eyes had searched her, questioning, demanding answers, trying persuasion before threats, before pain ... But before pain she had told nothing; it was during pain, after pain, that she had spoken, and told – what? Darkness rolled in on memory and mind, a confused, saving oblivion, swinging shut a door. (107)

The door that, in shutting, temporarily saves Barbary from the pain of remembering, serves to shut the reader out as well. She is opaque before any attempts at psychoanalysis. It would be convenient if this psychological opacity were simply the result of shortcomings on Macaulay's part, who, at least earlier in her career, was thought to be more interested in flippant character sketches than psychological depth. But other characters, including Helen, Richie, and Sir Gulliver, are given interior monologues that betray a more typically novelistic complexity of thought, and more importantly a direct readerly access to those thoughts; Barbary alone displays no equivalent transparency.

Barbary's traumatic shutting down of memories is most complexly rendered when she is propositioned by Jock, a denizen of the London ruins. Jock sees sex as a natural and pleasurable pursuit for two young outlaws. Barbary demurs. She calls sex "that stupid thing" and describes it as "silly and uncomfortable" (75). When Jock asks if she has even had any sexual experiences, she does not respond. In lieu of disclosure by Barbary, the narrative provides a brief and disjointed view of her memories from France:

> She was silent; she would not tell him. A thin, fair young face, the face of the enemy, the harsh, broken French of the conqueror, the smell of the forest in October, of wild apples and wood fires and heath ... later the maquis had killed him ... No one had known. They knew that she had been caught by the Germans, beaten a little, released with a warning. They did not know that she had met again in the forest the one who had ordered her to be beaten and released; met him three times, and the third time it was a trap. They had only known of the trap, and had praised her for her cunning. (77)

The passage marks a stylistic shift in the narrative: there is a sudden proliferation of parataxis, as impressions hang suspended without a clear order or hierarchy. The phrasing elides key details and therefore resists clear interpretation. She was "beaten a little," then released for unnamed reasons. Her subsequent meetings with the German soldier are not expanded upon; it is unclear who instigated them, and exactly what occurred in the first two meetings, before Barbary set her trap. The reader is left to puzzle whether Barbary felt, and acted upon, a desire for the human representative of her wartime oppression, or whether she was sexually assaulted. It is possible that the truth lies somewhere in between: under the pressures of war, she found herself dragged into the kind of sexually and ethically murky human contact that flourishes under conditions of political occupation. Whatever her initial thoughts on meeting the German soldier, Barbary commits herself bodily to the Resistance by turning a potential liaison into a political execution.

The Limits of the *Bildungsroman*

Beyond the fact of her assistance to the maquis with matters of theft and minor sabotage, Barbary's traumatic wartime experiences are never described in detail. For the most part, they serve as a murky justification for an otherwise obtuse insistence on perpetuating wartime resistance in the rapidly stabilizing British welfare state. This murkiness results in an uncanny sense of readerly detachment from Barbary, the character whose experiences ought to make her the most sympathetic in the novel. The ultimate limitation on her richness as a character may lie in her total lack of transformation over the course of the novel. This runs counter to Macaulay's other protagonists, most of whom, as Alice Crawford notes, struggle throughout their respective novels to achieve some form of compromise between their desires for self-actualization and the constraints imposed by external, social factors (112–13). Barbary never grows up; in this sense, as Beryl Pong has argued, *The World My Wilderness* is a distorted version of the conventional *Bildungsroman* (104–6). In Franco Moretti's formulation, the *Bildungsroman* is the genre through which the ideals of self-determination and socialization come to a kind of resolution; the classical novel of development traces the increasing alignment between individual self-fulfillment and social usefulness, arriving finally at what Moretti calls "the comfort of civilization" (15–16). While Moretti insisted that the *Bildungsroman* effectively collapsed with its earliest modernist incarnations, recent criticism has sought to map the evolution of the novel of development in an age in which national identifications are not as easily correlated with personhood. Slaughter has argued that one cannot reach the "comfort of civilization" in the absence of one's participation as a rights-bearing citizen of a political entity. "Both human rights law and the *Bildungsroman*," he writes, "posit the nation-state as the highest form of expression of human sociality and the citizen as the highest form of expression of human personality" (96). Read in this way, Barbary slips through the plot of the *Bildungsroman* precisely because of her non-integration with a conventional nation-state. An outlaw in France, she has not learned to subdue her rebelliousness in favour of integration with the more benevolent postwar welfare state; she is a socially disruptive force, unbound by responsibilities because unaccustomed to rights. Still stuck at an early stage of characterological development, she remains opaque to readers. The traumatic effects of occupation and resistance therefore appear to readers not only as Barbary's non-integration into civil society, but also as the non-fulfillment of a narrative expectation – the expectation of development towards a socially sanctioned form of adult personhood.

In linking the collapse of national structures of identification to the collapse of nation-centric forms of narrative, *The World My Wilderness* becomes what Jed Esty has called a metabildungsroman. Focusing on modernist novels whose protagonists' development stalls or is thwarted at the intersection of the metropole and its imperial periphery, Esty argues that twentieth-century novels of development chart the breakdown of the unity between self and nation that had characterized the *Bildungsroman* (6). But rather than reverse or destroy completely the arc of characterological and national development, the metabildungsroman critiques it from within, "laying bare the contingent elements of a progressivist genre formed inside the framework of the nineteenth-century European nation-state" (13). Although Esty's main concern is with the threat posed to a nation-based genre by imperialism and global capitalism, his argument might be extended to the breakdown of national affiliation in the wake of another total crisis: during the Second World War, the disruption of rights and the displacement of traumatized political subjects opens up another vein for critique of the *Bildungsroman*. *The World My Wilderness* therefore fails as a novel of development because its protagonist cannot move towards Moretti's "comfort of civilization." Barbary cannot live within the nations that lay claim to her because she cannot identify with their political, legal, and social codes.

Macaulay's critique of the necessary developmental parallels between child, family, and nation coalesce in the final pages of the narrative. Barbary is caught shoplifting in London. A police chase ensues through the ruins that are her urban maquis. She falls into a deep, exposed basement, injures herself badly, and passes into a coma. In the ensuing melodrama, Helen flies to London from France and takes a spare bedroom at Sir Gulliver's house, where Barbary is being treated. Once Barbary's recovery seems assured, her mother chides her for non-conformity: "Since you obviously don't know how to behave in Great Britain, I shall take you back to France" (230). Sir Gulliver, who has legal custody over Barbary, is harder to convince. He wants to send her to a British boarding school so that she might grow up to be a law-abiding member of society. As a final revelation designed to loosen Sir Gulliver's hold on Barbary, Helen informs him that Barbary is not, in fact, his child; she was fathered by a Spanish artist with whom Helen had a brief affair in 1928.

As Helen had hoped, Sir Gulliver's response is an immediate and total renunciation of any responsibility for Barbary. "I don't want ever to see her or hear of her again," he declares. "By all means take your Spanish daughter with you, and do exactly as you like with her; it has nothing to do with me" (247). His instant withdrawal of love and support is striking; having no biological connection to and no fiduciary responsibility for Barbary, he relinquishes any love born of the parenting he did in Barbary's first decade. In this regard, the novel draws a parallel between the rights of natural-born children to the protection of their parents and the rights of citizens born into the protection of a sovereign state. To some extent the narrative naturalizes Barbary's resistance to British life and laws, even as it illustrates the suffering inflicted on those displaced by the struggles of interwar and wartime Europe. Barbary has had little protection, support, or guidance from either parent, nor from the French, British, or Spanish governments; her development as a citizen, and as a character, has suffered. It has been, in all senses, a rather ungoverned bringing up.

At the close of the novel, Helen plans to take Barbary to Paris to study. Even at this late moment in the narrative, there is no indication that Barbary has transformed in any significant way. Helen intends to keep Barbary's Spanish ancestry a secret from her. Wherever she ends up, she will have only nominal ties to anyone or any place. Her future is not without possibility, but it holds little promise of emotional and psychological security. Unable to assimilate herself to the demands of postwar British life and of psychological realism, Barbary is exiled from the final chapter of what has been, up to this point, her story. Attention shifts to her brother Richie, the returned warrior who, at twenty-three, is firmly Tory and Anglo-Catholic. Though out of step with the emerging welfare state, he is prepared to move forward with the nation emerging out of the rubble. He surveys the wreckage around St Giles Cripplegate and imagines reconstruction: "Before long, cranes and derricks would make their appearance, sites would be cleared for rebuilding, tottering piles would be laid low, twisting flights of steps destroyed" (253). Whatever Britain's chances are at building something new, Barbary would only be out of place; indeed, she has already left the scene.

3

Not of National Importance: Sylvia Townsend Warner, Women's Work, and the Mid-Century Historical Novel

MELANIE MICIR

What do you do, as a self-sustaining writer of political and historical fiction, when your duty as a citizen conflicts with the rights you thought you had as an individual? What do you do when you find out that these rights might depend on whether you are married or not, whether you are a mother or not, whether you are, at least implicitly, a God-fearing, king-saving, heterosexual citizen – or not? How do you react when your government decides that your life's work is not, as Sylvia Townsend Warner puts it in a 1944 letter to Nancy Cunard, "of national importance" (*Letters* 84)? In *The Corner That Held Them*, Warner implicitly considers the precarity of civilian rights during wartime, especially the rights of women. Ostensibly a historical novel about fourteenth-century nuns, *The Corner That Held Them* nonetheless addresses conditions of life in England around 1945. Specifically, it speaks to women's work, the historicity of forgotten and insignificant people, and the place of queer individuals and couples within the nation. In order to show how Warner's novel is contemporary with the time of its writing, I will discuss the effect of Warner's national service – first voluntary, then mandatory – on her writing during the war; next, I will situate it alongside mid-century theorizations of the historical novel and contemporary theories of queer temporality; and, finally, I will read Warner's mid-century turn toward historical fiction alongside Carolyn Dinshaw's recent recuperation of amateurism. One reason that "the woman's historical novel" was almost completely left out of early and mid-twentieth-century theorizations of the genre is that it was too often considered amateurish or escapist (Wallace ix). Yet this so-called amateurism, I will argue, opens a productive way to read *The Corner That Held Them*.

Pithily described by Janet Montefiore as a "provincial lesbian communist" (39), Warner spent most of her life in Dorset, England, with her partner, the poet Valentine Ackland, and their several cats. Extremely prolific, she produced seven novels, one biography, fifteen collections of short stories, and a great number of pieces for the *New Yorker*, *Time and Tide*, and other publications. Several collections of her correspondence, two collections of poetry, and a few additional story collections have appeared since her death in 1978. Of the seven novels, five – everything published from 1929 onward – are usually considered historical fiction.

Warner suspected that *The Corner That Held Them* might be her best work, but it was not a bestseller, and it is virtually unknown today.[1] She herself wrote that she was nearly "incline[d] to call it People Growing Old. It has no conversations and no pictures"; as if that were not enough, she added, "it has no plot, and the characters are innumerable and insignificant" (qtd in Harman, "Introduction," v). In other words, between its historical distance and the banality of its formal difficulty, it is not fully or easily legible to us. It is only a slight exaggeration to describe this as a novel without a protagonist in which nothing really happens. It is a novel in which people grow old, slowly, from one year to the next, without much excitement or fuss, and which challenges its readers to accept its slow, chronicle-like pacing rather than racing through page-turning plot twists. For this reason, like so many of Warner's stealthily sexy novels but unlike many texts now considered mainstays of mid-century queer fiction, it was never scandalous. As Jane Garrity notes in *Step-Daughters of England*, "none of Sylvia Townsend Warner's texts that engage the conjunction of homoeroticism and Englishness were ever censored or denounced as notorious" (142), whether they were published before the *Well of Loneliness* was successfully prosecuted for obscenity in 1928, like *Lolly Willowes* in 1926 and *Mr. Fortune's Maggot* in 1927, or afterward, like *Summer Will Show* in 1936 or *The Corner That Held Them* in 1948. Despite the recent resurrection of much of the Warner canon through the NYRB Classics series, and despite the increasing frequency with which Warner appears in critical accounts of the British mid-century, ongoing interest in Warner's work has been sustained by a relatively small but dedicated audience of largely non-academic, "amateur" readers.[2]

The Corner That Held Them is both a wartime and a postwar novel. Starting in 1942, Warner worked on it intermittently for six years before it was eventually published in 1948. The novel chronicles the rise and near fall of a self-contained and secluded cloister of medieval nuns. It does not offer a particularly flattering portrait of the nuns or of anyone with whom they come into contact, and some early readers found the representation of the nuns irreverent and insulting.[3] Dedicated to Saint Leonard, the patron saint of prisoners, this ramshackle convent – Oby it is called – was founded to memorialize a twelfth-century adulteress who detested her husband. Moreover, Oby is located in the Fenlands, so the nuns who live there have even less contact with the rest of the world than might otherwise be expected. It is an insular community. Although the novel begins with the endowment and installation of Oby in the middle of the twelfth century, continues through the spread of the Black Plague and the beginning of the Hundred Years War, and ends sometime after the Peasants' Revolt of 1381, these major historical events register only as the nuns might have known them, namely in bits and pieces, distorted by rumour and speculation, transformed in the telling from one person to the next. For the most part, the nuns go about their daily routines and ignore the larger world. The virtue of women, the novel implies, leaves no historical trace:

> A good convent should have no history. Its life is hid with Christ who is above. History is of the world, costly and deadly, and the events it records are usually deplorable: the year when the roof caught fire, the year of the summer flood which swept away the haystacks and drowned the bailiff, the year when the cattle were stolen, the year when the king laid the great impost for the Scotch wars and timber for five years had to be felled to pay for it, the year of the pestilence. (7)

This list of impersonal events could continue indefinitely. The exploits of men – theft, war, and other "deplorable" events – are recorded in this history "of the world, costly and deadly," but the daily, domestic lives of women are all but forgotten.

This may be why Warner emphatically denied that *The Corner That Held Them* should be considered a "historical novel" at all. She explained in a letter to her friend Paul Nordoff that, although she set the novel in the English past, it simply could not be a historical novel because "it hasn't any thesis" (*Letters* 79). She worked hard to keep it free of what she called the "arthritis of antiquarianism" (qtd in Harman, "Introduction," vii). Yet this authorial protest has not stopped critics from reading it as both a historical and an allegorical novel. For example, Jenny Hartley builds an explicit analogy between the culture of fear governing fourteenth-century Oby and twentieth-century England. After describing the nuns' perpetual fear of "labour shortages, bad weather and unfriendly bishops" (46) alongside the larger threats of the Black Death and the Peasants' Revolt, she cites a diary entry from 1940 in which Warner explicitly claimed that "people here [in England] would be much more frightened if the Germans were the Black Death. Then the news the Black Death has arrived in Rouen, is in the Channel Ports, has appeared in Paris, would set people thinking: 'Soon I may catch it and die'" (qtd in Hartley 47). For Hartley, Oby "represents the beleaguered fortress of England in war, simultaneously sanctuary and prison" (47). As Montefiore has argued, however, *The Corner That Held Them* "differs politically from [Warner's] previous historical novels," which "belong to the genre of the politicized historical novel in which contemporary writers engaged with present conflicts through a semi-allegorical return to the past" (49). This novel is different from Warner's earlier work, but it does engage with contemporary conflicts. Just as it is impossible to read *Summer Will Show* without reference to both Warner's love affair with Ackland and their involvement in the Spanish Civil War, the medieval nuns in *The Corner That Held Them* cannot be separated from their provincial counterparts during the Second World War.

Citizenship, Women's Work, and the Question of National Belonging

Written by a woman who is avowedly interested in what links this fourteenth-century community of women with postwar Britain, *The Corner That Held Them* is not a strict historical novel – or, at least, it is not only a historical novel. Events unfold slowly; the plot plods along from one year to the next. Focused on an obscure community of women, the novel is unconcerned by History with a capital H. Relatively insignificant characters bide their time in an out-of-the-way convent. Yet Oby is an imaginatively reconstructed portrait of an insular, aging community during an era of intense social change. As Wendy Mulford and Jenny Hartley have suggested, Warner's historical novel mirrors the period of social and economic transition that England experienced in the mid-twentieth century. What some early readers found to be a rather disrespectful representation of a religious order is also a darkly funny indictment of the time that Warner spent in her own obscure community of women while she volunteered for the Women's Volunteer Service (WVS) during the war.

The WVS was founded in 1938 in order to assist civilians during and after air raids. It still exists as the Royal Voluntary Service, though its services greatly expanded in the postwar years. By 1943, the WVS had over a million volunteers and was "involved in almost every aspect of wartime life from the collection of salvage to the knitting of socks and gloves for merchant seamen."[4] Beginning early in the war, Warner volunteered twice each week at the Dorchester chapter of the WVS, which was primarily occupied with the task of organizing rest centres for urban evacuees (Harman, *Sylvia Townsend Warner* 185–6). As many critics have noted, Warner's interactions with other local women volunteering in the WVS and other civil service organizations during this time fuelled her keen observations of the relationships between ambitious, yet relatively powerless, women in *The Corner That Held Them*. In one exasperated letter to Nordoff, she wrote, "It is becoming my belief that if our local villages were invaded, nobody would have time to notice the enemy, they would all be too busy taking sides over Mrs Tomkins and Mrs Bumpkin" (*Letters* 80). Rather than remaining focused on the larger historical fact of war, the women surrounding Warner in the WVS were primarily attentive to smaller, more local concerns.

For Warner, at home in rural England during the war, the horror of war was "tantamount to the horror of boredom ... being compelled to attend to things that don't interest one" (qtd in Mulford 150). She felt that there was no place in the war effort for her particular talents as a writer and intellectual, and, especially in contrast to her earlier work during the Spanish Civil War, it frustrated her to have so much of her time taken up with the often ineffective and only questionably necessary activities of the WVS. Comparing the two wartime environments, she mused: "Strange how there was room for one in that war: and in this – none. This war has not issued a single call for the help of intellectuals. It is just – your money and/or your life" (*Diaries* 106). If, as philosopher Étienne Balibar has claimed, citizenship may be understood "in its strict sense as the full exercise of political rights and in its broad sense as cultural initiative or effective presence in the public space (the capacity to be 'listened to' there)" (724), it is clear that Warner felt like a second-class citizen during the war. As both a woman and an intellectual, she was not fully "listened to" in the public sphere, which demanded only her "money and/or [her] life." For Balibar, "the exercise of citizenship appears inseparable from belonging to a nation" (726). By contrast, Warner's inability to contribute meaningfully to the war effort through her writing added to the distance she sometimes felt from her English compatriots.

Nonetheless, she and Ackland managed to continue their literary work, however sporadically, alongside volunteer shifts until changing wartime national service laws required them, as legally single women, to take up work of national importance.[5] There were several possible exemptions from this mandatory national service, including students, the elderly, clergy, blind people, married women of child-bearing age, and women who had children under fourteen years old living at home with them. Nearing fifty years old, Warner was exempt from this required war work (for the time being), but Ackland, who was nearly thirteen years younger, was not. And since they were not officially married, and they did not have any children, she had no choice but to begin a regime of daily work in the local office of the Territorial Army, where she was, in Warner's outraged words, "surround[ed] with ugly faces and loud voices and hearts like linoleum" (Harman 199). The work was tedious and unfulfilling – hardly satisfying for a poet or intellectual – but Ackland could not request a different position without risking a transfer that might take her a great distance away from the life she shared with Warner. As a legally single, unattached woman, she could be transported virtually anywhere in the country. The impossibility of being considered a legitimate couple in the eyes of the state infuriated Warner, who had publicly referred to Ackland as her "wife" for many years. As she wrote to Cunard, "If I had taken myself a husband, lived on him and made his life a misery (as undoubtedly I should have done, as no man has ever been able to bear me as a continuity) I should not be troubled with any of this. Being kept by a husband is of national importance enough. But to be femme sole, and self-supporting, that hands you over, no more claim to consideration than a biscuit" (*Letters* 84). Had Warner married, or had Ackland remained in the misguided marriage of her early youth, the state would have recognized their domestic, procreative work as wives and mothers as the adequate, honourable fulfillment of national duty. And while Warner's age allowed her to avoid compulsory war work during the early years of the war and focus all her rage on the unjust treatment of Ackland, she, too, was eventually given a part-time job as a secretary-dispenser to a local doctor in early 1944, which meant that she had less time for both the WVS and her own writing. There had been "no call for intellectuals," and her writing – even writing explicitly about the war – was not recognized as legitimate work.

Warner's responses to the emergency infringement of civil liberties during wartime overlap with her reaction to the patriarchal system of values behind the labour laws set in place during the war. Other prominent intellectuals also questioned why writers should not be counted among those serving the nation; in 1941, a manifesto entitled "Why Not War Writers?" appeared in the fourth issue of *Horizon*. Demanding special wartime exemptions for creative writers – like the exemptions already granted to journalists – the manifesto was endorsed by Cyril Connolly, George Orwell, Stephen Spender, and others. The petition failed to garner widespread support. Similarly, Warner's and Ackland's work as writers was not deemed to be "of national importance," but Warner's frustration at this lack of state-sponsored respect for intellectual and artistic work was compounded by her sense that their queerness was also being punished. To the state, the importance of their writing paled in comparison to the reproductive work of wives and mothers.

Angered by this legalized heteronormativity, Warner thus began work on a book that sidelines the very notion of national importance – a book that would "have no history." In *The Corner That Held Them*, world-historical events and people deemed to be important to the nation are not central to the narrative. They are scarcely present at all. The nuns fear the Black Plague, but those fears live and die within a single chapter; the fraudulent priest infected with the plague eventually recovers. The Hundred Years War approaches obliquely through a series of spoken complaints about rising taxes, as when a rector exclaims that "Kings should pay for their own wars, [as] it was too much to ask the poor man both to fight in the king's armies and to pay for them" (271–2). The Peasants' Rebellion, passing the monastery, leaves behind only a few broken windows. Historical information is generally absent – or obscured – from the narrative. "If more deeds of heroism could just fall flat," Warner wrote during the war, "there would be more hope for humanity" (*Letters* 80). In *The Corner That Held Them*, she refuses to include "deeds of heroism," just as she refuses to include anything like a heroic protagonist or plot arch. In this regard, she rebuffs the dominant wartime narratives of derring-do, escape, and heroic triumph. Warner even refuses to recognize heroes: "How often must I tell you," intones one prioress, "that I am not concerned with individuals?" (18). Embedded in the concept of the individual, the heroic is nowhere to be found in a narrative decentralized through the steady proliferation of protagonists. The national interest, reconceived not as heroics but as collective action, is most fully served by a group of undifferentiated women who go about their routines of daily life.

While she and Valentine were compelled, as committed but not legally married wives with no children at home to tend, to perform work "of national importance," Warner found time, here and there over the years, to defy this government command by writing this chronicle of cloistered old women who are powerless and nearly forgotten. "Why do I write about old people when I write about war," she wondered in her diary. "Because they have more independence, a freer play of reaction? – or because it seems, down here, so much an old persons' war?" (*Diaries* 119). In writing about the old women of fourteenth-century Oby while war ravaged twentieth-century Britain, she was writing about both independence and seclusion in a queer community of medieval women. These women are queer in that they are both non-reproductive and non-productive by vocation *and* by choice. They are non-reproductive because they are nuns; they will neither marry nor have children. They are non-productive because, in addition to the ever-increasing age of their population, which Warner stresses throughout the novel, the religious work to which they devote themselves is not valued by the surrounding community. As one poor traveller to Oby exclaims:

> You will stir your white fingers for God's altar, but when did you ever prick your fingers for God's poor? We go in rags. And you waste on one yard of your fancywork as much gold as would clothe and feed ten of us for a year's length. Where are the words of Christ, when he said, Clothe the naked? When do you sit down and spin for us? Spin! You cannot as much as spin for yourselves, you are not worth as much as spiders. (249)

Indeed, the nuns are so accustomed to hearing such accusations that they refer to themselves as "we idlers" and "us worthless nuns" (250). Like Warner's own work as a writer rather than a mother or a labourer in a munitions factory, the devoted artisanship of the nuns is not considered to be important work.

In this way, women's work is devalued from one century to the next. Even the nuns' supposed devotion to God does not exonerate them from the obligation to feed, clothe, and shelter men. In an angry tirade against medieval masculinity, one prioress complains that "all men are alike":

> If one asks a direct question they reply with a treatise. Edmund Gurney the mason had been just the same, wrapping himself in long discourses about the natures of different kinds of stone. That is how men are made, and that is what they expect women to put up with. Yet if she had failed to supply Sir Ralph with a dinner, replying to his hunger with a discourse on the breeding of cattle and the difference betwixt beef and mutton, he would scarcely be contented. Beef and mutton, clothing and firing, that is the life-work for a prioress. Not souls. Not even spires. (94–5)

The reported value of women's work in a world run by men is "not worth as much as spiders." Even prioresses are not allowed to build churches or save souls.

Instead of a historical novel "of national importance," which would follow Georg Lukács's formula for a staged interaction between world-historical events and the lives of regular working folk, Warner offers a defence of the "femme sole," a sustained representation of a single community dominated, though not entirely controlled, by women. She explores how such a community functions economically. What were the material conditions of this life? How did these nuns support themselves? How did they keep going when faced with a world that neither supported nor acknowledged them? In these questions is an understanding that a vocation, especially a woman's vocation – whether as a fourteenth-century nun or a mid-twentieth-century writer or something else entirely – must be economically viable. As Warner realized, economic viability does not always square with matters of national – or historical – importance.

Queer Peoplehood and the Historical Novel

As biographer Claire Harman points out, Warner was much more interested in "what links us with the fourteenth century than what separates us from it" ("Introduction," vii). In a 1939 lecture on "The Historical Novel," Warner emphasized the responsibility of the historical novelist to analyze the impact of changing material conditions upon what she understood to be an otherwise constant human nature. "Human nature," she claims, "does not change ... but human thinking alters a great deal, is conditioned by what it has been taught, what it believes, or disbelieves; what it admires in art or nature; at what age it marries ... what careers are open to it; whether it reads Aristotle or Plato; whether it believes in witches or planets" ("Historical Novel," 55). As an early material feminist, Warner is convinced that material conditions change human thinking (rather than human nature). If human nature does not change, then the past – with a bit of decoding – is always a recognizable past, a usable past, a past that can help us to understand the present and steer the way forward into the future. In sociologist Immanuel Wallerstein's theorization of "peoplehood," he understands "the temporal dimension of pastness" to be central to the idea of a people:

> Pastness is a mode by which persons are persuaded to act in the present in ways they might not otherwise act. Pastness is a tool persons use against each other. Pastness is a central element in the socialization of individuals, in the establishment of or

> challenge to social legitimation. Pastness therefore is preeminently a moral phenomenon, therefore a political phenomenon, always a contemporary phenomenon. (78)

The past is thus both preserved and adapted as it is passed down from one generation to the next, and histories of a shared past become markers of national belonging. For both Wallerstein and Warner, the past is always political. In *The Corner That Held Them*, Warner uses the past as "a tool" against her own contemporary moment as she lays claim to an alternate national past – a lineage of queer peoplehood – shared by both queer feminist women in the twentieth century and the fourteenth-century nuns of Oby.

In this empathy with those who lived centuries before her there is also a resonance with contemporary theories of queer temporality which seek to "touch across time" in order to imaginatively construct a kind of trans-historical queer community – or, in Wallerstein's terms, a queer peoplehood.[6] The nuns of Oby, isolated from national concerns and grand historical narratives, remain visible to Warner, a relative outsider in her own time. The same impulse to recognize a queer temporality that unites isolated people across centuries is operative in other historical fiction of the postwar, such as Marguerite Yourcenar's *Memoirs of Hadrian* (1951), about the Emperor Hadrian's love for Antinous, and Mary Renault's *The Last of the Wine* (1956), about a love affair between an ephebe and an older man in ancient Athens. For Warner, radical empathy across time distinguished her from people who, as she put it in a letter to a friend, "prefer their fourteenth century at a more gothic degree of perspective" (*Letters* 79). In her view, even the lost histories of the fourteenth century had to be legible, imaginable, and narratable.

If Warner did not think *The Corner That Held Them* was a historical novel because it had "no thesis," then what does that tell us about the kind of historical fiction she imagined writing? In a few passages, her theory of the genre sounds startlingly similar to the historical novel theorized by Lukács, who, in 1936–37, was building a theory of the genre upon the work of Sir Walter Scott. For Lukács, the classical form of the historical novel revolves around the lives of average, relatively minor characters who embody "historical-social types" (35), rather than famous, world-historical individuals. Any "hero" of Scott's, for example, is "a more or less mediocre, average English gentleman" (33).

According to Lukács, this English gentleman "generally possesses a certain, though never outstanding, degree of practical intelligence, a certain moral fortitude and decency which even rises to a capacity for self-sacrifice, but which never grows into a sweeping human passion, is never the enraptured devotion to a great cause" (33). With the protagonist as mediator, the historical novel stages the interactions between world-historical events and, in Fredric Jameson's later phrase, the "collectivity ... whose 'history' is here in question" (280). The genre depicts the epic transformation of social and political life in a progressive vision of the past that upholds, even while sometimes implicitly questioning, the historical necessity of the authorial present. The best historical novels thus allow readers to understand the past as "the prehistory of the present" (Lukács 53). In such a formulation, temporality is understood as teleological; it progresses towards and shapes the present.

Warner, too, imagines the historical novel to have an explanatory function. She wants the genre to be full of working-class rather than world-historical characters and inclusive of women rather than dominated by men. "When it comes to a piece of plain common sense," she argues in her lecture on "The Historical Novel," "it is the ruled who speak" (54). Common sense though this principle may be, it is hardly the norm that the ruled speak in historical fiction. Furthermore, in Warner's novels, as in her criticism, she emphasizes the significance of gender in the making of history. Gender, it must be said, is one of the serious blind spots in Lukács's theory of the historical novel. Scott's "more or less mediocre, average English gentleman" is still a man. As such, his outlook and position cannot be assumed to be universal; to narrate the prehistory of women's lives requires some knowledge – or at least imaginative speculation – about actual women's lives. The medieval nuns, as some of "the ruled who speak" in Warner's historical fiction, become part of the prehistory of twentieth-century British women's lives. And Warner herself, as a queer woman who chose to devote herself to a life of artistic production rather than biological reproduction, is positioned as the imaginative kin to the nuns of Oby.

The circumstances in which Warner wrote *The Corner That Held Them* indicate that she resisted commonplaces about historical fiction and mounted an oblique defence of the rights of women – particularly single female writers and artists – during wartime. In an interview given later in her life, Warner reflects that *The Corner That*

Held Them is her "most personal book probably," though she explains that she began writing it on "the purest Marxian principles":

> If you were going to give an accurate picture of the monastic life, you'd have to put in all their finances, how they made their money, how they dodged about from one thing to another and how very precarious it all was, how only the rich orders had any sort of financial security. The smaller houses just dodged about on the edge of the abyss: they were nearly always bankrupt, except just three or four and they were so rich that everyone wanted their money. But it's a strictly capitalist story. (qtd in Mulford 197)

This preoccupation with money pervades the novel. Religion appears inasmuch as the setting is a convent, but these nuns are nearly always too impoverished to be concerned with strict religious observance. They bend religious principles more often than they uphold them. "On the edge of the abyss," they just try to get by year in, year out. From prioress to prioress, under one bishop and then the next, they talk about money: how to keep it, how to raise it, and how, without substantially more of it, to maintain control of the peasants who live on the manor surrounding Oby. In one exchange, several nuns debate how they might stay on good terms with the peasants, "lest they should take part in the rebellions which were jumping up here, there, and everywhere, like a fire in the stubble":

> "There is one way [of pleasing people that is not costly]. We can teach their children. That would cost very little except time and trouble. People like you to make a fuss over their children, nothing pleases them so surely."
>
> "Teach them? Teach them what?"
>
> "Really, as little as you wish. A few hymn tunes, the names of the patriarchs, a little hearsay Latin, how to wipe their noses ... it is the attention that pleases, the learning is no matter." (243)

Pedagogical "attention" would stand in as currency for the nuns, except that education is immediately determined to be too dangerous. "If we teach them," another nun argues, "they will all go off the manor to become friars and clerks, nuns and jugglers, they will never stay at work once they begin to think themselves scholars" (243). And so it goes. Nothing happens. No one learns. Finances at the nunnery remain precarious.

Warner began this novel on "Marxian" principles; she called it a "strictly capitalist" story. Yet there is no major crisis, despite occasional reports of rebellion. Moreover, the threat of the Black Death is confined to a single chapter. The peasants outside Oby do not rise up and murder the nuns in their beds, as is sometimes feared. Instead, they cheat the nuns when possible and wise up in their negotiations over working conditions. Revolution happens elsewhere. At this half-forgotten monastery, everyone complains about their lot, yet, with precious few exceptions, everyone simply continues on, day by day, season by season. *The Corner That Held Them* is like a medieval version of *Waiting for Godot*. It is fundamentally about changelessness and temporal suspension. One prioress reflects on the life she has spent in a convent filled with old women: "And here I am, she thought, fixed in the same corner, always beleaguered by the same shadows; and in the end I shall burn out and another candle will be fixed in my stead" (80). Structurally, this book enacts the prioress's sense of tedious progression through time: the chapters move from the reign of one prioress to the next, and it is sometimes difficult to determine which is which, and when is when. The plot, such as it is, is not powered by reproductive time: neither the heteronormativity of the *Bildungsroman* nor the standard biographical structure of birth-education-marriage-children-inheritance-death have any purchase in the fictional world of Oby's nuns. This is why this peculiar historical novel, with its slow, circular, sometimes stalled temporal structure, is the genre in which Warner implicitly comments on both the value of women's work and the necessity of queer citizenship.

Amateurism, Obscurity, and Women's Writing

Just a few years earlier, Virginia Woolf called for novelists, historians, and biographers to take up the work of writing about the "extremely obscure" lives of women, particularly poor and working-class women. In a long endnote in *Flush*, her playful biography of Elizabeth Barrett Browning's cocker spaniel, Woolf demonstrates the "impossibility" of women's history. Writing about the Brownings' maid, Lily, she notes how intensely this figure "excites our curiousity and baffles it":

> Her Christian name was Lily, her surname Wilson. That is all we know of her birth and upbringing. Whether she was the daughter of a farmer in the neighbourhood of Hope End … or whether she was a Cockney; or whether she was from Scotland – it is impossible to say […]. Since English fiction in the 'forties scarcely deals with the lives of ladies' maids, and biography had not then cast its searchlight so low, the question must remain a question. (n6)

Professional, academic historians were only just beginning to develop interest in women's history, from the lives of medieval nuns to "the lives of ladies' maids."[7] And neither the novels nor the biographies of the mid-nineteenth century tended to investigate these obscure women's lives. From the intentionally marginalized position of a footnote, Woolf describes the difficult historical project that confronts her, Warner, and other women writers in the twentieth century: in the absence of an equivalent historical record, how can writers tell the stories of those unproductive citizens or gendered subjects deemed unimportant by the states in which they live?

The historical novel, given that it necessarily draws upon both fact and fiction, is one possible solution to this question of how to represent the lives of the obscure. The genre has been taken up throughout the century precisely by those who need to write themselves – and their ancestors, both biological and affiliative – back into a historical record that has excluded them. As Wallace demonstrates, "women writers turned to the historical novel at the beginning of the century, at a moment when male writers were moving away from the genre, with the result that it has come to be seen as a 'feminine' form, a view damagingly reinforced by its association with the 'popular'" (3). This explanation goes some way toward explaining why Warner's five historical novels suffer from relative critical neglect, especially in comparison with the reception Woolf's work has long received: general lack of interest in the historical novel, Wallace argues, has led "directly to the marginalization of Warner" (70).

Warner shared Woolf's interest in the "extreme precariousness" of women's lives. She chose to live in the country rather than the bustling modernist metropolis. She hardly flinched when her work was associated with "the feminine," "the popular," or even "the provincial," as long as it kept the bills paid. Her writing was her livelihood, at least until the state determined that it was not "of national importance." Despite her status as a professional, self-supporting writer, Warner's chronicle of the lives of a group of cloistered women, especially given their historically illegible lives, required her to become something of an amateur medievalist.[8] I use "amateur" not as a pejorative word, but in the spirit of Carolyn Dinshaw's recuperation and celebration of "amateurism."

Dinshaw suggests that the amateur "operat[es] outside regimes of detachment governed by uniform, measured temporality" (5). Furthermore, the amateur works from the position of "affect and attachment" (5) rather than specialization, professionalization, and detachment. One of her examples is Hope Emily Allen, the first modern editor of the *Book of Margery Kempe* and a near contemporary of Warner's. Dinshaw characterizes Allen as an amateur both because she "worked outside of the academy" and "because of the particular bond of contemporaneity she felt with Margery" (108–9). Allen's "particular bond of contemporaneity" with Margery is strikingly similar to Warner's sense that there was far more connecting her with the nuns of Oby than separating her from them. Allen and Warner share a devotion to the recovery of women's lives – whether archivally or imaginatively reconstructed. Official histories and what would later come to be considered "real" historical novels did not represent women's lives, so these two women – relative amateurs though they might have been – decided to take up the challenge. There is something deeply admirable, in this reading, about the amateur, the off-centre researcher, and the unrecognized devotee.

Amateurism often implies a lack of access to knowledge, services, resources, and even rights, while professionalism indicates the accumulation and recognition of specialized education and training. But which group – amateurs or professionals – should hold the power to shape historical narrative, to construct and wield the pastness of a people? Dinshaw asks us to consider the possibility that amateurism brings an undervalued affective charge to the writing of history. The amateur feels the "bond of contemporaneity" with, and attachment to, her subject that the professional has been trained to dismiss. In this sense, the women's historical novel is a form of amateur history that is also a corrective history. And the queer women's historical novel, in particular, is a revision of the past that builds a sense of belonging, a sense of queer "peoplehood," in the contemporary moment.

Dinshaw's reading of amateurs "operating in off-hours," out of love rather than professional obligation, equally applies to Warner's wartime work on *The Corner That Held Them*: expansive, ambitious, undertaken out of attachment, squeezed in around other obligations and what she called an "endless series of interruptions, distractions, and destructions" during the war. As readers, we should continue to read this novel on the model of the amateur by taking seriously these intimate, affective attachments rather than matters of specialized, professional, or national importance.

NOTES

1 In a diary entry on 15 January 1945, approximately three years after she began work on the novel, Warner reported: "Sometimes I suspect that I am writing my best book, but we do not seem to notice it" (*Diaries* 127).

2 As one recent reviewer noted in *The Telegraph*, Warner's novels have "gone on commanding the attention of a small public" (Hensher) over the course of the twentieth and twenty-first centuries. For examples of Warner's presence in recent accounts of mid-century British literature, see Kristin Bluemel, ed., *Intermodernism: Literary Culture in Mid-Twentieth-Century Britain* (2009); Jane Garrity, *Step-Daughters of England: British Women Modernists and the National Imaginary* (2003); Jenny Hartley, *Millions Like Us: British Women's Fiction of the Second World War* (1997); Phyllis Lassner, *British Women Writers of World War II: Battlegrounds of Their Own* (1998); Heather Love, *Feeling Backward: Loss and the Politics of Queer History* (2007); and Gill Plain, *Women's Fiction of the Second World War: Gender, Power and Resistance* (1996).

3 In response, Warner insisted that her depiction of convent life was accurate, if not overly generous: "Even allowing for a perceptible male bias against houses of women … the evidence of contemporary ecclesiastical records makes it inescapably plain that the monastic establishments (of either sex, but we will keep to nunneries) displayed all the characteristic faults of community living – as well as grosser faults. On this evidence I could have made Oby a much worse place, and still have had the support of contemporary ecclesiastics" (qtd in Harman, "Introduction," viii).

4 For more information about the history of the Royal Voluntary Service, see the "Our History" page on their website: http://www.royalvoluntaryservice.org.uk/about-us/our-history.

5 The Emergency Powers (Defence) Act, first passed in 1939 and expanded during later years of the war, allowed the government to pursue whatever domestic regulations it deemed necessary for the war effort. According to Roger Broad's history of conscription in Britain, "when war came there were 1.6 million men and women enrolled for all forms of civil defence, but the pattern was patchy and this total was 400,000 less than required ... Even the Battle of Britain and the Blitz the following winter did not produce enough volunteers and from January 1941 compulsion began to be applied. Defence Regulations 26A, 27A, and 27B gave the Minister of Home Security power to compel men and women to undertake part-time civil defense duties ... Use of the Defence Regulations was followed in April by an NSA that extended to men and women the obligation to undertake some form of National Service" (223–4). For further information about how these new wartime laws changed daily life for Warner and Ackland, see Harman's biography of Warner (190–200).

6 For discussions of queer temporality, see Dinshaw et al. Also see Freeman.

7 Cambridge historian Eileen Power's pioneering *Medieval English Nunneries* (1922) was the first academic monograph to engage the social history of these nunneries. Several earlier studies had already dealt with the subject of medieval English monasteries.

8 Warner was only really an amateur *medievalist*; her historical novels vary widely in setting and period. The historical novelist must become a kind of temporary specialist of whatever time she chooses to write about.

4

Citizens of World Photography

EMILY HYDE

Edward Steichen's 1955 photographic exhibition *The Family of Man* has been well seasoned in the barrel of critique. This mid-century blockbuster premiered in 1955 at the Museum of Modern Art (MOMA) in New York and circled the globe until 1962; its syrupy liberal humanism was so obvious that the United States Information Agency teamed up with Coca-Cola to sponsor its travels. In studies of photography and Cold War culture alike, *The Family of Man* is an "ultimate bad object" (Solomon-Godeau 29). It seems to stand at the beginning of the contemporary era, but just far enough away that we think we can see it clearly. This clarity of vision, this availability in an object of study, rests upon the assumption that the photographs Steichen selected for the show are as easily and immediately legible as his intentions.

Viewed in the context of citizenship and human rights at mid-century, the photographs in *The Family of Man* demand another look. Rather than reading them as objects of critique, I see these photographs as actively making claims. Critique looks backwards; it has the prerogative of hindsight (Felski). A claim, by contrast, makes a demand upon the future. Ariella Azoulay's approach to photographs as open encounters rather than closed representations suggests a new way of reading *The Family of Man* as it travelled the mid-century world. Seen as active encounters, the photographs in *The Family of Man* – and the photographs it occasioned on its journeys – reveal a specifically mid-century model of citizenship, one that overruns national boundaries. Azoulay likens citizenship, as "a framework of partnership and solidarity among those who are governed" (*Contract* 23), to the photographic relation, but at mid-century *The Family of Man* shows how the circulation, reproducibility, and seriality of photography could also model a more participatory and proliferating form of citizenship and belonging.

Claiming citizenship and rights at mid-century, the photographs in *The Family of Man* also suggest how to read the photographs and visual images that crowd mid-century literature, especially early post-colonial literature. From Steichen's work in the mid-fifties and the global travels of his photographic exhibition, this essay will turn to V.S. Naipaul's novel *The Mimic Men* (1967), with its representative use of a snapshot as a narrative device for the novel as a whole. *The Mimic Men* captured its mid-century moment and also provided a key term for later post-colonial critique. But the post-colonial model of critique too often rests upon reading visual images and the mid-century novels that contain them as closed representations, sealed into naively realist or Eurocentric literary modes. Then as now, these visual images demand to be read as open, active encounters: they too make claims on the future. These are claims to citizenship and to belonging that proliferate forward in a series and thereby exceed the national and critical boundaries that tend to govern views of the mid-century.

The Universal Family of Man

The Family of Man was the creation of Edward Steichen, a photographer who started out in the early twentieth century as a pictorialist and member of the Photo-Secession, then moved into celebrity portraiture for *Vogue* and *Vanity Fair*, and aerial photography during both world wars. In 1947 he became the head of MOMA's relatively new department of photography. Steichen organized *The Family of Man* from his position at MOMA, then ceded direct control to the United States Information Agency, which sent the show around the world. The United States Information Agency (USIA) had just been established in 1953, and its mission was to "submit evidence to peoples of other nations by means of communication techniques that the objectives and policies of the United States are in harmony with and will advance their legitimate aspirations for freedom, progress, and peace" ("Report to the National Security Council"). A key actor in the Cold War diplomacy of culture and information, the USIA was all too happy to promote a universal vision of family life that purported to rise above Cold War ideological disputes. Yet, as Eric Sandeen has shown, *The Family of Man* was sent around the world at the bidding of the American government: "wherever the national presence needed to be felt, the exhibition could be counted upon to reassure that American values were local values" ("Road to Moscow," 62). It was the USIA that made *The Family of Man* a global phenomenon.

Steichen's liberal humanism and the ease with which the undisguised universalism of the exhibition was put at the service of the USIA has provided fertile ground for critique.[1] Nonetheless, as Lydia Liu has shown, the idea of "the universal" at mid-century did not necessarily serve neo-liberal and neo-colonial aims. In an essay on the great human rights debates in and around the year 1948, Liu argues that critical discussion too frequently rests upon proprietary, Eurocentric arguments about the geopolitical origins and the history of the idea of universal rights. Her essay brings to light the fact that at mid-century non-Western peoples and diplomats frequently elaborated and articulated universal norms and principles in order to oppose the West's assessment of the status of colonial and non-self-governing peoples. Rather than the imposition of a Western regime of universal rights, the mid-century saw a participatory, "universalizing process" (Liu 414). Viewed as part of a universalizing process, the travels of *The Family of Man* also suggest reasons to modify our understanding of citizenship and rights at mid-century. According to Azoulay, citizenship is also "an unfinished event that will remain unfinished" (*Contract* 166). Rather than defining a citizen as a legally recognized subject who has been granted certain rights, privileges, and duties by virtue of her citizenship within the closed container of the sovereign, territorial state, citizenship designates a continuing and proliferating process, one that produces, in Lynn Hunt's words, a "cascade of rights" (212).

The Family of Man cascaded around the world. It stopped in thirty-seven countries on six continents. Cleveland, Toronto, Mexico City, Nairobi, London, Paris, Delhi, Tokyo, Kabul, and even, in 1959,

Moscow were on the itinerary. The exhibition also resulted in a best-selling book. For the show, Steichen selected 503 photos from a pool of over two million; he included 273 photographers from 68 countries. In an NBC interview in 1955, he declared that the exhibition was meant to be "an article of faith" (Sandeen 57). As Steichen himself put it, he had faith that photography was "the best medium for explaining man to himself and to his fellow man" (Sandeen 8). Despite his position at MOMA, he was no longer interested in photography as autonomous art in the modernist tradition. He practically banned abstract images from the show. A few years later he claimed not to "give a hoot in hell" about photography as a fine art (Christopher Phillips 41). His predecessor at MOMA, Beaumont Newhall, put this aesthetic doping down in a different way. He objected to Steichen's promotion in 1947 because he was only interested in "the illustrative use of photography, particularly in the swaying of great masses of people" (Phillips 40). Steichen would not have objected to this characterization. *The Family of Man* was very clearly meant to illustrate and to sway. Steichen continued in the NBC interview: "How can anybody be satisfied [with] ... photographing the horrible monstrosity we call 'war'? ... I don't see how any artist can be satisfied ... People look at the pictures; they are exciting pictures; and occasionally they shed a tear at some tragic thing, and they tell me it was a wonderful job, and then they go out and have some drinks. That is a negative approach" (Bezner 138). His positive approach would illustrate the argument against war as viewers proceeded through images of courtship and childbirth, children at school and at play, family life and work, religious worship, and death. The MOMA show ended with an image of the UN General Assembly, a back-lit colour transparency of a hydrogen bomb explosion, and W. Eugene Smith's "Walk to Paradise Garden," a sentimental shot of his two children making their way in the world. Steichen intended *The Family of Man* to be constructive, rather than deconstructive, to illustrate rather than to critique.

The mass cultural appeal of illustration cloaks *The Family of Man*'s simultaneous balancing act with modernist aesthetics. Steichen, retaining the role of modernist author, shored fragments against ruin: he solicited and selected the individual photographs, then removed their original titles, framing, and context. He enlarged images and changed their formats, a few drastically. He equalized tonal values and edited for formal similarities. His well-known arrangement of eighteen photographs of children playing "Ring around the Rosie" into a circle best exemplifies his photographic formalism. Difference might exist on the surface of the image, but nothing could distract from the universal human family or, in this case, from the universal visual language of photography.

The language that accompanied these photographs as they traversed the planet frequently emphasized the role of the photograph in seeing, mirroring, and universalizing the world. In the prologue to the book, Carl Sandburg addresses viewers directly: "You travel and see what the camera saw. The wonder of human mind, heart, wit, and instinct, is here. You might catch yourself saying, 'I'm not a stranger here'" (2). In his introduction to the book, Steichen himself writes that the exhibition "was conceived as a mirror of the universal elements and emotions in the everydayness of life – as a mirror of the essential oneness of mankind throughout the world" (4). Nelson Rockefeller, as Special Assistant to the President for Psychological Warfare, opened the show at MOMA in a way that typifies how primitivism is often used to prove the universal.[2] The show, he remarked, "demonstrates that the essential unity of human experience, attitude and emotion are perfectly communicable between all peoples through the medium of pictures. The solicitous eye of the Bantu father, resting upon the son who is learning to throw his primitive spear in quest of food, is the eye of every father, whether in Montreal, Paris, or in Tokyo" (2). It is no mistake that Rockefeller imagines he can see an eye, solicitous or otherwise, in Nat Farbman's photograph (fig. 4.1). The eye is his own, and it gazes at a photograph that is "perfectly communicable," perfectly transparent, and thus becomes the perfect evidence of the universality of *The Family of Man*. It was this language – this unguarded, unhistorical way of reading a photograph – that animated the harshest criticism of the show.

Roland Barthes went to the show in Paris in 1956 and included it in *Mythologies* (1957). "Everything here," he argued, "aims to suppress the determining weight of History" (101). But Barthes, who, less than ten years later, wrote pages about a single photographic advertisement for Panzani pasta, has nothing to say about the individual photographs as they were presented in *The Family of Man*: "the failure of photography seems to me to be flagrant," he remarks, because

4.1 | From Edward Steichen and Carl Sandburg, *The Family of Man.*

"to reproduce death or birth tells us, literally, nothing" (101). Susan Sontag continued this line of attack in *On Photography* (1973); she too fails to mention any specific photograph. For her, the photographs are not just stripped of their titles and context, they are "stripped of all demands" (31); they deny "genuine and historically embedded differences, injustices, and conflicts" (33). Her most unforgiving line homes in on the universalizing that passes for democratization: "Steichen set up the show to make it possible for each viewer to identify with a great many of the people depicted and, potentially, with the subject of every photograph: citizens of World Photography all" (32). Sontag assumes identification is the primary mode of interacting with a photograph. Like Barthes, she objects less to the individual photographs than to Steichen's mirror, to Sandburg's "I am not a stranger here," and to Rockefeller's "solicitous eye." The photographs these men describe are too legible, too strenuously natural, too easy to identify with; therefore, their claims about universality and humanity are spurious and deceptive. She goes on to say that the humanity they depict is "a quality things have in common when they are viewed as photographs" (111). For Sontag, those who celebrate *The Family of Man* take the ease with which one can identify with these photographs for humanism itself.

In addition, Sontag's criticism reveals her anxiety about photographic reproducibility and proliferation in mass culture. Photographs without history, without captions or context, simply proliferate; by doing so, they blind viewers to the world around them. Allan Sekula makes a similar point. He argues that while the show "claims to fuse universal subject and universal object in a single moment of visual truth and visual pleasure, a single moment of blissful identity," in fact it is nothing but an "aestheticized job of global accounting" (20). All these critics abhor "the single moment of blissful identity" that a viewer might experience before these photographs because identification is the operating mode of a consumer culture of images. *The Family of Man* thus stands on the cusp between two worlds: between the photograph as high art sponsored by MOMA and the photograph as brought to you by Coca-Cola. It stands between a global audience imagined as political subjects and an audience conceived of as consumer subjects (Sekula, "Net," 26). Sontag does not, in fact, mean "*citizens* of world photography" at all – she means *consumers* of world photography. Nonetheless, if read with an eye to a participatory and proliferating form of citizenship and belonging at mid-century, the photographs in *The Family of Man* open themselves to forms of spectatorship beyond simple identification.

Photographic Encounters

In 1948, the Universal Declaration of Human Rights followed the formal model Lynn Hunt traces from the Declaration of Independence to the Declaration of the Rights of Man and Citizen: self-evident clauses beginning with "whereas" followed by "Now, Therefore THE

GENERAL ASSEMBLY proclaims THIS UNIVERSAL DECLARATION OF HUMAN RIGHTS." Joseph R. Slaughter treats this temporal structure as tautological. Crucial to my argument is that this self-evident model depends on recognition, not identification. The inherent rights of each human being are known before, but they must be acknowledged in the present and then proclaimed in a declaration that will serve as "a common standard of achievement for all peoples and all nations" in the future. This is an encounter between knowledge and acknowledgment, not a "single moment of blissful identity," to use Sekula's words. It is a temporally open model – it makes a set of claims upon the future.

In her work on *The Family of Man*, Ariella Azoulay describes it as a new genre: a visual universal declaration of human rights. For her, the photos in *The Family of Man* are not descriptive but prescriptive – they target universal human rights. After all, one cannot take a photograph of universality – a photograph intended to show an abstraction will always divulge the particular as well.[3] Steichen's photos are not, therefore, presented as documentary in their particularity. Rather, they document degrees of realization or violation of universal rights (40). This argument elevates *The Family of Man* in the hierarchy of genres at the same time that it discredits its critics. I want to retain the history of critique that the show as a whole provoked but add Azoulay's innovative approach to the individual photographs. For Azoulay, the photos in *The Family of Man* adhere to the same temporal structure as the declaration itself: they make a claim upon the future. She comes to see this because her very definition of photography differs from critics like Barthes, Sontag, and Sekula. First, for Azoulay, the photograph is not a black and white print on paper or a set of pixels on a screen. In *The Civil Contract of Photography*, she describes it as an encounter between the "users" of photography: the person holding the camera, the subject in front of the lens, the spectator they each imagine in that moment, and the infinite number of spectators that will view the photograph as it travels in space and time. This is the citizenry of photography, bound by mutual recognition and mutual obligation. Citizens sign on to the plurality of positions possible in the photographic encounter. You have the right to be an image, to make an image, to view an image, but you also have the obligation to defend photography, to "make it available for others to enter and intermingle" (113). This plurality undermines the seemingly stable and hierarchical relations of photographer, subject, and viewer. Photography is an encounter where none of the participants possesses a sovereign status.

While Azoulay's approach captures important temporal links between the UDHR and *The Family of Man*, her lexicon makes photography stand in the place of the nation, as the closed container that grants citizenship and rights. Blake Stimson likewise argues that at mid-century *The Family of Man* carried forth "the dream of public life – of nation" (7) through the medium of photography itself. Photography "realized itself as a nation" (24) in the affective sense – it creates a sense of belonging to a collective life. While Azoulay's model of photography-as-nation depends upon a contract among its citizens, Stimson's relies upon the model of identification, especially the "flow of identifications" that the viewer experiences as she moves through the photos in Steichen's exhibition (82–5). Both Azoulay and Stimson enrich critical understanding of *The Family of Man* by reading its photographs in their mid-century milieu, yet both readings seem to downplay the violence that can be inflicted by the camera when it is wielded by those in power.[4] Retaining Azoulay's idea of the photograph as a temporally open encounter and Stimson's work on the serial flow of the exhibition, I offer a series of readings of individual photographs from *The Family of Man* in which recognition, rather than identification, becomes the primary mode of interacting with the photograph. Seriality, as a result, reveals itself to be an important element of mid-century universality. Serial form depends upon conjunction rather than hierarchical ordering, variation rather than replacement. This additive form proliferates forward in time but never fully subordinates its starting point. The visual image in early post-colonial literature operates in the same way: read as one in an open series of encounters, it depicts and critiques the violence of colonial modes of representation at the same time that it moves forward into the future.

If, as Azoulay argues, Steichen's removal of captions and historical context from the photos in *The Family of Man* results, paradoxically, in each photo opening itself up to the "traces of an encounter of multiple participants" ("The Family of Man," 32), Steichen is deprived of his sovereign authority over the show. For example, Azoulay reads two photos identified only by location and photographer that were paired on the page of the book and grouped in a series in the exhibition (fig. 4.2). "Bechuanaland, Nat Farbman, *LIFE*" faces off against "USA, Nina Leen, *LIFE*." These are portraits that clearly aim to illustrate the fact that we are all kin, despite our racial differences and our attainment of modernity. The universal value of the family unit makes us all alike, according to the primitivist argument. On the one hand, taking these two photos as objects of critique would emphasize the fact that the American family has access to photography and the media and displays its ancestors proudly on the wall. The family in Bechuanaland, on the other hand, is being subjected to the camera for the first time. But reading these photos as claims allows Azoulay to make a simple point: except for the little boy who has become distracted by something on the ground, the members of the family in Bechuanaland all stare straight and firm into the camera's lens. They are engaging with the camera, perhaps making some sort of address. By contrast, many of the members of the American family clearly have either been told to "say cheese" or have so absorbed the protocols of photography that they automatically produce little grins, grins that would be wholly foreign to their ancestors on the walls. As a result, Azoulay points out, *they* seem more passively subject to the camera than do their neighbours on the page (26). This close reading does not attempt to redeem Steichen's politics, but it does, perhaps surprisingly, reflect more closely the original publication context of these two photographs.

Nat Farbman's 1947 photo essay in *LIFE* magazine was titled "The Bushmen: An Ancient Race Struggles to Survive in the South African Deserts." Four more primitivizing images from this essay appeared in *The Family of Man*. But Nina Leen's photographs accompanied an article, again in *LIFE*, called "An American Family in Trouble," which uses the Russells of Bellview, Missouri, as an example of the type of sturdy, American family that was dying out in 1948, when their photograph was published. In this article, *LIFE* looked at American families with an ethnographic eye, categorizing them into the trustee, domestic, and atomistic varieties and providing photographs as visual evidence. As they were originally conceived and presented, both families were on the brink; they did not represent a singular, timeless humanity. And in *The Family of Man* they appeared as two photographs in a

4.2a | From Edward Steichen and Carl Sandburg, *The Family of Man*.

series of four, a series that also included formally posed families from Sicily and Japan. Thus, as Stimson points out, the visual experience of these photographs must include the jump, the partition; they create an experience of difference rather than sameness (55).

This mode of reading can also enrich one of the most difficult series of photographs in *The Family of Man*. After a long sequence

4.2b | From Edward Steichen and Carl Sandburg, *The Family of Man*.

of kids playing, learning, and participating in family life, the book includes a two-page spread that seems to depict delinquent, dangerous behaviour. Interpretations abound. "Kids will be kids," the world over; they will grow out of this phase to perpetuate the universal family of man. At the same time, all these photos originate in the same place: the United States. Perhaps Steichen is making a political

4.3 | From Edward Steichen and Carl Sandburg, *The Family of Man*.

comment on childhood in the shadow of atomic war. If Steichen's intentions are put aside, what do these photographs depict? In the photo labeled "W. Eugene Smith, USA," for example, one child has grabbed an object from the other (fig. 4.3). The object itself is not important to the camera lens – it is soft and blurred in the lower corner of the image. The desperate expression on the girl's face contrasts with the fact that we cannot see the face of the perpetrator, if that is indeed what this boy is. The framing and perhaps the physical space that these children occupy are compressed, and motion predominates within the tight frame. The photographer himself seems to be caught up in this motion, almost to the point of vertigo. This is more than "give me back what's mine" or "but I had it first" – the multiple participants in this photographic encounter are caught up in the depiction of injury, part of the vertiginous point of view, and its viewers are experiencing, perhaps, what it feels like to participate, indeed, to have citizenship, in this photograph.

The original publication of this photograph both undermines and supports this reading. In 1953, W. Eugene Smith published a photo essay titled *My Daughter Juanita* that chronicled the "many moods" of his eight-year-old girl. (This essay also includes a younger Juanita in "Walk to Paradise Garden," which came to epitomize the show as a whole.) The photograph of injury and intention to harm comes in a section called "A Make-Believe Party and a Rude Intruder," which describes Juanita's older brother ruining her tea party by making off with a stuffed monkey called Bong-Bong. As the text makes clear, Juanita's imaginative play sparked her brother's rage. The description is heavily gendered. The photographer, then, *is* caught up in the action – he is abdicating the role of father and protector in order record this scene, and in order make his daughter's distress public in the pages of *LIFE*. This photograph's referential content – the abduction of Bong-Bong the monkey – recedes in importance as we continue to imagine the plurality of roles, points of view, injuries, and claims that inhere in this single image. Whereas the UDHR opens with the "recognition of the inherent dignity and of the equal and inalienable rights of all members of the human family," this photograph can be imagined to recognize the dignity and privacy of the imagination, and to make a claim for it even, or perhaps especially, within family life.

The Family of Man generated another set of photographs as it travelled the globe. This epiphenomenal photograph album is held in the USIA archives. In order to demonstrate to Congress the success of the world tour, the USIA collected photographs of people viewing the photographs in *The Family of Man*. These images depicted celebrity and VIP visitors as well as the subjects of photographs identifying themselves or those they knew. There are even photographs of Steichen taking photographs among the photographs at the show in Moscow in 1959. Other images show ordinary visitors, pointing and posing: couples in front of the portraits of couples, families in front of the photographs of families. Eric Sandeen, who understands these photographs as part of the story of *The Family of Man*, argues that these publicity shots were meant to "show how individuals from other cultures were drawn into this American depiction of the world" ("The Show You See with Your Heart," 348). But equally this epiphenomenal photo album shows how these images could be unmoored from their American Cold War context as they circulated. Sandeen also points out that the exhibition was often sent to global hot spots and was therefore situated in "particular local histories, [and amid] the flow of contemporaneous events" (349). In other words, the images that make up *The Family of Man* should be read as encounters between the timeless universality proposed by Steichen and the timely, historically specific circulation of his images. These photos should be read as encounters between a universalizing Cold War narrative and the unpredictable chains of meaning generated by encounters with that claim to the universal.

Sandeen's reading of these photographs hews too closely to Steichen's model of photographic accessibility and universality, which fit the USIA's purposes all too well. In November 1955, an employee of the USIA wrote to his colleague in Munich to request some of these publicity shots: "Now, may I ask that you carry out one important request? Ask Paul if he will assign a very fine human interest photographer to go to the show in Munich and get us a truly good coverage on the showing [...] faces looking at faces [...] seeing themselves mirrored [...] there will be so many, many wonderful shots [...] no one needs to write a shooting script" ("The Show You See with Your Heart," 107). The USIA employee proposes a model of identification: faces perfectly mirrored in photographs. This publicity request is so sure of how these photographs will be interpreted that a shooting script is not even necessary. The captions that Sandeen appends to his archival discoveries follow this model. In one, the photograph "envelopes" its audience in Paris; others "encourage an identification," "break through the plane of the image," or depict "respectful, almost reverential communion with the engaging photographs."

4.4 | *The Family of Man* exhibition in Washington, DC, 1955.

Spectators "become a part of the crowd" or "make eye contact" with a photograph (110–13). In one image, taken in Washington, DC, in 1955, the daughter of a Chinese diplomat looks at a photograph of herself originally taken in New York in 1941 and published in *LIFE* (fig. 4.4). This is clearly a staged publicity shot, but is it really an image of identification, as the USIA intended it to be? Her expression looks entirely skeptical – perhaps because the subject of the original *LIFE* photo was the bubble, not the child. (It was part of a spread meant to promote the photographer's high-speed camera technique.) Or perhaps she looks skeptical because she has also been forced to hold another print of the photo in the book in her hands. She is inundated with glossy simulacra of herself. This image captures photograpic reproducibility and cascading excess, not a singular moment of identification.

4.5 | *The Family of Man* exhibition in Munich, 1955.

Reading for photographic encounters and for photography's proliferation – its reproducibility and seriality – raises similar questions about another USIA shot. Sandeen captions this image, which was taken in Munich in 1955, "One couple views another" (109) (fig. 4.5). But is this couple really being pulled into the American world view by identifying with another such couple? This photograph actually depicts almost every anxiety inherent in photography: it is an image of reproducibility and contingency. Why the couple on the swing? Why not this couple from Munich? Why not any couple at all? The shot is set up so that we read from left to right, and these couples appear in serial form, just like the rest of *The Family of Man*. The couple from Munich has perhaps entered the show, but only to demonstrate the show's tendency to proliferate, to reproduce itself. This is not the many merging into the universal, but an image of the recognition of difference and the contingency of serial form. It is the tendency of the photographs in *The Family of Man* to produce an epiphenomenal album that demonstrates the importance of reading these images as encounters, or, rather, as images that form a series and thereby make claims upon the future.

The Mimic Man and the Snapshot

Visual images crowd the pages of mid-century post-colonial novels – they are paratexts and illustrations, narrative devices and ekphrastic objects. But rarely do these visual images provoke critical engagement – they seem too clear, too obvious, just like the photographs in *The Family of Man*. At mid-century, the Cold War was toughening modernism into abstraction and realism into socialist propaganda: New York became the capital of difficult, high art and appropriated modernist international ambitions, leaving realism to be associated with nationalist ardour in the era of decolonization. But approaching these visual images as either realist or modernist too often denigrates them entirely. A realist image in a mid-century post-colonial novel is, at worst, mere local colour. At best, it is a sharply referential image that willingly adheres to the descriptive protocols of English realism. A modernist image may serve as a destabilizing device by defamiliarizing the protocols of realism. Yet such an image must seem necessarily belated in terms of its modernism. Cascading like the photographs in *The Family of Man*, travelling the world as open encounters rather than closed representations, these visual images evade the critical categories that tend to govern mid-century post-colonial literature: realism versus modernism, representation versus misrepresentation, inclusion versus exclusion, the particular and the universal, the perceiving subject and the passive object. The context of citizenship and human rights at mid-century shows another way of describing how images work upon us in the present and promise to make claims upon us in the future.

Naipaul's *The Mimic Men* is structured around two photographs, or, rather, two photographic encounters. First, the narrator, Ranjit Kripalsingh (who long ago on the Caribbean island of Isabella renames himself Ralph Singh), repeats the idea that from a young age he felt marked by a celestial camera. He is superbly sensitive to the assurances of the camera: "a celestial camera recorded my every movement, impartially, without judgment or pity. I was marked; I was of interest; I would survive" (114). According to this perception, the impartial celestial camera documents the protagonist's confident progress through his own narrative. But the novel does not follow that narrative model at all. Rather, it opens with an unremarkable snapshot. This snapshot haunts the narrator and structures his story. In the opening scene, the narrator wanders up to the attic of his London lodging house to witness the first snow that he has ever seen. The moment is described photographically: the light is "dead, but seemed to have an inner lividness" (8); the snow defines everything in black and white. The narrator feels disenchanted and forlorn: "I had seen. Yet what was I to do with so complete a beauty?" (9). He is disconnected, shipwrecked, and separate from the photographically rendered metropolis. In his landlord's abandoned writing table he finds "a creased photograph of a plumpish girl in a woollen skirt and a jumper. The photographer's hand had shaken, so that the photograph, like the photograph in some magazine article on great events, seemed rare, as of a person who would be photographed no more" (9). She stands in a back garden, "her familiar home," the narrator imagines, but her image is preserved in this attic "among the chimneypots of what to the girl from the back garden must have seemed like a foreign country" (10). For a moment, the narrator seeks to enter this photograph imaginatively – he seeks to identify with the girl by reading his own exile and alienation into her image. The chimney pots that surround him are assumed to be foreign to her as well.

That impulse does not last. Rather than tempting the narrator into identification, the snapshot becomes an image of displacement. He thinks, "let it not happen to me ... Let my relics be honored. Let me not be mocked" (10). But of course it does. The story Ralph Singh tells of his rise and fall as a mimic man of the New World (175) forms another in a series with the girl in the back garden. As the photograph circulates throughout the novel – Ralph Singh refers to this snapshot repeatedly, especially towards the end of his story – he associates this impulse towards identification with order, "the order which, as I thought, expressed its sweetness in young girls and especially in one in a jumper in a sunny back garden" (184). As Ralph Singh seeks to impose his own narrative order on his experience of colonial education, politics, and finally exile, he articulates his difficulty via this visual image of displacement. He remembers "holding the creased photograph of an unknown girl and wishing for an instant to preserve it from further indignity" (220). The instinct to preserve – which is a large part of his impulse to write his own story as well – operates not in the mode of identification but through recognition. The celestial camera does not seek out, mark, and identify Ralph Singh for survival, as he assumed. Instead, the photograph survives to encounter the narrator and to make a claim upon him.

The temporal structure of recognition and the seriality of the form of the novel do not depend upon the referentiality of the snapshot. The content of the image is not important – we never find out the story of the girl in the back garden – and neither is its form or medium, though we know that the snapshot is creased, blurred, and secret. Neither realist nor modernist, neither particular nor universal, Ralph Singh and the girl in the back garden do not function as perceiving subject and passive object. Do they, then, adhere to the structure of mimicry so crucial to post-colonial critique? In the well-known essay "Of Mimicry and Man," Homi Bhabha assigns Ralph Singh to a line of literary descent in which colonial subjects desire to emerge as "authentic" through mimicry and, in particular, through a process of writing and repetition (126). In this formulation, mimicry, like seriality, is structured around a "displacing gaze" (123). It continually produces "its slippage, its excess, its difference" (122) as it operates along the horizontal axis of metonymy (128). Bhabha concludes with the idea that "the *founding objects* of the Western world become the erratic, eccentric, accidental *objets trouvés* of the colonial discourse" (132). In this reading, the celestial camera, as a founding mode of narration in the Western world, can only be indicated in Ralph Singh's story by the lost, forlorn, creased snapshot. But this would assume that Ralph Singh identifies with the plumpish girl and therefore imperfectly mimics her Englishness, or that the image of the girl reveals the ambivalent desire at the heart of colonial discourse itself. Identification is, indeed, his first impulse. But then comes the impulse to preserve the girl's snapshot "from further indignity," to allow it to survive and to accumulate meaning in his narrative. Rather than being a closed representation, the snapshot is open in time, and Singh is open to encountering it.

This is spectatorship beyond identification. It is a serial form without mimicry. Azoulay would call it citizenship – Ralph Singh, for a brief moment, recognizes his solidarity with the girl in the back garden and feels a resulting obligation to protect her from indignity. He is open to the snapshot as claim, and that claim proliferates forward in time and across many national and political boundaries. At the same time, the violence of colonial representation – the certainty with which the celestial camera tracks its protagonists – remains. This violence is not ignored or erased by the snapshot, but the snapshot does join it in serial form and therein comes to govern the form of Naipaul's novel as a whole. Visual images in mid-century postcolonial literature, operating as one in an open series of encounters, depict and critique the violence of colonial modes of representation at the same time that they move forward into the future.

NOTES

1 For a range of approaches to the political aims and outcomes of *The Family of Man*, see Bezner, Garb, Roberts, Stimson, and Turner.

2 In his piece on the notorious 1984 show at MOMA, "'Primitivism' in 20th Century Art: Affinity of the Tribal and the Modern," Hal Foster points out that "affinity" is a kinship word, and thus the recognition of difference joins the "Family of Art" under the sign of Western universality (53). Primitivism, in other words, is explained with a contemptuous nod to *The Family of Man*.

3 Azoulay reads the 1950 UNESCO photograph "kit" that illustrated selections from the UDHR as selectively universal and therefore beholden to its own particular time and place. See "Palestine as Symptom."

4 Azoulay has described the right announced by such violent images to the citizens of photography as "the right not to be a perpetrator." See "Palestine as Symptom."

PART TWO

VIOLATIONS

5

The Human and the Citizen in Joseph Conrad's *The Secret Agent*

JANICE HO

What is the relationship between the human and the citizen? Political theory offers at least two seminal accounts, the first classical and the second biopolitical. The classical separation of the human from the citizen, as Giorgio Agamben reminds us, originates in the Greek distinction between *zoē*, "the simple fact of living common to all living beings ([whether] animals, men, or gods)," and *bios*, "the form or way of living proper to an individual or a group" (1). This opposition counterposes biological existence to political life, an opposition fuelling a series of binaries that has structured the occidental tradition of politics: to wit, nature versus culture; the materiality of the body versus the abstraction of citizenship; the *oikos*, the private home, versus the *polis*, the public sphere. But if classical political thought regards the human and the citizen as conceptually distinct entities, their histories have intertwined in practice. After all, as Nikolas Rose observes, "biological presuppositions, explicitly or implicitly, have underlain many citizenship projects, shaped conceptions of what it means to be a citizen, and underpinned distinctions between actual, potential, troublesome, and impossible citizens" (*Politics* 132). In this view, derived from Michel Foucault's theory of biopolitics, physiological and political life, far from being separate, are intimately connected insofar as anthropological definitions of the human circumscribe who might or might not be deemed a citizen; under a regime of biopower, the human is subjected to myriad forms of political control designed to produce the proper citizen.

This essay maps the diverse relations between the biological human body and the political realm of citizenship in Joseph Conrad's *The Secret Agent* (1907), a novel that takes a disabled body – the "idiot," in the medical terminology of the time[1] – as its central focus. Conrad's novel, I argue, offers a useful aesthetic corrective to the way political theories have construed the relationship between the human and the citizen: rather than seeing the human as an apolitical species-being as classical political thought regards it or as a perpetual target of sovereign control and violence in a biopolitical reading, Conrad instead shows how the corporeal body is capable of functioning as a subject and an agent of politics. The representation of disability in *The Secret Agent* expands conceptions of what it means to be human and consequently challenges classifications of citizenship predicated on biologically normative definitions of the human. Put differently, the literary sphere acts as an epistemological alternative to political theory by constructing an imaginative space in which we might rethink intersections between the embodied existence of the human and the abstract life of the citizen. My analysis proceeds in three parts: first, taking Hannah Arendt's writings on human rights and Giorgio Agamben's elaboration of sovereign power and bare life (that is, human life stripped of political rights) as exemplary instances of classical and biopolitical frameworks respectively, I briefly discuss how these theoretical accounts delineate the relationship between *zoē* and *bios*. Second, I turn to the late nineteenth- and early twentieth-century rise of eugenics and fears of degeneracy that saturate *The Secret Agent* to explore how these discourses historically mobilized forms of biopolitical control that transformed the mentally disabled into bare life (*zoē*) by systematically excluding them from the rights of citizenship (*bios*). Yet, as I further suggest, Conrad's depiction of terrorism offers a countervailing reading of bare life as a potential site of political praxis in place of Agamben's totalizing definition of it as life that can be destroyed with impunity. Third, I argue that Conrad's turn to sentimentalism as a literary mode to represent idiocy challenges biopolitical categorizations that treat mental disability as a form of degeneracy. In *The Secret Agent*, the idiot Stevie is simultaneously the object of sentimental perception by his sister, who views him as a singular being irreducible to a typology of abnormality, and the subject of sentimental feeling whose bodily perception of social injustice is itself a potential force of politics. Sentimentalism thus allows Conrad to rewrite the disabled human body in ways that link it back to the realm of political citizenship from which it has been expelled.

Zoē and *Bios*

Hannah Arendt's analysis of "the perplexities of the rights of man" in *The Origins of Totalitarianism* (1951), which meditates on the condition of stateless refugees displaced during the interwar years, fundamentally turns on the Greek distinction between *zoē* and *bios*, biological life and political citizenship. When deprived of the rights of citizenship, the stateless, writes Arendt, are reduced to the condition of being merely human, forced to appeal to natural human rights that, although "supposedly inalienable," nevertheless "proved to be unenforceable" (293). But Arendt is not just referring to the logistical difficulties inhering in the idea of human rights which were – and still remain – legally unguaranteed by sovereign nation-states and whose lack of juridical authority had led to Jeremy Bentham's dismissal of natural rights as sheer "nonsense upon stilts" (53). More importantly, the loss of citizenship results in the loss of a political community that sees the refugee thrown back onto the "nakedness of being nothing but human," nothing more than a "specimen of an animal species called man" (300, 302). When one is removed from political association, one is banished to the natural realm of the body and the private sphere, rendered merely human and consequently, if paradoxically, not quite human, undifferentiated from the pure biology of animal existence. When Arendt suggests that "only the loss of a polity itself expels him [the refugee] from humanity" (297), she equates the dispossession of citizenship with the deprivation of humanity altogether. Elizabeth Anker rightly notes that Arendt's reflections on human rights "betray ... [an] aversion toward embodiment" insofar as the "realm of nature and the private" is systemically subordinated to "the achievements of politics, public life, and culture" (*Fictions* 27). This aversion stems from the separation between *zoē* and *bios*: Arendt sees human rights as a conceptual paradox since they posit natural rights as political rights, thereby confusing the realms of private and public, the human and the citizen; human rights prove ineffectual for guaranteeing the protections of the stateless precisely because they are *human* rights and not the rights of the citizen.

Arendt's idealization of Greek political praxis means that, for her, *zoē* is non-coincident with *bios*: the human qua biological being is a non-political entity that cannot realize the true humanity of being a citizen. Michel Foucault's theory of biopolitics, by contrast, posits modern modalities of power that alter the classical relation between physiological and political life. As he writes in the first volume of *The History of Sexuality*, "For millennia, man remained what he was for Aristotle: a living animal with the additional capacity for a political existence; modern man is an animal whose politics places his existence as a living being in question" (143). Foucault charted new operations of power over biological life by analyzing both instrumental technologies that produced the "docile bodies" of normal citizens at various institutional sites and fields of knowledge that sought to classify populations in order to regulate them.[2] Under a regime of biopower, any separation between *zoē* and *bios* is impossible since life itself becomes both the subject and object of politics. Arendt had likewise observed the expansive intrusion of private issues of biological necessity – the social concern with hunger and poverty, for instance – into the public domain in modern times, but saw the intermingling of these two spheres as a debasement of classical political life.[3] Biopolitics, whereby biology is politicized and politics biologized, conversely treats this intermingling not as defective practice, but as a new political rationality that acts on individual bodies and collective populations.

Drawing on Foucault's thesis of biopower to reframe Arendt's reading of the condition of refugees, Agamben in *Homo Sacer* argues that the plight of the stateless, of those voided of their citizenship rights, exposes the central logic behind the exercise of sovereign power. Sovereign power is nothing more or less than a biopolitical power grounded in the ability to decide on "the value (or nonvalue) of life as such," to distinguish between "life that does not deserve to be lived ... [and] life that deserves to be lived" (137). Biopower produces the unstable threshold between *zoē* and *bios*, human and citizen: it determines which life belongs to the sphere of *bios* and is conferred citizenship and its juridical protections, and which life is mere creaturely or human existence – what Agamben calls "bare life" or "nude life" – and can therefore be killed with impunity. As he reminds us, before Jews were sent to concentration camps to be exterminated, they first had to be denationalized: made into refugees, expelled from political association, and reduced to bare life, to the "nakedness of being nothing but human," in Arendt's formulation. Whereas classical politics had seen *zoē* and *bios* as ontologically separate spheres, biopolitics reads these as domains structured by a flexible and moving border produced through a sovereign authority who decides on the distinction between the human and the citizen.

Idiocy and Bare Life

Agamben's conceptualization of biopolitics provides a useful lens for understanding the way late nineteenth- and early twentieth-century discourses of eugenics and national degeneracy constituted the distinction between *zoē* and *bios* by excluding certain populations from citizenship and transforming them into bare, or biologically expendable, life. This process of differentiation is at the heart of *The Secret Agent*, a novel centred on a mentally disabled character, Stevie, who is made an unwitting instrument of his brother-in-law Verloc's attempts to engineer a bombing at the Greenwich Observatory and who ends up killing only himself when he inadvertently trips with the bomb. Conrad's interest in the historical figure of the idiot comes as no surprise: the novel was published in the same year as Francis Galton's establishment of the Eugenics Education Society. The modernist era witnessed the rise of numerous ways in which mental disability was subjected to biopolitical regulation in fields as diverse as immigration law, education, and criminal psychology; in all these emerging social science disciplines, the question of who was a citizen was deeply contingent on what kind of human one was.

Indeed, if Agamben takes the refugee as the paradigmatic figure of bare life denuded of political rights, the idiot presents us with a different incarnation of the refugee after the passing of the 1905 Aliens Act. As David Glover documents in his cultural history of the legislation, the Aliens Act was "the first recognisably modern law that sought permanently to restrict immigration into Britain according to systematic bureaucratic criteria that were initially administered and interpreted by a new kind of public functionary: the immigration officer" (1). The act was driven by growing domestic unease about foreign anarchism and the influx of Eastern European Jews fleeing Russian pogroms; *The Secret Agent* is invariably read as an ironic response to such fears since Conrad presents us with a large cast of lazy and singularly unthreatening anarchists and a cosmopolitan London that belies any belief in an autochthonic Englishness.[4] But what has been less remarked on is how the act defines citizenship through the parameters of biological health by specifying that "an immigrant shall be considered an undesirable immigrant ... if he is a lunatic or an idiot, or owing to any disease or infirmity appears likely to become a charge upon the rates or otherwise a detriment to the public" (qtd in Henriques 185). The determination of un/desirability was placed under the purview of an immigration official and a medical officer accompanying the official on his inspection of ships, with the latter asked to certify that the "Alien Immigrant" in question was not a "lunatic or idiot." By proscribing the idiot from the nation-state, the Aliens Act codified citizenship through a biological norm of the human that rendered the idiot a refugee. Insofar as the act placed jurisdiction over the conferral of citizenship under the authority of state officials, it also sought "to insulate the routine work of this new apparatus of control from the wider legal system, and particularly from scrutiny by the higher courts" (Glover 2). If Agamben defines sovereignty as the biopolitical power to distinguish between "the value (or non-value) of life as such" (137), the extralegal authority of these officials might be read as the historical instantiation of the state's power to produce the disabled body as bare life, banished from the political realm of *bios* into the merely human realm of *zoē*.

The mechanisms of biopolitical control did not operate solely at the exterior borders of the nation-state, since the mentally disabled were also domestically dispossessed of rights as a consequence of social science disciplines that sought to taxonomize idiocy in ever more specific ways. As Matthew Thomson explains in his history of mental disability: during this period, "mental defectives became defined as the central eugenic threat facing the nation ... [by] seem[ing] to provide a biological explanation for social failure[s]" occurring in the diverse areas of the school, the workhouse, and the prison (20–2). The field of education, by mandating compulsory elementary schooling in the 1870 Education Act, first sharpened the focus on mental disability as a national problem, since enforced schooling brought to light a population who, although not "idiots" or "imbeciles" in the medical sense because they were not, strictly speaking, incapacitated, was nevertheless unable to advance from year to year and required special classes. This resulted in the introduction of the category of the "feeble-minded," a liminal space between normalcy and the established medical-cum-legal categories of the idiot, the imbecile, the lunatic, and the unsound of mind. *The Secret Agent* briefly alludes to the Education Act when the narrator observes, "Under our excellent system of compulsory education he [Stevie] had learned to read and write, notwithstanding the unfavourable aspect of the lower lip" (7). At the same time, Winnie, Stevie's sister, complains, "I wish he had never been to school," given that Stevie has a penchant for "always taking away those [anarchist] newspapers from the window to read" (44). He is unable to assess their contents critically, responding to them with uncontrolled excitement and outrage.[5] Idiocy as a "social hygiene" issue, to use a popular term at the time, thus initially revolved around the question of whether or not idiots could be educable – and if so, to what extent.

Conrad's portrayal of Stevie's idiocy, however, is influenced not primarily by the field of education but of criminology: it is well known that the novel draws largely on the writings of Cesare Lombroso, the nineteenth-century anthropologist who believed that criminality was identifiable through physiological traits. Idiocy had likewise become a concern in the penal system, with prison doctors labelling habitual offenders who appeared impervious to reform as "weak-minded criminals" with a natural predisposition to crime and whose mental degeneracies were thought to be visibly inscribed on a pathological body (Thomson 17–19). Upon examining Stevie, the anarchist Ossipon, a former medical student, pronounces him a "[v]ery good type too, altogether, of that sort of degenerate. It's enough to glance at the lobes of his ears. If you read Lombroso – " (34–5). Ossipon inspects Winnie with the same physiognomic template when he discovers she has killed Verloc: "he gazed scientifically at that woman, the sister of a degenerate, a degenerate herself – of a murdering type.

He gazed at her, and invoked Lombroso, as an Italian peasant recommends himself to his favourite saint" (217). Ossipon's faith in the veracity of Lombrosian criminology is satirized since he is compared to a gullible peasant in thrall to religious principles, but, as many critics note, even as Conrad subjects this pseudo-science to trenchant irony, he repeats this discourse in his narration. The most striking instance occurs when Winnie stabs Verloc after she learns of his role in Stevie's death: "Into that plunging blow, delivered over the side of the couch, Mrs Verloc had put all the inheritance of her immemorial and obscure descent, the simple ferocity of the age of caverns, and the unbalanced nervous fury of the age of bar-rooms" (193). Winnie's body replicates Stevie's stigmata as "the resemblance of her face with that of her brother grew at every step, even to the droop of the lower lip, even to the slight divergence of the eyes" (192). Not only are criminality and idiocy written on the body, the language of "inheritance" and "obscure descent" conforms to a eugenic vision of heredity that Foucault has described as the "background-body ... behind the abnormal body" – "the parents' body, the ancestors' body, the body of the family" that is seen as the cause and origin of pathology (*Abnormal* 313–16).

The biopolitical classifications of these growing disciplines stoked fears that national degeneration was on the rise: the addition of the category of "feeble-mindedness" into a 1901 national census caused a statistical inflation in the estimated number of mentally disabled – from 97,000 in 1891 to 133,000 ten years later – since it included those who would not previously have been considered mentally "defective." In response to such fears, the government in 1904 appointed a Royal Commission on the Care and Control of the Feeble-Minded, which presented its report in 1908. Following the report's recommendations, parliament passed a Mental Deficiency Act in 1913 mandating the permanent segregation of the mentally disabled in institutional colonies – a law not repealed until 1959 – thus effectively stripping them of their civil rights of citizenship.

In *The Secret Agent*, the political rightlessness of the idiot leads directly to Stevie's victimization by Verloc and his consequent death. When interrogated by Inspector Heat, Verloc explains that Stevie's idiocy makes him the ideal carrier of the bomb because "the lad was half-witted, *irresponsible*. Any court would have seen that at once.

Only fit for the asylum. And that was the worst that would've happened to him if – " (155; emphasis added). Verloc points not to Stevie's gullibility but to his lack of legal personality, which renders him incapable of being tried as a criminal altogether. The distinction Hannah Arendt draws between the criminal and the refugee is worth recalling here: "It seems that a man who is nothing but a man has lost the very qualities which make it possible for other people to treat him as a fellow-man. This is one of the reasons why it is far more difficult to destroy the legal personality of a criminal, that is of a man who has taken upon himself the responsibility for an act whose consequences now determine his fate, than of a man who has been disallowed all common human responsibilities" (*Origins* 300). Arendt returns to the opposition between *zoē* and *bios*, between the merely and therefore not quite human and the political citizen. Criminals may be deprived of rights through juridical punishment, but their capacity to be held responsible for their actions is still a sign of their place in the political order. By contrast, legal irresponsibility denotes a lack of personhood and is a fundamental marker of rightlessness: Stevie cannot be tried because he does not in the first place possess any rights to be confiscated. The idiot is not to be conflated with the refugee to be sure; yet they might be read as structurally analogous figures of statelessness at this time – the one internal and the other external – in light of the Aliens Act barring the idiot from the nation-state's borders and the Mental Deficiency Act physically segregating him or her. Stevie's situation encapsulates Agamben's notion of bare life in that he occupies "a threshold beyond which life ceases to have any juridical value and can, therefore, be killed without the commission of a homicide" (139).[6] In Verloc's eyes, Stevie's rightlessness means he is superfluous in every sense, as symptomatically revealed in the language of inutility employed to assess Stevie's place in the household. Winnie seeks to justify his worth by telling Verloc, "It isn't that he doesn't work as well as ever ... He's been making himself very useful"; but her assertion of Stevie's value is undermined by Verloc's belief "that his wife's brother looked uncommonly useless" (135), a uselessness reflecting his status as bare life "unworthy of being lived" (Agamben 138).

Yet *The Secret Agent* does not merely replicate Agamben's presentation of bare life as life unremittingly subject to extinction by sovereign violence, for an alternative vision of idiocy emerges in Conrad's depiction of Stevie's uncanny double: the Professor.[7] Like Stevie, the Professor is described via the stigmatic tropes of degeneracy: "His flat, large ears departed widely from the sides of his skull, which looked frail enough for Ossipon to crush between thumb and forefinger ... The lamentable inferiority of the whole physique was made ludicrous by the supremely self-confident bearing of the individual" (46).[8] More importantly, whereas Stevie is killed after being tricked into becoming an unintentional suicide bomber, the Professor is the terroristic foil to Stevie's ineffectuality, a resolute suicide bomber who walks the streets with a detonator in hand, ready to explode himself and everyone around him if he is apprehended by the police.[9] The Professor's revolutionary extremism is a function of his Sorelian embrace of violence and his desire to make "a clean sweep and a clear start for a new conception of life" (55). His willingness to be a suicide bomber leads Inspector Heat to regard him as a "lunatic" (72), a diagnosis linking the Professor to Stevie yet again insofar as he too is seen to suffer from a mental affliction. (In the Aliens Act, the proscription of anyone who was "a lunatic or an idiot" reflects the interrelations between these categories.) And terrorism is repeatedly troped in the novel in the language of idiocy: when instructing Verloc to blow up the Greenwich Observatory, the ambassador Vladimir describes the planned "outrage" as combining "the greatest possible regard for humanity with the most alarming display of ferocious *imbecility*" (26; emphasis added). The Professor's lunacy is hence a mirror of Stevie's idiocy, but Conrad draws this parallel only to invert it since the Professor is no simple victim of biopower but is instead a threat to the social system. Disability, then, is refigured in the text as a potential source of political action, not just as vulnerable bare life.

After an encounter with the Professor in an alleyway, Inspector Heat offers a eugenic explanation for the Professor's use of his body as a weapon of destruction: "To the vigorous, tenacious vitality of the Chief Inspector, the physical wretchedness of that being, so obviously not fit to live, was ominous; for it seemed to him that if he had the misfortune to be such a miserable object he would not have cared how soon he died" (70). Because the Professor's degeneracy marks him as "a life unworthy to be lived," to use Agamben's phraseology, his death should be a matter of indifference. This is the biopolitical logic of sovereign power that leads to Stevie being casually sent to his death by Verloc. In this scene, however, Heat's judgment of the non-value of the Professor's life – that he is "not fit to live" – is not an expression of authority by a state representative but one of fear, since this worthlessness paradoxically allows the Professor to weaponize his body into an "ominous" bomb. Indeed, the Professor insists he is superior to the police because they "depend on life" whereas he "depend[s] on death, which knows no restraint and cannot be attacked" (51). The terroristic threat posed by the Professor's devalued biological existence turns bare life into a space of struggle that revises Agamben's insistence that it remains perpetually the target of sovereign power. The Professor occupies the "zone of indistinction," the liminality of the "living dead man" who is the emblem of bare life, given that the Professor lives at every moment ready to die (Agamben 122, 131). In Conrad's novel, however, this liminality is not a manifestation of state power but its attempted negation. The figure of the suicide bomber presents us with a radical reorientation of the relationship between the human and the citizen, with human life turned into a political weapon of protest. For the suicide bomber, writes Achille Mbembe, "the body does not simply conceal a weapon. The body is transformed into a weapon, not in a metaphorical sense but in the truly ballistic sense" (36). In the Professor's threat of suicide bombing, the disabled and degenerate body – banished from the political realm into bare life – re-enters the field as the secret agent of politics.

Ewa Ziarek has argued that Agamben's understanding of biopower is flawed because he reads bare life as a static ontological state rather than "a site of contestation and political possibility," thus foreclosing the question of resistance and of "whether bare life itself can be mobilized by emancipatory movements." Ziarek cites the hunger strikes of suffragettes in the early twentieth century as a historical instance of how the biological human body (*zoē*) can insert itself into the topos of politics (*bios*), even when legally excluded from the rights of citizenship. The Professor's readiness to suicide bomb the entire social order into destruction is not easily assimilated to the "emancipatory movements" that Ziarek identifies, especially since the iconography of terrorism and suicide bombing historically figures these acts as outside the scope of politics altogether: "Aristotle's definition of man as '*zoón politikon*', a political animal, certainly did not extend to 'terrorists' as far as the popular media was concerned. Viewed as being devoid of politics, they were cast simply as animals, or rather *anti-human* life-forms" (Houen 32; original emphasis). Houen's analysis is revealing; the belief that terrorism is "devoid of politics" rather than a different form of politics is a consequence – especially in the case of suicide bombing – of its reliance on a vehicle conventionally viewed as apolitical, that is, the physical body. Because the human body classically belongs to the realm of *zoē*, to bare life, and not to *bios*, political life, the use of it renders suicide bombers mere "animals" or "*anti-human* life-forms." Conrad's depiction of terrorism as idiocy conforms to some extent to this classical distinction, but he also transforms the bare life of the body into a potential force of politics insofar as the Professor's degenerate physiology, deemed valueless by a biopolitical discourse of eugenics, opens up the threat of "a clean sweep of the whole social creation" that might be the prelude to a new political order (24).

The Sentimentalization of Idiocy

In *The Secret Agent*, then, bare life is not just the product of a biopower dispossessing the disabled body of political rights, but also a fraught site in which resistance to sovereignty may be staged: in the figure of the suicide bomber, the human acts as a political animal even when unrecognized as a citizen. Conrad's deployment of sentimentalism as a mode for portraying idiocy further enacts a literary rewriting of the biopolitical discourses of eugenics that constructed disability as degeneracy. In this respect, the novel qua novel might be seen to partake in an epistemological competition occurring in the modernist era between literature and the emerging social science disciplines: "The contention between a literary intelligentsia and an intelligentsia devoted to the social sciences ... was accentuated ideologically through the confrontation of cold rationality and the culture of ... feelings" (Lepenies 1). As we saw earlier, the stigmatization of idiocy was fuelled precisely by the social science fields of educational psychology and criminology, which deemed the mentally disabled unfit for citizenship through classifications derived from "cold rationality." Conrad's recourse to sentimentalism, by contrast, seizes on "the culture of ... feelings" to offer a competing lens through which the disabled body may be regarded as both human and a political subject, thus facilitating a literary reconfiguration of the relation between the corporeal body and the practice of politics.

It may be strange to think of Conrad, invariably perceived as the master practitioner of irony, as a sentimentalist. Yet Wendy Lesser has observed that *The Secret Agent*'s indebtedness to Charles Dickens's London novels means that "Conrad's irony is in fact an outgrowth of Dickens's complex form of sentimentality" (185). James Chandler has also situated *Lord Jim* (1900) within a tradition of sentimental fiction, which suggests that sentimentalism is not an exceptional mode in Conrad's broader oeuvre. In *The Secret Agent*, sentimentalism emerges most clearly in two ways: first, in how Stevie's disability is perceived by his sister, Winnie, in familial and not biopolitical terms; and second, in how Stevie's idiocy is a corollary of his own sentimental and visceral response to social injustice. In other words, Stevie is made into both the object and subject of sentimental feeling in the text.

Winnie's perception of Stevie is contrasted to the eugenic gaze embodied by Ossipon, who apprehends Stevie and Winnie only as "types" – a "very good type" of degeneracy and a "murdering type" (35, 217). Against this classificatory impulse, Stevie's physiognomy appears quite different to Winnie's sentimental gaze, a gaze borne of their familial intimacy: "She cast a swift glance at the boy, like a young man, by her side. She saw him amiable, attractive, affectionate, and only a little, a very little, peculiar. And she could not see him otherwise, for he was connected with what there was of the salt of passion in her tasteless life – the passion of indignation, of courage, of pity, and even of self-sacrifice" (128). In his "Author's Note," written thirteen years after the publication of *The Secret Agent*, Conrad suggested that the novel's central focus was the story of Winnie's "maternal passion" (231). He may overstate the case, but it is nonetheless true that the tragic dimensions of the narrative are largely experienced through Winnie's devastation at her brother's death after her life's work of caring for him. The narrator describes it as "a life of single purpose and of a noble unity of inspiration" (178), and Conrad extensively catalogues Winnie's trials and tribulations to achieve the full effects of tragedy, from her defence of Stevie as a child against their abusive father to her abandonment of her impoverished young lover so she can marry the wealthier Verloc to guarantee Stevie's security. Winnie's "maternal passion" denotes her suffering for her brother, much like the passion of Christ. The reasons for Winnie's single-minded devotion are never explained. They are the self-evident givens of her familial bond with Stevie: because he is her brother, Winnie sees Stevie as "only a little, a very little, peculiar," and otherwise "amiable, attractive, [and] affectionate." His deficiencies are interpreted not through the medical category of idiocy, but as a unique idiosyncrasy. Nobody else reads Stevie's disabled body this way, a disjunction that becomes painfully evident when Verloc fails to comprehend why Winnie might grieve for the death of an idiot: "The mind of Mr Verloc lacked profundity. Under the mistaken impression that the value of individuals consists in what they are in themselves, he could not possibly comprehend the value of Stevie in the eyes of Mrs Verloc" (172). We encounter again the language of worth, but Stevie's eugenic inutility as an idiot is juxtaposed here against Winnie's care for him in all his singularity.

The novel counterposes the biopolitical determination of "the value or nonvalue of life as such" (Agamben 137) to the private domestic family that dispenses with the question of value altogether. This reflects one of the key differences between the public and private spheres that Arendt has delineated. She writes: "the public sphere is as consistently based on the law of equality as the private sphere is based on the law of universal difference and differentiation"; citizenship makes us equal, but it is only in the private sphere of human life that "the disturbing miracle contained in the fact that each of us is made as he is – single, unique, unchangeable" – can be affirmed (*Origins* 301). Arendt unsurprisingly treats the public and private as distinct and irreconcilable modalities of existence, yet her account implicitly anticipates what has become a common critique of such a separation, namely, that the abstraction of citizenship fails to consider the embodiment of human difference. The formal equality of citizenship means that material differences – including physical disability, social inequality, or cultural diversity – are structurally banished from the public sphere (*bios*) into the apolitical space of private life (*zoē*). To be sure, Winnie's kin-based view of Stevie's unique personhood has no public or political consequences since no one else shares it. She imagines that Verloc might see Stevie as she does when she invents a bond of filiation between them – "Might have been father and son," she thinks – but Conrad's implacable nihilism describes this as "the supreme illusion of her life" (179). Winnie's apprehension of Stevie is literally idiotic, then, if we recall the etymology of the word: according to the Greeks, "a life spent in the privacy of 'one's own' (*idion*), outside the world of the common, is 'idiotic' by definition ... The privative trait of privacy, indicated in the word itself ... meant literally a state of being deprived of something" (Arendt, *Human* 38). Winnie's sentimental gaze belongs solely to the site of the family, to the private and domestic sphere of *zoē* that is invaded and destroyed by the realm of *bios*, but fails inversely to have any impact on public life. If this is the case, Arendt may be right in her contention that the affirmation of human difference does not exist beyond private spaces: outside the confines of the family unit, Stevie's disability can no longer be regarded as individual peculiarity but only as medical idiocy.

On the other hand, *The Secret Agent* is also the literary vehicle by which idiocy – in its etymological sense of privacy – enters the public sphere of letters through Conrad's portrayal of Winnie's "maternal passion," which offers readers a sentimental view of Stevie's disability that is distinct from the biopolitical gaze categorizing him as unfit for citizenship. This is the work of sentimental fiction that proceeds, argues Philip Fisher, via an "experimental extension of humanity to prisoners, slaves, madmen, children, and animals, [and] exactly reverses the process [... of] the withdrawal of human status from a part of humanity" (100). The representational space of literature both compensates for and challenges the denial of humanity of these figures who, by virtue of being excluded from the political realm of *bios*, are otherwise regarded as bare life. By foregrounding the relationship between Winnie and Stevie, Conrad employs a paradigmatic convention of the sentimental novel, which not only turns on the family unit but, more specifically, on the parent–child relationship. The parent–child relationship is

> the fundamental social example of compassion: that is, of the correct moral relation of the strong to the weak. The political importance of the family for the sentimental novel's version of history lies in the fact that throughout human history the family is the only social model for the relations between

> non-equal members of a society, relations based on dramatically different and unequal contributions to the group and equally dramatically different and incomparable needs ... No other unit regularly provides for helplessness, whether in childhood or old age ... No other solidarity is so indifferent to contribution. (Fisher 102)

Winnie's care for Stevie does indeed consist of the "moral relation of the strong to the weak," or, as the narrator puts it, of "the consolations administered to a small and badly scared creature by another creature nearly as small but not quite so badly scared" (178). In this novelistic world, Conrad offers an alternative "social model" in which bodily weakness and disability remain untranslatable into the biopolitical rationalities of eugenics, degeneracy, and social hygiene that go into producing anthropological distinctions between valued citizens and valueless non-citizens. Sentimentalism as a literary practice is, of course, frequently criticized for recasting systemic political issues into personal and domestic ones.[10] Yet in *The Secret Agent*, the semi-autonomy of the private sphere of the domestic family – a sphere in which Stevie is still appreciable as a "single, unique, [and] unchangeable" biological being (Arendt, *Origins* 301) – provides a textual landscape in which disabled bodies figure differently, hence opening up the political possibility, however momentary or unrealized, of thinking otherwise.

By staging Stevie's disability as an object of sentimental compassion, the novel enacts an "experimental extension of humanity" and confers a literary plenitude that opposes itself to the political rightlessness characteristic of bare life; the depiction of the human qua human is the means by which exclusionary forms of citizenship are reversed. But, importantly, Stevie is also represented as the subject of sentimental feeling, not just an object to be pitied, for his idiocy is defined by his innate susceptibility to emotional response. Indeed, the most distinguishing attribute of his mental affliction turns out to be his inability to keep his excessive emotions in check: he is unemployable because he is too often distracted by "the dramas of fallen horses, whose pathos and violence induced him sometimes to shriek piercingly in a crowd" (7). Winnie dislikes his overhearing anarchist conversations about socio-economic exploitation because "he isn't fit to hear what's said here. He believes it's all true. He knows no better. He gets into his passions over it" (44). The cause of his emotional responsiveness is specifically attributed to his disability, to the fact that he "isn't fit." The word "passions" to describe Stevie's affective state is significant, for this word recurs most frequently in association with both Stevie and Winnie. The latter's passions emerge solely in connection with her brother as Conrad's observation about Winnie's "maternal passion" in his "Author's Note" implies (231). When she discovers the news about Stevie's death, for instance, "her tearless eyes [grew] hot with rage, because she was not a submissive creature ... She had battled for him [Stevie] – even against herself. His loss had the bitterness of defeat, with the anguish of a baffled passion" (181). Stevie's passions, on the other hand, are most strongly stirred by the sight of social injustice. This reactiveness is amply evidenced in a key chapter when he enters a "metropolitan hackney carriage," with a "maimed driver on the box" whipping an infirm horse, an outfit resembling a "Cab of Death" (114, 125). Horrified by the whipping, Stevie pleads with the cabdriver to stop. "I've got my missus and four kids at 'ome," the driver tells Stevie. Life is "'Ard on 'osses, but dam' sight 'arder on poor chaps like me" (115, 122–3). The cabdriver's reply prompts Stevie's socialistic epiphany – "Bad world for poor people" – and a visceral sympathy for and anger at the adversities that have beset the cabman and his horse: "In the face of anything which affected directly or indirectly his morbid dread of pain, Stevie ended by turning vicious ... Supremely wise in knowing his own powerlessness, Stevie was not wise enough to restrain his *passions* ... Being no sceptic, but a moral creature, he was in a manner at the mercy of his righteous *passions*" (124, 126; emphasis added). Although never explicitly stated, the novel implies that Stevie's susceptibility to Verloc's anarchist propaganda is strengthened by this encounter, which materializes for him the plight of social suffering.

How should we read the word "passion" as a recurring attribute of Stevie and Winnie's affective lives? One answer takes us back to Cesare Lombroso and the discourse of biological degeneracy: in 1878, Lombroso published an updated edition of *Criminal Man* where he added a brief chapter on "criminals of passion." He defined these as virtuous people who nonetheless commit "crimes of impulse" because they are "people of full-blooded or nervous temperament"; "the criminal by passion displays exaggerated sensitivity and excessive affections" (105). According to Lombrosian psychology, Stevie and Winnie are criminals of passion who end up impulsively committing different crimes. But Conrad's description of Stevie being at the "mercy of his righteous passions" because he was "a moral creature" also points us towards an alternative intellectual genealogy of the term, one going back to the eighteenth century, when "passion" – the archaic word for emotion – was part of a language of sensibility that referred to moral feelings experienced via the body. These ethical reactions were also, properly speaking, aesthetic responses, given that "aesthetics is born as a discourse of the body," with the word "aesthetics" stemming from the Greek *aisthesis* which, in turn, refers "to the whole region of human perception and sensation" (Eagleton 14). From Francis Hutcheson's *Essay on the Nature and Conduct of the Passions and Affections* (1742) to Adam Smith's *Theory of Moral Sentiments* (1759) to David Hume's *Dissertation on the Passions* (1777), eighteenth-century philosophers outlined the possibility of a moral sense grounded in sentiment, feeling, and passions, elements of the body that would allow persons "to experience right and wrong with all the swiftness of the senses, and [that would thus lay] the groundwork for a social cohesion" based on instinctive morality (Eagleton 34). One does the right thing because it feels right and it feels right because it is right. The eighteenth-century thesis of moral sentimentalism thus attempts to unite the central oppositions of political philosophy – *zoē* and *bios*, the human and the citizen, nature and culture, the private and the public, the body and the body politic – into an organic and a harmonious whole, since the corporeal body that feels is no longer excluded from political life, but is instead the very ground on which ethical action and the public good are to be constructed. In this world view, "the body's affections are no mere subjective whims, but the key to a well-ordered state" (34).

Conrad's portrayal of Stevie as the subject of sentimental feeling takes on a different significance in light of this genealogy, for Stevie's passions are recoded not as mere mental afflictions but as innate moral sensibilities. His impassioned response to the cabdriver and the horse's suffering is figured first and foremost as a reaction of the body that instinctively apprehends the injustice he is witnessing:

> "Poor! Poor!" stammered out Stevie, pushing his hands deeper into his pockets with convulsive sympathy. He could say nothing; for the tenderness to all pain and all misery, the desire to make the horse happy and the cabman happy, had reached the point of a bizarre longing to take them to bed with him ... Stevie, though apt to forget mere facts, such as his name and address, for instance, had a faithful memory of sensations. To be taken into a bed of compassion was the supreme remedy, with the only one disadvantage of being of difficult application on a large scale. (123)

Stevie's "convulsive sympathy" speaks of a sentimental reaction that is also political insofar as it registers what is fundamentally wrong with the social order that he inhabits; he likewise attempts to imagine a solution borne of the body, calling on his "memory of sensations" to "remedy" the poverty with which he is confronted. But Conrad and *The Secret Agent* belong, of course, not to the eighteenth-century age of Enlightenment and progressive optimism, but to the modernist era of anti-humanist skepticism. Because Stevie's emotional responsiveness is both represented in the novel and perceived by others as a mental and somatic disease rather than as an internal ethical sensibility, we might say that Stevie's idiocy consists of being a moral sentimentalist in an age of irony. No longer are the responses of the body seamlessly contiguous with the political order, the human unified with the citizen, since private feeling no longer coheres with a public world of impersonal bureaucratization and rationalization. Stevie himself recognizes that his sentimental solutions are impossible to apply "on a large scale." Moral passion is hence shown to be politically ineffective in the modern world.

On the other hand, *The Secret Agent* repeatedly suggests that the real failure underlying the socio-political landscape inhabited by the characters is, in fact, the failure to feel – a moral and an aesthetic failure that reinforces an unjust status quo. Vladimir, for instance, justifies the need for a sensational terrorist attack because "the *sensibilities* of the class you are attacking are soon blunted ... You can't count on their emotions either of pity or fear for very long" (24; emphasis added). The London denizens of the novel uniformly exhibit what Georg Simmel has described as the "blasé attitude" of "indifference" that pervades the mental life of the modern metropolis (106). Looking at a crowd, the Professor sees that "they swarmed numerous like locusts, industrious like ants, thoughtless like a natural force ... impervious to sentiment, to logic, to terror too perhaps ... What if nothing could move them? Such moments come to all men whose ambition aims at a direct grasp upon humanity – to artists, politicians, thinkers, reformers, or saints" (61). The Professor's terrorism grows out of his desire to make the impervious public feel – to "move them" into emotional response – even if they feel nothing more than sheer terror. Conrad's turn to the rhetoric of aesthetics – the catharsis of "pity and fear" – and his reference to "artists" suggest that the desire to move is also *The Secret Agent*'s project, an aim inseparable from the reinvigoration of politics when confronted by a public with deadened sensibilities. Stevie's visceral and bodily passions may be "idiotic" – because they are politically inconsequential – but they paradoxically also model an ideal political sensibility that the novel and its revolutionary characters wish to cultivate. Indeed, the novel's end returns to a desire and dream for passion. Ossipon, wracked with guilt after having abandoned Winnie and caused her suicide, asks the Professor: "Here, what do you know of madness and despair?" The Professor replies, "There are no such things. All passion is lost now. The world is mediocre, limp, without force. And madness and despair are a force" (226). The passion of "madness" seems to refer to Stevie's idiocy, and the passion of "despair" to Winnie's emotional state after her brother's death. If this is the case, all passion is indeed "lost" in the novelistic world of *The Secret Agent* because both characters are dead by its end. Nevertheless, the Professor does not see passion as an impotent weakness, but as a vital and necessary "force" capable of rejuvenating a "limp" and "mediocre" world. Stevie's idiocy – reinscribed by Conrad as a passionate moral responsiveness originating from the body – is consequently tied back to something like a program for political action, even if this possibility is neither dramatized nor realized in the text. The rendition of Stevie as a sentimental "man of feeling" allows Conrad to draw on the resources of the human – the private sphere of affective life – to imagine different ways of being citizens and being political.

In *The Secret Agent*, anthropological norms of the human – structured by a historical discourse of eugenics that drew distinctions between the fit and the unfit, the degenerate and the healthy, the normal and the abnormal – do indeed constrict and shape the scope of citizenship; yet the world of the novel simultaneously constructs a discursive space in which such distinctions may be resisted and challenged. Not only can the aesthetic sphere document other ways of reading the disabled body that expand and offer alternative conceptions of the human, but, as Conrad also shows, the singularity of the human body is itself the necessary ground from which we can rethink our ideas of the citizen.

NOTES

1 When historical accuracy is important, I use the circulating medical vocabulary of the time, which refers to the mentally disabled as "idiots," "imbeciles," or "mental defectives"; I return to the language of disability when historical context is less at issue.

2 The term "docile bodies" derives from Michel Foucault's *Discipline and Punish.*

3 In *On Revolution*, Arendt sees the French Revolution as flawed because of its focus on "the social question ... [and] the existence of poverty." She notes: "When they [the multitude of the poor] appeared on the scene of politics, necessity appeared with them, and the result was that the power of the old regime became impotent and the new republic was stillborn; freedom had to be surrendered to necessity, to the urgency of the life process itself" (60). In this reading, the "freedom" of politics is debased by the intrusive demands of human bodily "necessity" – of hunger and poverty – which are properly issues belonging to the private sphere of the *oikos*, not the public sphere of the *polis*.

4 For examples of such analyses, see David Glover's reading of the novel in *Literature, Immigration, and Diaspora in Fin-de-Siècle England: A Cultural History of the Aliens Act* and Rebecca Walkowitz's *Cosmopolitan Style: Modernism beyond the Nation*.

5 Peter Nohrnberg has read *The Secret Agent* as a satire of compulsory elementary education. This education, in Conrad's view, provides basic literacy to the masses, but leaves them unable to grasp what they have read in any meaningful way. Nohrnberg does not, however, discuss the

1870 Education Act in relation to its role in developing a discourse of "feeble-mindedness." For a detailed history of the interrelations between the study of psychology (including that of mental disability) and the field of education, see Nikolas Rose's *The Psychological Complex*.

6 In the chapter of *Homo Sacer* entitled "Life That Does Not Deserve to Live," Agamben cites the writings of Karl Binding, a specialist of penal law in the early twentieth century, who discusses the valuation of life in relation to the mentally and physically disabled, deeming these lives superfluous.

7 Doubling, of course, is a figure that haunts all of Conrad's fiction; in a letter written on 5 December 1903 to Kazimierz Waliszewski, Conrad also described himself as a "homo duplex" (*Letters* 89).

8 As many critics have noted, Conrad's anarchists are frequently described as abnormal bodies. Michaelis is corpulent, "round like a tub, with an enormous stomach and distended cheeks"; Karl Yundt possesses "a skinny groping hand deformed by gouty swellings" (31–2).

9 Conrad's exploration of the Professor as a suicide bomber is the main reason why *The Secret Agent* has been regarded as "the classic novel of the post 9/11 age" (Reiss).

10 Lauren Berlant's critique exemplifies such a view: "when sentimentalism meets politics," she writes, "it uses personal stories to tell of structural effects, but in doing so it risks thwarting its very attempt to perform rhetorically a scene of pain that must be soothed politically ... The political as a place of acts oriented toward publicness becomes replaced by a world of private thoughts, leanings, and gestures" (41).

6

Interventions: Haiti, Humanitarianism, and *The Girls of Slender Means*

ALLAN HEPBURN

While she was writing *The Girls of Slender Means* in New York in late 1962, Muriel Spark lived in an apartment at 310 East 44th Street, from which she had a view of the nearby United Nations building (Stannard 269). The UN and its global missions preoccupied Spark in the early 1960s. As background research for her novel, she collected documents about UN interventions in Haiti. While the principal action in *The Girls of Slender Means* adheres to a narrow calendar of dates between VE-Day and VJ-Day in 1945, it also leaps forward to the early 1960s, when Nicholas Farringdon is martyred in Haiti, and further still to an undefined future. In the last days of the war, Nicholas glimpses "the new future" (19), which may entail either the welfare state led by the Labour Party or global governance spearheaded by the United Nations. Although it concerns a lodging for destitute women called the May of Teck Club, *The Girls of Slender Means* represents Spark's thinking about the necessity, if occasional absurdity, of intervention, whether individual and charitable or international and humanitarian.

The Small Fact of Time

Spark obsessively took notes for her novels: outlines, phrases, character lists, dates, genealogies, vectors of plot. Some of these notes recorded fleeting inspirations; others reminded her of details that she wanted to incorporate into her prose. While planning *The Girls of Slender Means*, Spark developed a chronology that focuses tightly on international events in summer 1945: Ribbentrop is captured on 15 June; the World Security Charter is signed in San Francisco on 26 June; the Allies recognize the Polish government in Warsaw on 5 July; the Labour Party comes to power in the British general election on 26 July; more than one thousand aircraft bomb Tokyo on 30 July; the first atomic bomb falls on Hiroshima on 6 August, with an estimated death toll of 78,150; Russia and China sign a thirty-year treaty of friendship and alliance on 26 August.[1] In the final version of *The Girls of Slender Means*, Spark marks historical time by referring to several of these events. Nicholas mentions the capture of Ribbentrop and the Labour Party victory in casual asides (98, 111). Phrases from Winston Churchill's notorious "Gestapo" speech, broadcast over the radio on 4 June 1945, resound through the May of Teck Club like "Sinaitic predictions" (86). Although Spark draws parallels between global history and local events in London in the last days of the war to suggest that nations and individuals have a responsibility for far-flung political interventions, she notes that such calls to responsibility engender, more often than not, nothing more than indifference. No one at the club pays much attention to Churchill's castigation of Clement Attlee and the Labour Party.

In its precise chronology, *The Girls of Slender Means* heralds the transition from wartime coalition government to welfare state. As one state withers away, another takes its place. The women at the May of Teck Club, however, have other matters on their minds than statehood. They worry about clothing coupons, food rations, and coins for heaters. They take turns wearing a Schiaparelli dress, handed down from a rich aunt to one of the impoverished residents. The girls of slender means, many of whom date men in the RAF or Intelligence, think of the future in terms of better jobs and suitable husbands, rather than the consequences of peace. By and large, they remain unconcerned by the passage of time. Only when a UXB explodes in the garden and thirteen women are caught by a fire on the top floor of the May of Teck Club do they see temporality as meaningful. While the women wait to be rescued, the "question of time opened now as a large thing" in their minds (121). "It was all a question of time," they are told about unbricking a skylight for them to escape (117). As catastrophe looms, the narrator, nearly chortling with gleeful wickedness, tolls the minutes as they pass from 6:00 p.m., to 6:15, to 6:22, to 6:30.

In its obsession with counting and its central catastrophe – a bomb blast followed by a fire – *The Girls of Slender Means* closely resembles John Hersey's landmark book, *Hiroshima* (1946). Both books are centrally concerned with human responsibility and the confusion that reigns after a military intervention. Hersey's report on the devastation of the Japanese city by the first atom bomb dropped on a civilian population filled an entire issue of the *New Yorker* on 31 August 1946.[2] The report was syndicated in many newspapers (Hersey viii). Spark may have seen the 30,000-word article in the *New Yorker*, or she may have read it in book format, or she may have heard it broadcast in four instalments on the BBC Third Programme. In his account of the bombing and its aftermath, Hersey repeatedly draws attention to temporality. He begins his story on the morning that the bomb falls on Hiroshima, and he documents what six survivors did in the hours, then days, weeks, and months after the blast. Spark uses a similar technique of counting down the minutes until the UXB explodes in the garden and the time it takes to break through a bricked-up skylight, even as she measures the significance of that catastrophe from a moment in the early 1960s, when Jane telephones various old friends and, by doing so, dredges up the past. In *Hiroshima*, Hersey describes the general bewilderment that befalls the Japanese in the minutes and hours after the bomb explodes. No one knows what is happening. Similarly, the tenants in the May of Teck Club, frantic to escape the burning building, grope about in the smoke while waiting for rescue workers to reach them. In *Hiroshima*, Hersey reports that schoolgirls, trapped under a heavy wall, sing the Japanese national anthem until "smoke entered into even a crack and choked their breath" (116). Only one girl escapes to report how all the others suffocated to death. In the final chapter of *Hiroshima*, time decelerates. Hersey sums up what has happened to the six survivors "a year after the bomb was dropped" (114). Although the report breaks off in 1946, Hersey implies that the consequences of radiation sickness and fallout from the bomb will continue for years and years. In *The Girls of Slender Means*, by allowing a gap of time to intrude between the events in 1945 and the recollection of that disaster years later, Spark suggests that the consequences of 1945 really have not been dealt with at all. The ramifications of violent interventions go on indefinitely.

As a satirist, Spark doubts that time brings change to human behaviour or international affairs. She takes a cosmic view of human folly. Between 1945 and the early 1960s, shifts in global alliances became, for Spark, "metaphors for mankind's infinite capacity for humanist delusion" (Stannard 296). In her figuration of temporality, Spark's comedy dissolves human, as well as humane, connections; from the perspective of eternity, all human actions appear absurd. In *The Girls of Slender Means*, the narrator often withdraws to a remote location in space or time to assess human behaviour. As fire rages in the May of Teck Club, Joanna Childe, daughter of a clergyman, recites the Psalter for Day 27 in the Anglican order, which was

> held to be applicable to all sorts and conditions of human life in the world at that particular moment, when in London homing workers plodded across the park, observing with curiosity the fire-engines in the distance, when Rudi Bittesch was sitting in his flat at St. John's Wood trying, without success, to telephone to Jane at the club to speak to her privately, the Labour Government was new-born, and elsewhere on the face of the globe people slept, queued for liberation-rations, beat the tom-toms, took shelter from the bombers, or went for a ride on a dodgem at the fun-fair. (126–7)

Although this sentence embraces diverse activities in a global panorama, these events and people have no particular connection to each other. Those who take shelter from the bombers on 27 July 1945 are probably located somewhere in the Pacific theatre, where the war with Japan has not yet ended. In London, fire engines are observed with detached curiosity by homing workers. The allusion to Thomas Gray's *Elegy in a Country Churchyard* – "the plowman homeward plods his weary way" – opens up a gap between the eighteenth and twentieth centuries, a gap bridged by the historical continuity of human indifference to other people's suffering. The narrator, detached and aloof, sees all these activities and people in time and across time, yet leaves them all to their own devices. They do not help each other.

There is no implication of human attachment among those being bombed, those who starve, those who spy emergencies at a distance. In other words, there is no intervention, either by narrator or by characters.

In *The Girls of Slender Means*, Spark pulls temporality every which way. Various characters foresee the future. Greggie predicts that the UXB will explode (115). Jane foresees arrangements for a drive to Kew before they happen (75). Nicholas has intimations of his later fame (69). In a note for the novel, Spark mentions that Nicholas "carries within him the future" (Tulsa 24.4; notebook p. 13). He is gifted with an "excruciating foreknowledge" (Tulsa 24.5), just as other characters have hunches and intuitions about events to come. Working to patterns of destiny, the narrator fancies the verb construction, "had not yet," as a sort of future anterior tense (59, 60). At the same time, much of the novel is set in a fairy-tale vista of the past. "Long ago in 1945 all the nice people in England were poor, allowing for exceptions," the novel begins (7). The phrase "long ago in 1945" repeats with variations throughout the novel. "That is how things were in 1945" (131), the narrator says about austerity measures, as if with a shrug of resignation. In this ironic perspective, history cannot be righted, only mythologized. In part, Spark mocks nostalgia for the war: the tendency to cast the past as a rosy fiction obscures the continuity of the wartime past with the postwar present. If the narrator is to be believed, the girls waiting to be rescued may as well be flung into outer space: "There, in 1945, they were as far removed from the small fact of time as weightless occupants of a space-rocket" (118). The comparison is flagrantly anachronistic. In 1945, they could hardly be astronauts, let alone participants in the space race. The anachronism magnifies the temporal contradictions within the sentence: although anchored historically in 1945, the girls refuse "the small fact of time" that adds so much moral heft to their actions. The sly narrator, as is usual in Spark's novels, knows more than the characters ever will. Gifted with foresight, these prescient narrators speak from a perspective that encompasses all time – past, present, and future.

In Spark's version of history, the consequences of the Second World War extend indefinitely into the future. Mrs Gareth Dobell, just arrived from California when the UXB explodes at the May of Teck Club, imagines "that belated bombs went off every day in Britain, and, content to find herself intact, and slightly pleased to have shared a war experience, was now curious as to what routine would be adopted in the emergency" (115). To have survived one belated bomb after the armistice hardly counts as "a war experience." As Adam Piette points out, Spark often applies the chronotope of the "temporary moment" to political ends ("Muriel Spark and the Politics of the Contemporary," 56). In the case of *The Girls of Slender Means*, the chronotope of the temporary moment – the short transitional period between VE-Day and VJ-Day, as well as the more specific duration between the explosion and the death of Joanna – tracks "postwar British international relations in terms of traumatic residues of the war" (Piette 62). On loan from British Intelligence, Nicholas Farringdon works for the Americans in the last months of the war. In fact, American Intelligence occupies the hotel next door to the May of Teck Club. This arrangement facilitates Colonel Felix Dobell's stepping round to visit Selina Redwood, just as it later facilitates Nicholas's seduction of Selina on the roof of the May of Teck Club. In short, international relations turn out to be intensely personal. For her part, Mrs Dobell hopes to travel to Europe with UNRRA, the United Nations Relief and Rehabilitation Administration (79). Having a sixth sense that her husband is up to something, she prepares a lecture on "the Western Woman's Mission" (102). Hypocrisy and puritanism set the tone for postwar relations between Britain and the US. The war never stops happening, insofar as it has lasting consequences for statehood and Cold War alliances.

The distorted temporalities of *The Girls of Slender Means* figure the time of the sovereign state. Ian Baucom claims that the state "has yielded a thinner grammar of time [than the nation], in significant part because it has seemed to succeed in putting the question of time outside itself or, at most, in producing a simple binary code of before and after" ("Afterword: States of Time," 713). The state monopolizes all imaginable temporality by squashing alternative temporalities; whatever preceded the state was all-out warfare or, in a Hobbesian vein, a benighted state of nature, and whatever follows the state would be some version of same, or so flows the logic of the sovereign state. In Baucom's assessment, the temporality of the state contains the temporality of the nation, insofar as the state permits only a permanent present, "which sets itself off as guarantor of national culture and the sole measure of imaginable time" (714). *The Girls of Slender Means*, in its simultaneous disordering of time and restrictive chronology, takes place within the temporality of state sovereignty. The Second World War keeps happening as a recollection of the nasty, brutish state of nature from which the state delivers its subjects. In Spark's novels, characters are stuck in time, where past and future collide in a perpetual now, which is the time of the state.[3]

Imagined States

The trope of being stuck gripped Spark's imagination. In *The Only Problem* (1984), Harvey Gotham labours for years over a treatise about the Book of Job without finishing it. In *The Finishing School* (2004), Rowland Mahler makes notes toward a thwarted novel and suffers fits of jealousy when Chris, his star pupil, writes a historical novel about Mary Queen of Scots without any hesitation or self-doubt. While working on *The Mandelbaum Gate* (1965), Spark herself had an uncharacteristic block, so she turned to *The Girls of Slender Means* as a holiday from that more arduous novel. Writer's block is just one way of being stuck. In *Memento Mori* (1959), Jean Taylor, the sympathetic and intelligent conscience of the novel, is paralyzed with age and arthritis; she is stuck in bed in a ward for valetudinarian women. In *Robinson* (1958), a reimagining of statehood along the lines of *Robinson Crusoe*, January, the narrator and protagonist, is marooned on an island with other survivors of a plane crash. She fears that she will be stuck there indefinitely at the mercy of weirdos and power grabbers. Being stuck has ethical ramifications for January. Self-interest motivates the survivors, who only act when an action benefits them. Thinking about the selfishness displayed by the island inhabitants, January concludes, "there's no such thing as private morality" (161). January is stuck between two impossibilities: she can help others who act only for themselves, or she can do nothing, which does not help her out of her own dire situation.

In *The Girls of Slender Means*, being stuck has literal and metaphorical meanings. The women at the May of Teck Club, providing they are skinny enough, slither through a lavatory window that measures a mere seven inches wide by fourteen inches long. Several of them can do so without difficulty; others get stuck. Selina Redwood and Anne Baberton squeeze through by turning their hips at just the right angle at the right moment. Dorothy Markham manages for a while, but pregnancy causes her waist to thicken and her agility to decrease. Clambering through the window is a contest of thinness for the women. Nancy Riddle, after getting caught in the frame, has to be "released and calmed" (44). Tilly Throvis-Mew, despite taking off her clothes and covering her body with a "greasy substance" (108), is half an inch too big; she cannot wriggle forward and she cannot be shoved back. Only the bomb blast jolts her free. While fire rages round the girls, slithering through the tiny opening becomes a test of passing into the realm of the saved, like entering the kingdom of heaven through the eye of a needle.

Among her notes for *The Girls of Slender Means*, Spark saved a newspaper clipping, dated 16 July 1962 and entitled "Oxy-Acetylene Used to Free Prisoner":

> A 5ft. prisoner, John Hind, aged 17, of Upton Park, Slough, appeared at Slough Magistrates' Court today charged with housebreaking. He looked little the worse for a five-and-a-half-hour ordeal the previous evening when his head was stuck in the 10¼ in. window of a cell door at Slough police station.
>
> A doctor stood by while police, firemen, and a rescue team from a local factory tried without avail to separate him from the door. After the door had been removed from its hinges oxy-acetylene cutting gear was used successfully. Water cooling the metal as it was cut turned to steam and caused slight scalds on Hind's shoulders. He was treated later at hospital for scalds and shock.
>
> Chief-inspector A. Hailstone explained: "Hind was found with his head and shoulders through the aperture after his call for help had been heard. We tried to release him by holding him horizontal and turning him in various ways. Hind kept remarkably cheerful in spite of at times being in considerable pain."
>
> Hind was remanded to another cell for 24 hours today and will appear again tomorrow. (Tulsa 24.3)

This news item no doubt amused Spark for several reasons. A rescue team combines forces with policemen, firemen, and a doctor to free one petty criminal. With his head stuck in the door, Hind the housebreaker can neither proceed nor retreat. In recounting this *fait divers*, the anonymous journalist preserves a studied neutrality about the moral implications of freeing a criminal.

In *The Girls of Slender Means*, being stuck has implications for statehood and international governance: being stuck in the past prevents viable political action in the future. In this regard, the novel belongs among a series of British novels, published in the late 1940s and 1950s, that imagine the reciprocal responsibilities of individuals and states as, at best, incompatibility, and, at worst, unchanging devastation: Ivy Compton-Burnett's *Manservant and Maidservant* (1947), Aldous Huxley's *Ape and Essence* (1948), George Orwell's *Nineteen Eighty-Four* (1949), Graham Greene's *The Third Man* (1949), and Alan Sillitoe's *Saturday Night and Sunday Morning* (1958). Spark, unlike the majority of her peers who thought of statehood in terms of levelling down or nuclear catastrophe, dwells on the divergence between the ideal society and the heavenly kingdom. Among her notes for *The Girls of Slender Means*, she mentions: "The ideal society. To keep in mind. Thy Kingdom Come. How can you act if you have not an idea of what you want?" (Tulsa 24.4; notebook p. 29). The eternity of heaven rivals the non-time of the state. In *Saturday Night and Sunday Morning*, Arthur Seaton thinks of blowing the castle "to Kingdom Cum, so's nob'dy 'ud ever see it again" (72). State bureaucracy blocks Arthur's self-realization, or so he thinks. Nicholas Farringdon, sometime poet and anarchist, comes to a slightly different conclusion: by converting to Catholicism, he positions the heavenly kingdom over and against the sovereign state.

Spark's archival notes are filled with speculations on practical statecraft and varieties of governance. "Dreary utopia," she notes on one scrap of paper, without further explanation (Tulsa 24.5). As a way of working out Nicholas's political position, she developed a long sequence of extracts from his manuscript, which he calls *The Sabbath Notebooks*. Some of these extracts find their way verbatim into *The Girls of Slender Means*: "We in Britain have no need of government. We do not need members of Parliament. Parliament should dissolve and go home for good. We could manage very well, if only in a period of a transition to a complete anarchist society, with our existing great but powerless institutions" (Tulsa 24.5; cf. *Girls* 57). Channelling Nicholas's anarchism, Spark wonders about "the abolition of the State and the creation of a cooperative commonwealth" (Tulsa 24.5). She noticeably does not endorse Labour-sponsored welfare initiatives. While the destruction of the May of Teck building implies the destruction of an antiquated ideal of womanhood and wartime conservatism, no clear structure of governance asserts itself in the place of those ideals. Britain, during the transitional months of summer 1945, is stuck between the ruins of the past and the promises of the future.

As archival materials indicate, Spark considers varieties of statehood in *The Girls of Slender Means*: anarchist, libertarian, parliamentary, revolutionary, spiritual. The evolution of the welfare state out of wartime governance sets the parameters for Spark's thinking. Again and again, she returns to 1945 as the crucial moment in imaginings of statehood. That year, despite rationing and hardship, contained potential new forms of statehood for the future. In one of Spark's working notes, Nicholas reflects on postwar British governance:

> He saw them [the girls of slender means] as he saw the nation. Poor, reduced to nothing. A hope for innocence. His austere mind saw the possibility of a new social order. He rejoiced as rationing became stricter. Anarchism. MI5 incurious while concentrating on Commies & Fascists. Perhaps the most dangerous of all, because the most reliant upon individual goodness, which is enough to undermine any state. It held something of the menace of early Christianity. (Tulsa 24.4; notebook p. 8)

Spark explicitly links anarchism, as an opportunity for an improved social order, with a version of statehood guided by individual goodness and spiritual values, rather like early Christianity. In Spark's view, such a version of statehood could possibly rectify the ideological extremes of communism and fascism, which galvanize the attention, not to say the surveillance, of MI5. Anarchism, understood as personal goodness, could alter the social order for the better. A reform in statehood begins with a reform of the individual. As *The Sabbath Notebooks* further indicate, the return to peace in 1945 calls individuals to their responsibilities in a state that guarantees freedoms: "The opportunity of freedom, and the disposition on the part of individuals to use it, do not necessarily coincide. Freedom enforced is no freedom, but a new kind of slavery: fear and the distress of unaccustomed responsibility. Nevertheless, let our moment of opportunity be stated. Now that we have peace, in this year of special grace, 1945, we have the opportunity of constructing a free life from our poverty and our peace" (Tulsa 24.5). For Spark, 1945 is a chronotope of potential, one that she looks back on as a moment of missed opportunities.

With the perplexities of statehood on her mind, Spark fussed over the final sentence of *The Girls of Slender Means*. In an attempt to resolve the conundrums of statehood and personal obligation, she tried out multiple versions of this sentence. Most of these versions are clauses, not complete sentences. She initially intended to link the last line of the novel to the title. In one version, she aimed for cadence and allusiveness: "inherit the abundant earth on hopes so slender and means so tenuous" (Tulsa 24.4; notebook p. 15). In another note, she switches adjectives: "inherit the abundant earth on hopes that were so slender and by such unpredictable means" (Tulsa 24.5). Still another version attributes the inheritance of heaven and earth to Nicholas as an intimation of his sanctity: "Not suspecting in the least he too would come to inherit the abundant kingdoms of heaven and earth on hopes so slender and by serpentine means" (Tulsa 24.5). In this version, Spark also inserted "lethal" under "serpentine" as an alternate modifier. Yet another attempt, scribbled on the same sheet as the "lethal" and "serpentine" variation, establishes parallels between Haiti and the slender means that prevail in London at the May of Teck Club: "see *Haiti* // Island of W. Indies // Port au Prince // inherit the abundant [earth] on hopes so slender and by such extraordinary means" (Tulsa 24.5). In all versions, the hopes remain "slender," while the means vary from "tenuous" and "unpredictable" to "serpentine" and "extraordinary."

In a further version of this sentence, Nicholas walks in the park with Jane. In this iteration, meekness shifts from Nicholas to Jane: "At the time, he merely speculated humorously whether she might have possessed the gift of meekness, and so inherit the earth [...] – not suspecting in the least that he too would – might accomplish the feat on hopes that were so slender and by means so serpentine. The End" (Tulsa 24.5; p. 54). This version resembles the final sentence of the published version, in which Nicholas walks with Jane through roistering crowds in central London on VJ-Day. Jane stops to pin up her hair, which Nicholas remembers years later in the country of his death. In its temporal layering and complexity, the concluding sentence that appears in the published text is a tour de force of allusiveness, circularity, nostalgia, and temporal dislocation: "Nicholas marvelled at her stamina, recalling her in this image years later in the country of his death – how she stood, sturdy and bare-legged on the dark grass, occupied with her hair – as if this was an image of all the May of Teck establishment in its meek, unselfconscious attitudes of poverty, long ago in 1945" (142). A trace of meekness remains within the sentence, though now identified with the May of Teck Club and possibly with Haiti, where Nicholas dies. More startling still, Spark tosses aside all efforts to create a sentence that resonates with the title. She opts instead for the fairy-tale phrase, "long ago in 1945," that opens the novel. If any inheritance remains in the sentence, it is Nicholas's recollection, long after, of Jane pinning up her hair, emblem of austerity and unselfconsciousness.

To end the novel, Spark wanted to contrast human and heavenly states. Regardless of the variation, the sentence recalls the beatitudes: "blessed are the meek for they shall inherit the earth" (Matthew 5.5). On another allusive plane, it echoes Psalm 37: "the meek shall inherit the earth; and shall delight themselves in the abundance of peace" (Psalms 37.11). In the same psalm, lest the reader forget, the speaker predicts that "evildoers shall be cut off" and "the transgressors shall be destroyed together" (Psalms 37.9, 37.38). Spark spikes the likelihood of such an inheritance with doubt: no matter what happens, the hopes are slender and the means unpredictable for such an inheritance to come to pass. The word "peace," though everywhere implicit in the final scene on VJ-Day, never enters the concluding sentence. Jane, sturdy and energetic, is anything but meek. She affronts the future.

The year 1945 remains a chronotope for potential, not fulfillment. As the final sentence confirms, Nicholas glimpses a form of the ideal state in the May of Teck Club. Notwithstanding its appearance of being a self-regulating entity, the club may be just another dreary utopia. Nicholas imposes an "aesthetic and ethical conception" (86) upon the club, even though he knows that his conception is at odds with the good-time behaviour of the residents. The club intrigues and exasperates him because he wants it to live up to his ideal of a perfect society. For her part, Jane resists seeing the May of Teck Club "as a microcosmic ideal society" (62). At times, because she has a crush on him, Jane gives Nicholas tidbits of information that support his notions of the ideal society: "In fact, it was not an unjust notion, that it was a miniature expression of a free society, that it was a community held together by the graceful attributes of a common poverty" (84). In this instance, the narrator colludes with Jane, who supports Nicholas's view of the club, while also colluding with Nicholas, who lives in a squalid flat and praises poverty as a way of life. Poverty, in the Christian tradition, purifies the soul. At the same time, poverty, created by the war economy, may encourage the development of a new kind of statehood, one based on cooperation rather than self-interest. Nicholas urges Selina to "accept and exploit the outlines of poverty in her life. He loved her as he loved his native country. He wanted Selina to be an ideal society personified amongst her bones" (92). It is not clear how much Nicholas, an anarchist-serviceman evacuated from Dunkirk, actually loves his country. Rudi Bittesch reports that Nicholas was always torn between France and England, men and women, anarchism and Catholicism. If Selina personifies his native country, she does so only if she accepts her impoverishment, which is at odds with Selina's own aspirations for upward mobility.

Throughout *The Girls of Slender Means*, Spark sees correspondences between individuals and ideas, local incidents and global events. Such correspondences range over time and space. The UXB that explodes in the garden of the May of Teck Club on 27 July 1945 recalls the Blitz – the bomb has been concealed since 1942 – even as it forecasts the atomic bombs dropped on Hiroshima and Nagasaki. Indeed, Spark draws an equation between the UXB that goes off and the bombing of Japan: "The dropping of the bomb on Hiroshima & Nagasaki. [E]xtension of Selina's act" (Tulsa 24.4; notebook p. 25). In such equivalencies, the microcosmic substitutes for the macrocosmic, sometimes with the inappropriate consequence of belittling catastrophe. By the same token, human actions have large moral consequences. Selina's retrieving the Schiaparelli dress from the burning building has implications for the presence of evil in the world. While various reviewers and critics complain that Selina's act ought not to have triggered Nicholas's conversion to Catholicism,[4] for Spark, nothing more grand or definitive is needed for a decisive turn to faith.

In an intriguing preparatory note, Spark sees an analogy between "Selina's poise and that described in the ideal state by Simone Weil" (Tulsa 24.4; notebook p. 25). The extent of Spark's reading in Weil's works, many of which were published posthumously, is unknown. She praises Weil for her "consummate spiritual utterance[s]" (*Golden Fleece* 180). In a short review of Joseph-Marie Perrin and Gustave Thibon's *Simone Weil as We Knew Her* for the *Observer* in 1953, Spark expresses admiration for Weil "as an independent witness" to conflict (10). According to Spark in the same review, Weil belonged to "the order of independent Christians who seem expressly appointed as a living rebuke to Christendom, an embarrassment and stimulus to the Church" (10). As the analogy between Selina's poise and the perfect state presupposes, Spark had read Weil's writings on equilibrium within the state. "Poise is perfect balance, an equanimity of body and mind, complete composure whatever the social scene," recites Selina twice a day (50). Simone Weil, less concerned with taffeta dresses and immaculate grooming than Selina, often defines the ideal state in terms of equilibrium. In "The Power of Words," Weil writes about balance: "The essential contradiction in human society is that every social *status quo* rests upon an equilibrium of forces or pressures, similar to the equilibrium of fluids; but between one prestige and another there can be no equilibrium. Prestige has no bounds and its satisfaction always involves the infringement of someone else's prestige or dignity" (283–4). Selina should pay attention: her narcissism not only infringes other club members' prestige and dignity, but also leads her to ignore the girls trapped in the burning building. She refuses to recognize the suffering of others.

In pointing to the analogy between Selina's poise and political equilibrium, Spark may have been thinking of Weil's *Gravity and Grace*, published in English translation in 1952, during Spark's most intense phase of reading Catholic texts. In a series of maxims, Weil pursues the idea of equilibrium as part of social tussle: "Equilibrium alone destroys and annuls force. Social order can be nothing but an equilibrium of forces" (*Gravity* 150). Weil implies that equilibrium remains tenuous even while she holds out the possibility of permanent poise in the political register: "A well ordered society would be one where the State only had a negative action, comparable to that of a rudder: a light pressure at the right moment to counteract the first suggestion of any loss of equilibrium" (*Gravity* 151). Poise is therefore a political attribute.

The momentariness of equilibrium is illustrated by Weil's further observation that "one has to give in to the state as a necessity, but not accept it within oneself" (*Lectures* 160). The state cannot mandate freedom as it mandates subjection. Acting freely remains a prerogative of the individual, a liberty that can never be utterly regulated by the state. In *The Sabbath Notebooks*, Nicholas makes a similar point: "If the individual is deprived of the means to act freely – that is, to give and receive without thought of consequence, according to the conditions of the moment, the day, the hour, the year, the century, in which he lives, he cannot develop and expand" (Tulsa 24.5; looseleaf pp. 1–2). Strange to say, Nicholas Farringdon shares features with Simone Weil. Both think in aphorisms. Both write about statehood in relation to spiritual life. Both embrace Christianity awkwardly. Both may or may not be saintly. Nicholas dies a martyr's death in Haiti. Weil would have been canonized if she had only accepted baptism, Spark suggests in "Awkward Saint" (10).

Interventions

Having converted to Catholicism and become a missionary, Nicholas was "killed in a local rising in Haiti," as a Reuters news item puts it (18). The locale and the rationale of Nicholas's death remain nebulous. "He was trying to interfere with their superstitions," Jane tells Rudi: "They're getting rid of a lot of Catholic priests" (69). The narrative of the martyrdom becomes no clearer as Jane rings up all her friends to tell them the news: "Haiti, in a hut ... among some palms, it was market day, everyone had gone to the market centre" (85). Like Celia Copplestone, the holy woman in T.S. Eliot's *The Cocktail Party* who dies among heathens in Kinkanja, Nicholas could have died anywhere. Spark may have chosen Haiti because of its tumultuous political history and because of its status as a country subject to humanitarian interventions.

Among the papers that Spark assembled to write *The Girls of Slender Means* are two United Nations reports about Haiti. In all likelihood, she consulted these materials minimally; her copies show no underlining or marginalia. Nonetheless, she acquired these materials as background for her novel. The first document, entitled *Mission to Haiti*, is dated 1949. Written in the orotund, euphemistic language of international postwar development, this brief offers numerous recommendations from a team of experts for curbing illiteracy, developing imports and exports, building infrastructure, reducing malaria and yaws, shoring up administration, widening agricultural production – in short, remaking the country in the guise of an ideal society along the lines imagined by the United Nations. Emphasis falls on agriculture and fisheries, resources on which the Haitian economy relies. In passing, *Mission to Haiti* provides a brief history of the country from the declaration of national independence in 1804 to the US military occupation of the country from 1915 to 1934 (*Mission* 26). This history, albeit short, may have furnished Spark with some notions about Haitian uprisings and their suppression.

The second document that Spark collected, a report from the Technical Assistance Board, dated 5 October 1962, concerns failed UN interventions in Haiti. This brief, written in circumspect, bureaucratic language by Jean B. Richardot, UN director of Special Fund Programmes in Haiti, notes that the government has decreed a series of measures to collect funds "for the economic 'liberation' of the country" (Richardot 1). These measures include a lottery (all civil servants and employees in private Haitian enterprises had to buy a monthly allotment of tickets), a 20 per cent rise in import levies and a 10 per cent rise in export levies, a supplementary tax on vehicles, and so forth. Duvalier was elected to the presidency in 1957, then proclaimed himself "President for Life" in 1964. Yet the dictatorship of Papa Doc Duvalier receives no acknowledgment in Richardot's report. Nor does he mention the massacre of civilians by the Tonton Macoutes, Duvalier's paramilitary police forces.

Owing to the lamentable conditions in Haiti, an air of hopelessness wafts through the 1962 report. The US suspended aid to Haiti in 1961 because of Duvalier's misappropriation of funds. Money intended for schools and projects lined the pockets of the dictator. In Richardot's view, further humanitarian help with education, relief from poverty, and alleviation of hunger will have no positive benefits in Haiti. He cites specific examples of economic failure. For a rural normal school at Marfranc, for instance, the Haitian government did not contribute its share of expenses: "The Government contributed

$5,000 for buildings in 1961 but could not provide a larger sum. Approximately $20,000 in Government funds are needed to operate the school during the first year. UNICEF has approved an allocation of $15,000 in connexion with a nutrition programme in satellite schools. The project is not expected to continue in 1963 if the Government has not made its contribution available" (Richardot 8). The technical brief lists ILO, WMO, UNESCO, WHO, FAO, ICAO, and SNEM activities. UN optimism fizzles out in a tempest of acronyms. The fisheries project has to be suspended. A medical laboratory is created, but Richardot reports "no other progress" in health reform (11). Between the lines, one understands that UN interventions in Haiti conflict with national self-determination, as conceived by Papa Doc Duvalier.

Throughout her career, Spark was aware of the liabilities of humanitarian and cultural incursions. In 1949, she commented on the occlusion of native cultures – in Africa, not Haiti – in an essay called "African Handouts." She deplores glossy government brochures designed to lure migrants to South Africa and Rhodesia: "We have come to expect that Government handouts from English-speaking countries will convey the truth, but not the whole truth" (32). Photographs of beaches and gold mines pre-empt any image "of the overcrowded Native compounds and locations which lie on the outskirts of every large town" (32). In this essay, Spark dwells on the problems facing African artists – not Europeans who settle in South Africa or Rhodesia, but black writers born in Africa who have to figure out how to handle questions of race without ascribing to European attitudes. In short, she wonders about the efficacy of cultural interventions across national boundaries.

The Girls of Slender Means represents various interventions in terms of politics. As a "member of the Guild of Ethical Guardians" (73), Mrs Gareth Dobell hopes to rectify other women's lapses when it comes to preserving purity in the home. She exports American puritanism to Britain, in part to keep her husband mindful of his marital obligations. Other interventions are more immediate. On VJ-Day, Nicholas, walking among the crowds on The Mall, sees a seaman knife a woman. He cannot even draw attention to the crime because of the crowds. His failing to help the stabbed woman, paired with his aghastness at Selina's selfish rescuing of the Schiaparelli dress, drives him to convert, or so the narrative leads the reader to surmise. As a missionary, Nicholas subsequently intervenes in Haitian Vodou practices. He is killed, as far as anyone knows, for meddling with local superstitions. For Spark, intervention means a personal action for the benefit of someone else. Yet, on the principle that individuals' actions substitute for macrocosmic ones, she considers Nicholas's death in Haiti in terms of the well-intentioned interventions that end in futility and death.

Intervention is an acute issue in postwar fiction. It provides a way to think about the global balance of power, as well as a way to think about brinkmanship – being stuck in intransigent political positions – during the Cold War. In *The Quiet American* (1955), Graham Greene contemplates the egregious self-interest of American intervention in Vietnam; claiming to nurture democracy in that country, Pyle, a naive American, kills civilians by detonating a bomb in a public square. In Eric Ambler's *Passage of Arms* (1958), an American couple bumble into an arms deal in Singapore because they do not understand even the rudiments of foreign hostilities and alliances. Olivia Manning's *The Balkan Trilogy* (1956–64) assesses the war years as a series of diplomatic failures and fascist incursions in Romania. Nevil Shute's *On the Beach* (1957) represents nuclear war as the ultimate intervention that ends all human life. In *The Comedians* (1966), Graham Greene turns to the massacres in Haiti and the futility of international diplomacy in the face of Duvalier's assertion of sovereignty. "The Haitian government does not accept protests from foreigners," one character observes in *The Comedians* (111). Whether in isolated locations or in global theatres, these novels depict intervention as unhelpful, sometimes even catastrophic, in its consequences. At the same time, intervention for humanitarian reasons is morally inevitable and necessary.

Humanitarian intervention has elicited wide-ranging arguments from political theorists, who generally agree that an inherent contradiction between state sovereignty and universal rights limits the effectiveness of aid. Although some political theorists thought about intervention as early as the 1920s – Ellery C. Stowell, in *Intervention in International Law* (1921), likened declarations of war as structurally similar to international interventions, even as he upheld the distinctness of individual states and the right to self-governance – concerted thinking about intervention really only begins after the Second

World War. Intervention for humanitarian purposes has to surmount several paradoxes. Allegiance to a state that grants citizens' rights is at odds with an unenforceable allegiance to "the universal human community" (Parekh 49). Notwithstanding the sovereignty of states, humanitarian intervention is justified when a state has committed "a deliberate violation of that minimum of security and justice to which every individual in a civilized community is entitled," according to Stowell ("Humanitarian" 734). Stowell concludes that humanitarian intervention "tends to bind the whole world closer together in defense of elementary principles of justice" (736). Yet everyone demonstrably does not adhere to principles of justice, let alone the principle that "humanity, as a collective of human beings, is one and indivisible" (Fassin 518). According to Michael Ignatieff, the number of situations in which interventions could happen far exceed the number of situations in which interventions do happen. "The fact that we cannot intervene everywhere," Ignatieff argues, "is not a justification for not intervening where we can" (319).

Models of humanitarianism distinguish between military intervention and emergencies, such as natural disasters or epidemics, which require relief rather than armed intervention. Under the UN Charter, Chapter 7, coercion against a state is sanctioned when international peace and security are threatened. Military intervention, however, is rarely exercised in a "disinterested, neutral, and impartial manner" (Lu, "Humanitarian," 944). Intervention, on whatever scale and in whatever crisis, rests on the perceived value of human lives. As Didier Fassin claims, the lives of humanitarian workers, usually Westerners, are deemed to have more value than the populations that they help. Fassin calls this "an a priori differential evaluation of human beings" (513). Abducted aid workers in a conflict zone, regardless of their number, are perceived to have more value than local civilians, who may be slaughtered by the thousands. In theory, humanitarian intervention is premised on the indisputable value of every human life, yet that principle of dignity yields to quarrels about unnecessary risk and the limited payoff of intervention. Furthermore, intervention is premised on a dialectic of state and individual in which humanitarian intervention serves as a palliative, or sometimes as a mediation, of that dialectic. As Catherine Lu argues, intervention maps onto concepts of public and private spheres, so that the sovereignty of an individual state within an international arena is analogous to a zone of private governance (*Just and Unjust* 157). Thus sovereign states claim not to be accountable for abuses of citizens' rights: governance is a strictly domestic concern.

In many discussions of state or UN intervention, neighbourliness is invoked to clarify issues. "Should we intervene if our neighbour's husband beats up his wife?" Daniele Archibugi asks (3). By analogy, should a state intervene when its neighbour perpetrates aggression against its citizens or the citizens of another state? If so, when should intervention happen? At what moment does murder become a massacre, or massacres genocide? The analogy between violence perpetrated against an individual and violent conflict between states may cause misperceptions about the need for intervention. Good neighbours might call the police to intercede in domestic violence, or take matters into their own hands by knocking on the neighbours' door. In a domestic fracas or an international dispute, an intervention might have any number of motives. Building on the metaphor of neighbourliness, Ignatieff cautions against the assumption that "strong states [necessarily] have a clear interest in being good neighbours to weaker ones" (314). Ignatieff concludes that the long-term goal of humanitarianism ought to be the creation of sustainable nation-states: "Nation-building takes time, and it is not an exercise in social work. Its ultimate purpose is to create the state order that is the precondition for any defensible system of human rights and to create the stability that turns bad neighbourhoods into good ones" (321). Bad neighbours, Ignatieff implies, have a synecdochic effect like rotten apples in a barrel: in the long run, they ruin the whole lot.

Only with the ascendancy of international human rights laws after the Second World War does the idea of duties towards non-citizens create reasons for intervention in the ways that a sovereign state governs itself. And only in the twenty-first century, with the International Commission on Intervention and State Sovereignty and the 2005 World Summit, which adopted the humanitarian "responsibility to protect," has intervention affected state sovereignty ("2005 World Summit Outcome," ¶138–9). Under these UN-sanctioned provisions, states have the duty to protect their populations from genocide, war, ethnic cleansing, and crimes against humanity; the international community also bears the responsibility of acting in a timely fashion to prevent and stop genocide, war crimes, ethnic cleansing, and crimes against humanity. Unlike previous accords, this resolution allows for non-military, international intervention as a pre-emptive measure. The dichotomy of international versus domestic governance, like the dichotomy of public and private spheres, is effaced in the bid for human rights that transcend national borders. In *The Girls of Slender Means*, Spark explores intervention in very similar terms, namely as a disruption in the homology between state sovereignty as a zone of indisputable sovereign authority and citizens' rights as a zone of abuse.

In 1962, as she was writing *The Girls of Slender Means*, Spark's neighbourhood extended to the United Nations building. Her novel takes up postwar concerns about the necessity of intervention and the responsibility attached to such intervention. To what degree is one responsible for one's neighbours? When does one intervene with one's neighbours, or one's fellow man, on the grounds that intervention will make a difference? Selina Redwood does not intervene to help the women trapped by fire in the May of Teck Club. Nicholas can do nothing to help the woman stabbed on VJ-Day. Although Muriel Spark's great theme is suffering – "The problem of suffering is indivisible from life itself," she observes about the Book of Job (*Golden Fleece* 192) – nothing abates suffering in *The Girls of Slender Means*. That, at least, is how things looked to Spark, long ago in 1945, when all the nice people were thinking about the perplexities of world citizenship and the appropriateness of humanitarian intervention in the wake of the Second World War, allowing of course for exceptions.

NOTES

1 Muriel Spark Papers, McFarlin Library, University of Tulsa, box 14, file 4, notebook p. 27. Subsequent references to these papers will appear in the text in a shortened form, consisting of box and file number. Whenever possible, information about the exact location of a note is given. For instance, Spark numbered some pages in her notebooks, though she left other notes on unnumbered looseleaf pages. Spark habitually gathered materials for reference: life insurance pamphlets and transcripts of the Eichmann trial for *The Mandelbaum Gate*, for instance, or information about Benedictine monks and the Watergate tapes for *The Abbess*

of Crewe. In addition to showing what phrases Spark particularly cherished, the archives contain clues about what she was reading to prepare for the composition of any given novel.

2 *The Prime of Miss Jean Brodie* was similarly honoured: Wallace Shawn, editor of the *New Yorker*, devoted the entire 14 October 1961 issue to Spark's novel.

3 In *The Hothouse by the East River*, which takes place in the shadow of the UN building in New York City, Spark presents a counter-factual narrative about a group of Londoners killed in the 1944 Blitz. Being dead, the non-characters live out shadow lives that stretch into the indefinite future. "Oh God, what was 1944? It never happened to me," cries Katerina (74). As in *The Girls of Slender Means*, the narrator has access to information that characters do not: "Paul's jitters are not available to human eyes this afternoon in the early spring of England, 1944" (27). In this regard, Spark imagines state temporality as uniform and unchanging; it animates even those who have died decades earlier, as if they were stuck in a coma but sustained on life support.

4 Spark had clipping agencies that found, cut, and forwarded reviews of her works. She kept these among her papers. She therefore knew that reviewers understood *The Girls of Slender Means* in terms of evil and detachment. Simon Raven, writing in the *Spectator* on 20 September 1963, claimed that, "Of all contemporary novelists, Muriel Spark evinces the least confidence in morality. She encourages us neither to hope for good nor to deplore evil; indeed most of the time she is at few pains to distinguish between the two. True, some of her characters lead virtuous lives, are of modest and kindly disposition, are sincerely attached to the Christian faith; but whatever their intrinsic goodness, they do not emerge, on the evidence of their speech and actions, as being notably more commendable than those who traffic in sexual perversions or black magic. Mrs. Spark does not take sides, she deals neither in praise nor in blame; she merely records what occurs; and in so far as she lets us into motives, it is not to assess their worth but to show us how utterly irrational and undependable is the connection between motive and performance" (Raven 354).

7

Torture, Text, Human Rights: Beckett's *Comment c'est / How It Is* and the Algerian War

ADAM PIETTE

The torture scenes in Samuel Beckett's *Comment c'est / How It Is* test the limits of human rights. Article 5 of the United Nations Universal Declaration of Human Rights (1948) guarantees that "No one shall be subjected to torture or to cruel, inhuman or degrading treatment or punishment." With a minor modification – the word "cruel" was omitted – this protection was adopted as Article 3 of the European Convention on Human Rights (1950). Beckett wrote *Comment c'est* over eighteen months from the spring of 1959 to summer 1960; it is tempting to identify its compositional context in terms of late-1950s Cold War France, specifically, given the focus on torture and justice in the novel and the setting up of the European Court of Human Rights (ECHR). The first members of the ECHR were elected on 21 January 1959, and the first session was held 23–28 February in the same year. René Cassin was one of the judges at the first session – he had composed the UDHR from John Humphrey's draft – despite the fact that France had not even ratified the European Convention on Human Rights. Using Mikael Rask Madsen's work on the Cold War history of the ECHR, I read Beckett's novel as a response to and satire of the ambiguous French position. While Cassin advocated universal rights, the French abused those rights in its colonial policies, particularly through the use of torture in Algeria.

Henri Alleg's *La question* (1958), a grisly account of his torture at the hands of French paratroopers in the El-Biar camp during the Battle of Algiers in 1957, unleashed a stormy, public controversy. Jérôme Lindon at Éditions de minuit published Alleg's book as part of a long campaign against the abuse of power in Algeria; the English translation by John Calder appeared the same year. (Lindon and Calder were, respectively, Beckett's French and English publishers.) The title of Alleg's book is unambiguous. "La question" is the technical term used for torture in medieval and pre-Revolutionary France. Partly as a result of Alleg's exposé, intellectuals such as François Mauriac and Jean-Paul Sartre campaigned against the use of torture. The extraordinary impact of *La question* occurred while Beckett was writing *Comment c'est*. In February 1960, Beckett told Barbara Bray he was obsessed with the news from Algeria: "Ears glued to Europe no 1 up to a few days ago – news" (*Letters* 290). In *Comment c'est*, the conflict between colonial national interests and European (specifically Cold War anti-Communist) human rights legislation characteristic of French policy during the Algerian War is traceable in its dark satire of the relationship between torture and justice. The novel explores an extreme form of rights summoned by the plight of stateless victims of hegemonic violence and control.

The dialectic of victim and perpetrator in Beckett's novel materializes Sartre's critique of French torture in the Alleg case: "Anybody, at any time, may equally find himself victim or executioner" ("Preface," xxviii). The "dark twins" of torture and confession, to use Foucault's phrase (*History of Sexuality* 59), accompany the ghastly pseudo-couple of torturer and victim. Beckett's nightmare vision of the narrator torturing the story of his own life from his victim Pim stages the inseparability of torturer and tortured. In *Comment c'est* Beckett raises questions about the continuity between French Resistance victimhood during the Second World War and fascist-colonial perpetrator violence in the postwar. At stake for Beckett is the "right to have rights," as Arendt calls this foundational premise (*Origins* 296). Membership in the human species constitutes a fragile protection against colonial torture and appropriation of voice in the name of nation. In both *La question* and *Comment c'est*, resistance as an assertion of species rights arises from accounts of torture by witnesses who survive destructive interrogation.

Europeanization and Universalization of Human Rights

According to manuscript evidence, Beckett began writing *Comment c'est* on 17 December 1958. Before he worked on the manuscript proper, he alternated between manuscript and typescript versions in four bursts of text. The continuous manuscript, dated 13 March 1959, begins in the same notebook as the four initial bursts. A second notebook is labelled "Ussy 11.3.59." The whole manuscript occupies five notebooks plus a sixth comprising revisions, entitled "Pim I" to "Pim VI." The final notebook is dated 6 January 1960. During a major revision of the text in May and June 1960, Beckett began to fragment the prose; he split off each paragraph and left it surrounded by empty space (O'Reilly xliii–l). He submitted the complete manuscript to Lindon at Éditions de minuit by early October 1960, and the novel was published on 6 January 1961.

Another notebook, called the "Pim" manuscript, indicates that Beckett was thinking about the novel as early as summer 1956. His first thoughts help identify key considerations in the final text: "Pim: lui passais une main sur tout le corps, surtout le visage, c'était un homme, ç'avait été un homme" (O'Reilly 199). The torture theme is already present in this draft: "x communique avec Pim et [*sic*: en] traçant des mots sur son cul avec l'ongle de l'index?"; "bourreaux et victimes simultanément les cris" (201). Even at this incipient stage, justice is a key concern: "immobilité finale par couples échelonnés ce ne serait pas justice puisque une moitié privée de victimes l'autre de bourreaux" (202).[1] The plea for justice based on torture is resisted with a note that records a quotation from Hugo's *L'homme qui rit*: "Être un ver, quelle force!" (259).

L'homme qui rit has a torture subtext that turns on questions of mutilation and justice. A gang of perverse aristocrats torture the hero, Gwynplaine, while he is still a child by carving a ghastly grin onto his face. Hugo's novel contains several meditations on torture as a "supplice exquis": "ce triple sens terrible: recherche du tourment, souffrance du tourmenté, volupté du tourmenteur" (265).[2] *L'homme qui rit* is also about dark, mocking comedy – apparent in the rictus on Gwynplaine's face – and its relation to justice. In an address to the House of Lords, Gwynplaine harangues his laughing, mocking audience as oppressors of humanity and prophesies a liberating republic brought about by dissentient laughter: "Ce rire est un produit des tortures. [...] Je représente l'humanité telle que ses maîtres l'ont faite. L'homme est un mutilé. Ce qu'on m'a fait, on l'a fait au genre humain. On lui a déformé le droit, la justice, la vérité, la raison, l'intelligence, comme à moi les yeux, les narines et les oreilles" (623).[3] Gwynplaine's victimhood is revenged when Hardquannone, the artistocrat-torturer who kidnapped him, is himself tortured to reveal his crime. The floor of the vast cellar where he is being tortured, like the muddy world in *Comment c'est,* is damp and cold: "la terre mouillée et froide des lieux profonds" (Hugo 444). A judge interrogates Hardquannone; a clerk listens for any word from the tortured subject. Except to emit a burst of laughter when he sees Gwynplaine, Hardquanonne remains silent. If *L'homme qui rit* is understood as a source text or an intertext for *Comment c'est*, Beckett explicitly planned to explore the relation of torturer and victim within a "triple" system of justice that tests what it means to be a human being. The triple division of justice in Hugo's novel may in fact be a source for the three-part structure of *Comment c'est*. As both Hugo's and Beckett's novels imply, the powerless have a mystifying force that resists the mutilation of basic human rights.

As the allusion to *L'homme qui rit* further implies, the pseudo-couple of torturer and victim, created by the relation of power to subject, generates text. In Beckett's original notes for *Comment c'est*, Pim hears voices that are indistinguishable from his own. The narrator himself harbours several indistinct voices: "que le témoin dise de la voix de x ce que celui-ci de ~~la voix~~ celle de Pim" (201).[4] Voice splits into a sequence of questions that have the aspect of an interrogation: "fin sous forme de dialogue – questions et oui ou non rapellant fin de II" (202).[5] At the core of Beckett's novel, even from its inception, there is a relationship between extorted speech and torturing power as an act of violent appropriation of voice. A legal witness ("témoin") mediates a verbal transaction that probes the meaning of interrogation ("questions et oui ou non"). Beckett's allusion to Hugo clarifies the disturbing blending of extorted speech and the torturer's appropriation of voice. In the same chapter as "Être un ver, quelle force!" this dialogue appears:

> Un roi, cela obéit.
> A quoi?
> A une mauvaise âme quelconque qui du dehors lui bourdonne dans l'oreille. Mouche sombre de l'abîme.
> Ce bourdonnement commande. Un règne est une dictée.
> La voix haute, c'est le souverain; la voix basse, c'est la souveraineté.
> Ceux qui dans un règne savent distinguer cette voix basse et entendre ce qu'elle souffle à la voix haute, sont les vrais historiens. (259)[6]

The relationship of torturer to victim is the relation of sovereign to subject, locked into an ambiguous relationship not unlike Hegel's master to his slave. The voice of sovereign power is the product of an act of dictation as speech extorted from subjects. In this exchange, Hugo uses the question-and-answer form, as Beckett does in *Comment c'est.* Interrogation is a technique of torture, but it is also a transmission of collective dissentient voices from below that hum and buzz in the sovereign's ears.

By alluding to Hugo, Beckett opens up thinking about political events in republican France in the late 1950s. More specifically, by focusing on extorted speech, Beckett raises questions about sovereignty and human rights. In 1956, which Beckett explicitly records as the beginning date of the *Comment c'est* project, the European Commission of Human Rights published background material regarding the use of torture. Among other documents, the commission consulted the *Teitgen Report* tabled by the Committee on Legal and Administrative Questions (1949) before the Consultative Assembly of the Council of Europe, on the establishment of a collective guarantee of essential freedoms and fundamental rights. Labour MP Seymour Cocks spoke about the barbarity of torture in the preparatory work to Article 3 of the Convention of Human Rights: "this retrogression into barbarism [...] to maim and mutilate [the bodies of men and women] by torture is a crime against high heaven and the holy spirit of man" ("Preparatory Work," 4). Cocks asked the commission not to tuck away "such a terrible crime as torture ... almost casually at the end of the Report" ("Preparatory Work," 6). Cocks's impassioned speech resulted in the adoption of Article 3 as it stands: "No one shall be subjected to torture or to inhuman or degrading treatment or punishment." The Convention took some time to have any real effect on European citizens. The commission began receiving state petitions only in 1956, and it took until 1959 for the court to be established due to a long wait for a quorum of nations willing to allow international rulings to supersede national law. The court could only come into being if at least eight member states adopted its compulsory jurisdiction under Article 56 of the Convention (Kerson 181). The very first petitions received by the commission in 1956 and 1957 involved allegations of torture. Greece accused the British in Cyprus of using illegal emergency laws and submitted evidence of forty-nine cases of torture. As one academic noted in 1962, "Only France and Cyprus, of the sixteen nations which are members of the Council of Europe today, have not ratified the Convention" (Schindler 155).

According to Madsen, the Convention began as a form of limited Europeanization of the UDHR. Both France and England, Madsen argues, saw the Convention as first and foremost a Cold War instrument to distinguish the liberal democracies from the Communist totalitarian regimes.[7] The Convention lists rights to property, elections, and freedom of thought, a list that inevitably excludes the USSR and Eastern Europe. As Madsen points out, "the system was to protect Western European human rights rather than more generally European human rights" (140n3). More subversively, the Convention raised the problem of any potential extension of rights to colonial territories outside Europe. The *Teitgen Report* had already noted that certain members of the committee opposed extending rights "not only to all persons residing within its metropolitan territory but also to all persons residing within its overseas territories or in its colonial possession" (201). France had not ratified the Convention, Madsen states, "due to a general disbelief in supranational control of the area of *libertés publiques*, a sentiment only exacerbated during the colonial battles where the quest for sovereign control and nonintervention of the international community seemed paramount" (145). At the same time, the French government sent key jurists – Teitgen and Cassin – to Strasbourg to oversee the drafting of the Convention and, later, the setting up of the court. As Madsen remarks, the French position was an "imperialist balancing act consisting of both securing that colonial matters remained an issue of national politics and, simultaneously, continuing a tradition of supplying 'universals' to the international level" (145). As one contemporary observer noted, the reason that France – cradle of the Declaration of Human Rights, key player in the drafting of the 1948 UDHR, and member of the Council of Europe – refused to ratify the Convention "is attributable in part to French troubles in Algeria" (Kerson 175). Those "troubles" turned on torture.

Algeria and the Body in Pain

If Beckett wrote *Comment c'est* while the European justice system was being set up to outlaw torture, the French balancing act tottered over allegations that paratroopers systematically used "la question" in the crackdown against the Algerian Front de Libération Nationale (FLN). Rumours of brutal pacification tactics by the French government had been around since late 1951, when journalist Claude Bourdet, a Communist resistance fighter during the war, had questioned the interrogation methods used by French police against Algerians. In an article that appeared in *L'Observateur* under the title "Y a-t-il une Gestapo algérienne?" – which he based on evidence gathered by Pierre Stibbe, lawyer for tortured Algerian farmers – Bourdet compared the police to the Gestapo (Tétart 81; Beigbeder 110). After the uprising in 1954 and start of the Algerian War, accusations flew thick and fast. In "La question," an article published in *L'Express* in January 1955, François Mauriac denounced the army's use of torture in Algeria. The article takes the form of a dialogue between Mauriac and his witness-victim-informant, who speaks of various torture techniques: "coups de nerf de boeuf," "la baignoire," "le courant électrique sous les aisselles et entre les jambes," "l'eau souillée introduite par un tuyau dans la bouche."[8] Mauriac, appalled, compares "cette France qui a proclamé les Droits de l'Homme à la face d'une Europe enivrée" with the colonial power of the "bourreaux" (Beigbeder 110).[9] In April 1956, Henri Marrou, professor at the Sorbonne, exposed the practice of concentration camp torture in *Le Monde*: "camps de concentration, torture et répression collective. Je ne veux scandaliser personne et ne prononcerai pas à la légère les noms sacrés de Dachau et Buchenwald; il me suffira, hélas! d'en prononcer un autre, déjà bien lourd à porter: nous, Français, avions déjà sur la conscience le camp de Gurs."[10] Marrou shudders to remember the time he acted as representative of the French government "à une exposition organisée au musée Galliera, par l'Unesco, en l'honneur de la Déclaration des droits de l'homme; il y avait là tout un panneau consacré à l'abolition, et non, ô hypocrisie, au renouveau de la torture judiciaire."[11] When Beckett first started thinking about *Comment c'est*, voices were being raised in protest against the hypocrisy of a state that advocated universal human rights and practised torture in evil repetition of Gestapo brutality. At the same time, as Mauriac's article reveals, writing as dialogue between author and subject in the pursuit of the truth is shadowed by the Nazi inhumanity of "la question." There is no escaping political responsibility or the corrupting effects of state hypocrisy through art.

Perhaps the real trigger for *Comment c'est* was Sartre's article on French colonialism in Algeria, "Le colonialisme est un système," published in *Les Temps Modernes* in March-April 1956. In his coruscating attack on the unholy alliance of capitalism, exploitation, and colonial racism, Sartre argues that "Une des fonctions du racisme c'est de compenser l'universalisme latent du liberalisme bourgeois: puisque tous les hommes ont les même droits, on fera de l'Algérien un sous-homme" ("Colonialisme et néo-colonialisme," 44).[12] Sartre directly links universal human rights to French colonial control systems through racist legal clauses that exclude colonial subjects from human rights legislation. As Sartre further argued in a 1957 review of Albert Memmi's *Portrait du colonisé* and *Portrait du colonisateur*, "puisque l'indigène est un sous-homme, la Déclaration des Droits de l'Homme ne le concerne pas; inversement, puisqu'il n'a pas de droits, il est abandonné sans protection aux forces inhumaines de la nature, aux 'lois d'airain' de l'économie" (52).[13] Sartre regularly uses the term "sous-homme" to designate the subhuman. In his initial planning for *Comment c'est*, Beckett is explicitly concerned with the definition of a man ("c'était un homme, ç'avait été un homme") within relationships of power and subjection that extend to dehumanization.

Allegations of torture in Algeria were repeated throughout 1957. *Témoignage Chrétien* published the correspondence of Jean Müller, a soldier killed in Algeria in October 1956, with details of the torture perpetrated daily by a group of officers, non-commissioned officers, and conscripts (Beigbeder 110). In *Contre la torture*, published by Éditions de minuit, Pierre-Henri Simon agonizes over what he calls the "conversion" of French values into their Nazi fascist opposite, an assault "contre les droits des gens, et contre l'humanité": "Quant à nous, qui avons lutté contre la monstruosité raciste, nous étions donc des dupes et nous sommes aujourd'hui les vaincus d'Hitler, si notre patrie lui emprunte ses idées et ses moyens, et apostasie la foi humaine que nous avions crue immanente à son essence de nation" (Simon 123).[14] As Beckett worked on *Comment c'est* from December 1958 to summer 1960, allegations of torture became a national scandal that occasioned international outcry. Germaine Tillion, one of the leaders of Beckett's own wartime Resistance cell who had been tortured during interrogation at the rue des Saussaies before being sent to Ravensbrück, had investigated claims about torture in the camps as part of the "Comité international contre les régimes concentrationnaires." An ethnologist with expertise in Algeria, Tillion supported Simone de Beauvoir's "Comité pour Djamila Boupacha"; an FLN militant, Boupacha was imprisoned, tortured, and raped for a month in February 1960 (de Beauvoir et Halimi, *Djamila Boupacha*).

The most important text of this period is undoubtedly Henri Alleg's *La question*. Alleg was editor of the pro-FLN newspaper *Alger Républicain*; a pro-Communist paper, it was banned in September 1955. During the Battle of Algiers in 1957, the French began a terrifying crackdown on FLN activists and fighters in Alger. Alleg had gone into hiding in November 1956 but was arrested on 12 June 1957 while trying to trace the whereabouts of Maurice Audin, a Communist academic and activist who had been arrested the day before. *La question* details the month of torture that Alleg sustained at the hands of paratroopers. The half-built interrogation building at El-Biar where he was detained can only be described as a torture factory. Floor after floor, room after room of this five-story apartment block were filled with screaming victims. As Stephen Morton puts it, "the practice of torture had become an industrialised and almost banal technique of counter-insurgency" (157). After being tortured at El-Biar, Audin was killed.[15]

In *La question*, Alleg details the first twelve hours of electric shocks, water-boarding, burning, suspension by rope upside down, and injection of sodium pentothal. Alleg's writing is spare, controlled, focused, unflinching. It enters into the horrors of pain with an angry, satirical eye cast on his tormentors. Alleg describes the laughing soldiers who watch the horrible proceedings. Paratroopers secretly visit him in rest periods and compliment him on his resilience. One conscript, by asking Alleg if he had been tortured during the war, implicitly compares the French system to Gestapo brutalities (Alleg 65). At a further pitch of attention – despite the blinding, drowning, all-embracing destruction wreaked on his body – Alleg gazes upon the other victims, including Audin. Nods of encouragement from Algerians – quick gestures of solidarity – give him his only hope in the nightmare factory of pain.

Alleg somehow withstood the unbelievable assault and was eventually transferred to Lodi camp. Via his French lawyers, Alleg smuggled out an official complaint to the procurator at Algiers. When *L'Humanité* published the complaint at the end of July, authorities seized the entire issue. A huge press campaign ensued as rumours of his death in prison circulated. In November 1957, Alleg was put before a magistrate; he was charged with being a member of the Parti Communiste Algérien and a threat to national security. When Jérôme Lindon published *La question* in February 1958, it quickly became a bestseller despite government attempts to censor any reference to it in newspapers, including Sartre's trenchant commentary "Une victoire" in *L'Express* in March.[16] *La question* was banned, which only increased its clandestine circulation. As President de Gaulle talked about holding a referendum on Algerian independence, Lindon continued his campaign in 1959 and 1960 to convince the public that torture remained common pacification practice in Algeria. In June 1959, Les Éditions de minuit published *La gangrène*, an account by five Algerians of being tortured; they reveal that the Direction de la Surveillance du Territoire used "la question" on FLN dissidents in the heart of Paris at their quarters in the eighth arrondissement – the same premises where the Gestapo had its torture chambers and where Germaine Tillion had been interrogated. *La gangrène* was seized as soon as printed. Lindon sued; he subsequently published the minutes of the trial. In April 1960, Minuit published the novel *Le déserteur* by "Maurianne," pseudonym of Jean-Louis Hurst. The book was banned and Lindon was put on trial for inciting soldiers to insubordination and desertion. Published in October 1960, Noël Favrelière's *Le désert à l'aube* recounted his desertion from the French army and his joining the ranks of the FLN. Furthering the cause of anti-torture, Lindon actively supported philosopher Francis Jeanson, Sartre's colleague at *Les Temps Modernes*, when he and his fellow *inculpés* were charged with aiding and abetting the FLN in France as "porteurs de valises." They carried money for arms and documents for the organization and harboured activists (Ulloa 112). Sartre's letter of support, read out at the trial, argued that the war was corrupting France. The generalization of torture, along with the permanent insurrection of the military powers, Sartre claimed, qualified the regime as fascist (Péju 118). In 1960, Lindon published Jeanson's pamphlet *Notre guerre*, and followed this with the publication of a collective denunciation of the war by 121 intellectuals, the *Manifeste des cent vingt et un*. In a letter to Barbara Bray on 1 October 1960, Beckett noted the prevailing climate in France: "No talk of anything here but the Jeanson trial and the Manifesto of the 121. If I weren't a foreigner I suppose I'd be in it" (*Letters* 360). All in all, Éditions de minuit brought out twenty-three publications about Algeria between 1957 and 1962, twelve of which were seized by the authorities. Many were reprinted in Lausanne and recirculated in a campaign that Lindon compared to resistance work during the war: "J'ai aujourd'hui le sentiment d'être au moins [fidèle] à la tradition vivante de la Résistance" (Simonin 37).[17] In 1961, Lindon's flat was bombed by the Organisation Armée Secrète (OAS), the right-wing *pied noir* extremist group. Beckett signed and circulated a "manifesto" of support for Lindon at this time (*Letters* 450). Beckett was very concerned: "the director of Editions de Minuit, Jérôme Lindon, has been having a bad time on account of his anti-torture Documents and was dragged before the courts the other day for his publication *The Deserter*. Same night at midnight he was 'plasticated' – his private apartment. No one hurt but much damage to premises. Verdict day after tomorrow. Fine probably. And he goes in permanent personal danger" (*Letters* 452).

On 17 December 1958, at the end of a year dominated by Algerian news and the impact of Alleg's account of torture, in the middle of a feverish campaign by his own publisher which would include details of torture in the heart of Paris that took place that very month in the quarters used by the Gestapo during the war,[18] Beckett began to write *Comment c'est*. The title directs us to think about the contemporary moment. Sartre, while in the news, was also on Beckett's mind. Sartre's influence is visible in *Comment c'est* in the phenomenology of the interaction between the narrator and Pim. Moreover, the novel contains clear allusions to a Sartrean encounter. Crawling through mud in *Comment c'est* is a radical version of the slime or "visqueux" in Sartre's *L'être et le néant*, as Steven Connor has argued (67–70).

Sartre's article on Alleg's book, "Une victoire," which became the preface to the English translation and the Swiss edition, meditates on the relationship of victim and executioner, "victime et bourreau," as paradigmatic of the relation of the French to their own memories of Nazi torturers during the Occupation now inverted, as in a mirror, into the French as executioner gazing upon the Algerians as victims. The torturer and tortured, an internalized pair, are created by the horror of enemy torture during the war: "Victime et bourreau ne font plus qu'une seule image: et c'est notre image" ("Une victoire," 101).[19] In the nightmare, the torturer-tortured couple meet as hideous lovers in the night of the Gestapo torture cells: "[la victime qui parle] s'accouple avec son bourreau, c'est sa femme et ce couple enlacé s'abîme dans la nuit de l'abjection" (103).[20] That terrible night, Sartre maintained, returned during the colonial war in Algeria: "La nuit de l'abjection est revenue: à El Biar, elle revient toutes les nuits; en France, c'est la suie de nos coeurs" (102).[21] The Nazi chronotope releases sadistic energies in the colonial French that redefine torture as a struggle to destroy the victim's interiority. More than just death, torture aims to annihilate the humanity of those who are tortured, "de les humilier, de raser l'orgeuil dans leur coeur, de les ravaler au rang de la bête. On laissera vivre les corps, mais on tuera l'esprit" (119).[22] As Sartre defines it, torture is "cette étrange match," this strange contest of will between torturer and tortured: "le tortionnaire se mesure avec le torturé et tout se passe comme s'ils ne pouvaient appartenir ensemble à l'espèce humaine [...] celui que cède à la question, on n'a pas seulement voulu le contraindre à parler; on lui a pour toujours impose un statut: celui de sous-homme" (116–17).[23]

One might surmise that Sartre's preface to *La question* became so important to Beckett as he worked on his draft of *Comment c'est* because it binds the two histories we have been tracking: torture in French colonial space as a chronotopic and inverted replay of Gestapo terror, and the establishment of European human rights figured as a struggle between colonial sovereignty and universal rights. For Sartre, Alleg's book reveals the racial hatred written into colonial sovereignty. European hatred of the Arab-Algerian enters into the equation as a replay of European hatreds, namely the Gestapo's hatred of the French Resistance. The mirroring of the pairs is enabled because of the idea of fascist violence as an import from colonial racism into Europe, as argued by Hannah Arendt and later by Aimé Césaire. Arendt refers to this phenomenon as "boomerang effects of imperialism upon the mother country" (*Origins* 503). Torture in Algeria aimed at banishing the Moslem Arab nationalists from the human race, first by destroying their humanity through humiliation and mutilation, then by appropriating their mind and spirit through confessional extortion of voice. Sartre's observations chime with Alleg's own reading of the violence meted out to him. He is full of contempt for a young recruit who compliments him on his resistance, and who then a few days later is seen beating an Algerian on the stairs. For Alleg, El-Biar was both a site of torture for Algerians and "une école de perversion pour les jeunes Français" (*La question* 65).[24]

The phenomenology of Alleg's text raises a further consideration, borne of the Sartrean interpretation, about the torture pair. Alleg refuses speech to the torturer; yet the text of *La question* as published is a product of torture. In this sense it is "extorted speech," to use Beckett's form of words in *How It Is*. Extorted speech is transformed to include details of the horrors perpetrated on the victim's body as well as detailed descriptions of the torturers and what they say. For Sartre, Alleg's text is a liberating testimony because it reveals the workings of the system activated by racist hatred and colonial mimicry of fascist violence against human rights. In Beckett's *Comment c'est*, the narrator ponders the phenomenon of the narrative he is extorting from Pim: that voice is the text we read. That text is made up of Pim's account of the autobiographical visions said to be seen when the mud opens, like a theatre, upon remembered scenes. The text includes an account of Pim's torture, the questions and answers, as well as the torturer's reflections and detailed scripting of the relation between, and situations of, the bodies of both torturer and victim. The narrator says there are three notebooks: "one notebook for the body," "a second for the mutterings verbatim," and a third "for my comments" (70–1). The notebooks are coloured "blue yellow and red respectively" (71). The fiction of the notebooks is accompanied by the imagining of the bureaucratic recording of the torture by Kram the "witness" and Krim the scribe with his "ballpoint at the ready" (90). Beckett is clearly reflecting on his own compositional procedures: composition as an extreme form of self-torment, the writer split into self-conscious rememberer and scribal recorder. He is also reproducing the strange status of Alleg's *La question*. Alleg smuggled his text out of prison in bits and pieces, on pages torn from a notebook, as he told an Arab-American journalist:

> I did not write it in one piece, I had to evacuate these notes somehow and I wrote them on a school notebook four pages by four pages at a time. Then I had to somehow get the four pages out of there. Whenever a lawyer came to the prison and I had an opportunity to see this lawyer, I'd give him these pages, which I'd had hidden on my body, in my loafers or in my underwear until I had to pass the regular searches at the hands of the guards, some of whom searched you very carefully, others less carefully, but it was still quite risky. Anyway, somehow I managed to spirit out the entire book, bit by bit. (Bendib)

The "evacuated" notes that make up *La question* detail what happens to the body, what is said on both sides, what the torturer is thinking. Importantly they trump army torture methods by recording the whole system of voice extortion. The paragraphs of *Comment c'est*, strange in shape and form, mimic the extreme page-at-a-time bittiness of Alleg's text smuggled out from hellish incarceration.[25] Fragmentation and temporal disjointedness are thematized in *How It Is* as "my life in bits and scraps" (22). The novel also registers the irony that extorted speech is more about the torturer than the victim: "reread our notes pass the time more about me than him hardly a word out of him" (70). Torture, as an evil form of text generation, becomes, through the secret act of notebook evacuation that precedes published testimony, a text about the system, its hellish economy and industrialization of tortured-torturer intimacy.

Texts like *La question* and *Comment c'est* reverse the power dynamics of torture as analyzed by Elaine Scarry: "ultimate domination requires the prisoner's ground being increasingly physical and the torturer's increasingly verbal, that the prisoner become a colossal body with no voice and the torturer a colossal voice (a voice composed of two voices) with no body" (57). Two voices become three voices that drown out the colossal voice, just as Alleg's one notebook multiplies into Beckett's three notebooks: the body-text and the extorted-text trumped by the triple scening of the entire system by the victim-become-textual-agent representing, as plural testimony, all the voices, all of the torture's contexts, including the vile fictions and desires of the torturing regime.

The Extorted Voice and Loss of Species

In *Comment c'est*, Beckett adapts Lindon's "anti-torture [d]ocuments" (*Letters* 452) and fuses them with a Dantean staging of artistic composition. The compositional voice, even before the torture scenes in section II, is accompanied by "quelqu'un qui écoute un autre qui note ou le même" (10).[26] Composition is defined as interrogation, using "question" in the French as both Socratic prompt and inquisition. Paragraph after paragraph begins "questions si" or "question si," with hints that the environment of "shit and vomit" (*How* 12) is a space of punishment created by a mysterious "they": "they haven't left me that this time" (15). The space used to be a place of interrogation: "no one will ever come again and shine his light on me" (16). The text we are reading, made up of bits and scraps, may already be the voice that this narrator will be receiving from Pim the victim ("the speech I've been given") in the torture scenes of part II. This speech necessitates a more public scope than the narrator's solitary satisfaction, a *judicial* relationship: "all I hear is that a witness I'd need a witness" (19). The voice revels in the "rich testimony" (91) and in section III returns again and again to the notion of justice ("we have our being in justice" [135]). In the French, this mélange of legal, compositional, and punitive perplexities bears the mark of Mauriac's and Alleg's sense of the word "question": "voilà la parole qu'on ma donnée première partie avant Pim *question* si j'en use beaucoup on ne dit pas ou j'entends pas c'est l'un ou l'autre on dit qu'un témoin qu'il me faudrait un témoin" (22; emphasis added).[27] The speech has been given in an unfree space. In this extralegal environment, there are no witnesses, just recording agents, even though the space demands witnesses. The narrator possesses and is possessed by Pim's speech, then, so cannot freely disengage his own interrogative stance from his victim's. Consequently

Pim, inhabiting the interrogative role, begins to loom large: "he lives bent over me [...] all my visible surface bathing in the light of his lamps" (19). The narrator's life is actually Pim's story. Or curled up within its more inclusive frame of exposure, it is a story extorted by the extreme interrogation of the "question." Yet the story contains a counter-interrogation concerning the narrator's own existential dependence on that voice: "the words of Pim his extorted voice he stops I step in all the needful he starts again I could listen to him for ever" (23). The interrogation rebounds upon the inquisitorial narrator, despite his rebuff: "how I got here if it's me no question" (23). This extorted speech turns the narrator-narrated relationship upside down and inside out in ways that mimic the inversion of victim and torturer in Sartre's preface, "Une victoire." This inversion is accomplished through a procedure that renders that relationship judicial beyond the bare extra-judicial interrogative and within a legal textual space that is all to do with exposure, witnessing, and right to speech. "Parole" in French is a slippery term. "La parole qu'on ma donnée" can mean, and does begin to mean with "témoin" nearby, the right to speak in a deliberative assembly, as in the locution, "vous avez la parole" ("you have the floor"). Pim's extorted speech, if that is what we are reading, is given to the narrator through an interrogation that turns out to be an act of torture in part II. At the same time, the speech becomes a word given to a deliberative assembly, where we are witnesses to the whole story of extorted speech beyond its torturous scripting and recording. The story of torturer and tortured, recorded in bits and scraps of text within a twisted history of inversions and mirroring repetition, is in the end about loss of species, "perte d'espèce" (33): "soudain comme tout ce qui arrive ne plus tenir que par le bout des ongles image alpestre ou spéléologique à son espèce celle des rieurs du vendredi instant atroce c'est ici que les mots ont leur utilité la boue est muette" (*Comment* 31). Beckett renders this passage in English as follows: "suddenly like all that happens to be hanging on by the finger-nails to one's species that of those who laugh too soon alpine image or speluncar atrocious moment it's here words have their utility the mud is mute" (*How* 28). Those who laugh summon up the spectres of the mocking aristocrats in Hugo's *L'homme qui rit*, who laugh at the victim of torture. They also resemble the paratroopers in Alleg's *La question*, jeering and laughing while he suffers. They mock him in their "comic" role of milice-fascists returned again, as killers of words, who expose "how it is" in the torture chamber:

> [Érulin] hurlait: "Tu vas parler! Tout le monde parle ici! On a fait la guerre en Indochine, ça nous a servi pour vous connaître. Ici, c'est le Gestapo! Tu connais le Gestapo?" Puis ironique: "Tu a fait des articles sur les tortures, hein, salaud! Eh bien! maintenant, c'est la 10ᵉ D.P. qui les fait sur toi!" J'entends derrière moi rire l'équipe des tortionnaires. (Alleg 26)[28]

Just as the laugh of power becomes the enabling rictus of another denunciatory satire and text, so the narrator-torturer's extorted speech becomes a divine comedy that judges and condemns the interrogation and "question" within another more radical space of judgment: the text we are reading, and the judgment given freely on those who seek to banish fellow creatures beyond species.

According to Tyrus Miller, Beckett's interest in interrogative violence supports Scarry's view that torture is less about confessional extortion than about destroying the world of the victim. Indeed, Miller claims, the "confessional structure" of torture is exploited "for destructive ends" (266). Beckett's texts turn this around, however, or try to. They "restore the rights of the immediate 'aesthetic body' – the body that senses and feels pleasure and especially pain – over the mediate artistic discourse that appropriates it, communicating it at second hand to spectators and readers" (Miller 262). It does so, but it also, I would argue, doubles up the "artistic discourse" as always already the other's, the victim's, despite the mocking jeers of the fascist torturers: as indeed not only counter-satirical as Gwynplaine before the House of Lords, but as summoning another assembly, another space of judgement, something approaching a court of human rights. The torturer may seek, as Scarry argues, to appropriate extorted speech as his own: "The torturer tries to make his own not only the words of the prisoner's confession but all his words and sounds" (49). But the text we read has another frame and an uncontrollable, extra-extra-judicial set of witnesses, judges, jurors. As Sartre argues, *La question*, when read by a public beyond the silencing, torturing, and propagandist colonial powers, has a satirical effect directed against the torturers: "Mais Alleg nu, tremblant de froid, attaché à une planche encore noire et gluante des vomissements anciens, réduit tous ces manèges à leur pitoyable vérité: ce sont des comedies joués par des imbéciles" (107).[29]

For Beckett, the torturer fears the exposure of his own criminal extortion to such an extent that he pretends he will be the next victim in an endless "chain-like structure of torment" (Sheehan 97). In the end, the whole structure of rationalizations, even the structuring binary of the torturer and the tortured, collapses. There is a last, desperate attempt at radical appropriation of the victim's voice: "a formulation that would eliminate him completely" (*How* 157). The text is beyond him, beyond even Pim. It occupies "another world" (158), where the attempt to strip the victim of his right to have rights, the right to be part of the species, is judged. The reader as witness will read with Pim's radical satire in mind: "someone in another world yes whose kind of dream I am yes said to be yes that he dreams all the time yes tells all the time yes his only dream his only story yes" (158). The narrator tries to reduce rights to the mere expression of the tortured body qua extra-species subject of extortion, short of death ("a true corpse untorturable" [101]), capable of text generation ("rich testimony I agree questionable" [91]), and ceding voice, tears, and eyes to the torturers ("he turns his head tears in the eyes my tears my eyes" [83]). The word "right" inhabits this hellish world only as the victim's right side. Beckett repeats the word to an insane degree: "I let go the sack let go Pim that's the worst letting go the sack and away semi-side left right leg right arm push pull right right don't lose him round his head hairpin turn right right" (83).[30] The multiple meanings of "right" also apply in French, which Beckett reinforces with heavy rhyming on the sound of the words "droit" and "droite":

> je *lâche* le sac *lâche* Pim c'est ça le pire *lâcher* le sac et hop en avant demi-flanc gauche pied *droit* main *droite* pousse tire à *droite* à *droite* ne pas le perdre devant sa tête épingle à cheveux à *droite* toujours puis redresser par-dessus son *bras droit* le long du flanc serrer et stop la tête contre ses pieds les siens contre la mienne long repos *angoisse croissante*. (*Comment* 92)

The lyricism of the damned sings in this passage. The torturer adheres to the creed that "right" is a right-wing reactionary imposition of violence on the body of the victim stripped of all other rights. "Right" and "droit" are functions of the position of the bodies of torturer and tortured. Rights are subject to the documentary farce of the vicious recording technology of pain – a "little book" – that reduces the victim to a non-human creature: "little private book these secret things little book all my own the heart's outpourings day by day it's forbidden" (*How* 92). What phenomenologically occurs is not a scripted reduction of rights to tortured creaturely body possessed: its right side made right by the extreme right-wing paratroopers and its righting of the victim stripped of species rights. What occurs, rather, is this text beyond the world-destroying ambition of the torturing regime. The roles are reversed again, as we have seen, from the very beginning of this doubled-up, screwed-inside-out text of pain and extortion. Vision moves from right(s) to the humane. The narrator seeks to control Pim's arms and hands. He does not quite succeed by using the "right" method of torturous control, for he cannot see: "his right way off the right axis of the clavicle or cross Saint Andrew of the Volga mine about his shoulders his neck I can't see good so much for the right arms and their hands I can't see" (99). Weakened by something outside his scope of vision, the narrator seeks to control the victim's hand with a clasp: "clasp but how clasped as in the handshake" (99). Suddenly something else happens. Other means are revealed beyond the command and control structure of the torturing, beyond the positioning technology of the act of violent colonizing appropriation: "it's the position [the hands] have finally adopted clear picture of that good and parenthesis the vision suddenly too late a little late of how my injunctions by other means more humane" (99). There is guilt and disgusting special pleading, as he seeks a "different set of signals quite different more humane" (100). Yet a legal forum of injunctions is revealed, one that cannot be positioned by fascistic parenthetical command and control. This more humane forum is based on species recognition and acknowledgment (the handshake), and on lucidity of ethical judgment ("clear picture of that good" [99]). This revelation may operate only as an irony, a Pim accent to the torturer's creed and rationale. At the same time, the vision reverses the roles according to other mean(ing)s to rights: "right for you they are warm Krim to Kram roles reversed" (102). Not the narrator but Pim, "hanging on to humankind" (103), retains species rights in this reversal.

The muddy world the torturer and tortured occupy is the worm's world beyond rights, beyond the state, beyond the law. The Dantean origins of this world may obscure its contemporary force as a space of statelessness and rightlessness, with no future or past beyond the sovereign powers of the torturing and colonizing state of exception. Hannah Arendt argues that it was imperialism that allowed for abusive dissolution of nation-state forms of justice and helped to generate the extra-judicial sovereignty of the colonial powers within as well as outside Europe. As Seyla Benhabib argues in *The Reluctant Modernism of Hannah Arendt*, it is a melancholy paradox that the very agents of the denaturalization, discrimination, and disenfranchisement of stateless peoples, the colonial nation-states, are the protectors of the rights of those reduced to abstract nakedness (xix). For Arendt, torture aims to "manipulate the human body – with its infinite possibilities of suffering – in such a way as to make it destroy the human person as inexorably as do certain mental diseases of organic origin" (*Origins* 199). For this reason, torture is the violent act of choice for regimes set on destroying rights-based resistance to the colonizing mission. The manipulation of the body is an indirect consequence of colonizing imperialism and its destructive effect on human rights, especially with the totalitarian boomerang effect of importing colonial abuses into Europe. It is also in effect an act of colonization of the victim's body for destructive ends, especially when independence movements inspire colonized peoples to assert their rights. As Sartre argues, the colonizer resorts to torture as an assertion of dubious claims to being human: "Dompter, dresser, châtier, voilà les mots qui l'obsèdent: il n'y a pas assez de place en Algérie pour deux espèces humaines; entre l'une et l'autre, il faut choisir" (119).[31] Only by exposure of violations, advocacy of rights, and legal redress can the species-destructive aims of a torturing imperialism be unpicked; moreover, this righting of rights can be achieved only by way of a legal forum that is linked to but not dominated by nation-states. As Amartya Sen has argued concerning the practical ways in which human rights can both be defended and asserted, there are three prerequisites: recognition, agitation, and legislation (342–5). The UDHR assures that rights are recognized as binding and not simply viewed as a product of laws; NGOs and their activism and acts of exposure of violations are necessary; and a legal space is needed in which judgments can be enforced through channels that respect, within the parameters of the UDHR, nation-state principles of law and citizen rights. Sen cites the ECHR as an example of a legal framework that is sensitive both to the recognitions inspired by the UDHR and to the exposure and advocacy of NGOs and rights. Those who fought for human rights in Algeria aimed to assert the right to have rights for the Algerian people. They publicized violations with texts such Alleg's *La question.* They sought redress for violations not only by pushing back against censorship in court but also by putting pressure on the French state while the European Court of Human Rights was emerging. The fact that France was effectively asserting a colonial clause to the Convention of Human Rights by not ratifying the treaty, while sending René Cassin to become judge at the European Court of Human Rights, speaks to France's Janus-faced status as beacon of universal rights and militarist advocate of metropolitan-colonial sovereignty over rightless, subjected peoples. Article 63 of the 1950 Convention allowed nation-states to wriggle out of the extension of the rights to non-metropolitan territories. As Leopold Senghor argued at the Consultative Assembly of the Council of Europe: "In adopting article 63, the Assembly would transform the European Declaration of Human Rights into the declaration of European Human Rights. This would be to deny the same rights to other men. This would mean betraying the spirit of European civilisation which – as Valéry has written – made man the 'measure of all things'" (qtd in Vasak 1208). Alleg's *La question* and Beckett's *Comment c'est* bear witness to the abuse of torture at the heart of the state of exception justified by the colonial clause. Both texts go some way to recording, at key moments in the Algerian War, the need for recognition, agitation, and legislation.

The European Court had its flaws, which the ambiguity of the French position foregrounded. Nevertheless, like other supranational bodies, it was meant to be a space that fostered and protected the right to have rights. To invoke the torturer's text in *Comment c'est / How It Is*, such a space should be "somewhere merciful enough to shelter [...] where no one ever abandons anyone [...] by the mere grace of our united net sufferings from west to east towards [...] peace" (156).

NOTES

1 All translations from French texts are my own. The four quotations from the "Pim" notebook read as follows: "Pim: hand feels over whole body, especially the face, this was a man, this had once been a man'"; "x communicates with Pim [~~and~~] tracing words on his arse with fingernail of index finger?"; "torturers and victims simultaneous cries"; "final immobility of staggered couples would not constitute justice since half would be deprived of victims the other of torturers." The Hugo phrase translates thus: "To be a worm, what strength."

2 "This terrible triple sense: the seeking of torment, the suffering of the tormented, the voluptuousness of the tormentor."

3 "This laugh is the product of torture [...] I represent humanity, what its masters have made of it. Man is a mutilated creature. What was done to me has been done to Man. They have disfigured Man's law, his justice, truth, reason, intelligence, just as they disfigured my eyes, nostrils, ears."

4 "Let the witness say of x's voice what [...] it said of Pim's voice."

5 "End in the form of dialogue – questions and yes or no recalling end of [part] 11."

6 "A king obeys. / Obeys what? / Obeys some evil soul that lies outside of him buzzing in his ear. Dark fly of the abyss. / This buzzing commands. Sovereignty is an act of dictation. / The voice above is the sovereign; the lower voice is sovereignty. / Those who in a reign can distinguish between this low voice and hear what it whispers to the voice above, are the real historians."

7 According to the *Teitgen Report*, "the Committee thought that the racial restrictions on the right of marriage made by the totalitarian regimes, as also the forced regimentation of children and young persons organised by these regimes, should be absolutely prohibited" (199).

8 "blows by cosh," "drowning in bath," "electric current applied to armpits and between legs," "dirty water introduced by tube into mouth."

9 "this France which proclaimed the Rights of Man in the face of an intoxicated Europe"; "executioners/torturers."

10 "concentration camps, camps of torture and collective repression. I do not seek to scandalize anyone and would not pronounce lightly the sacred names of Dachau and Buchenwald; it is enough, alas!, to pronounce another name, already heavy enough to bear: we, the French, already had on our conscience the camp at Gurs."

11 "at an exhibition organized at the Galliera museum, by UNESCO, commemorating the Declaration of the Rights of Man; there was a whole

board dedicated to the abolition, and not, o hypocrisy, to the revival of judicial torture" (*Le Monde*, 5 April 1956).

12 "One of the functions of racism is to compensate for the latent universalism of bourgeois liberalism: since all men have the same rights, we will turn the Algerian into a subhuman."

13 "Since the native is subhuman, the Declaration of Human Rights does not concern him – conversely, since he has no rights, he is abandoned without protection to the inhuman forces of nature, to the 'steel laws' of the economy."

14 "against people's rights, and against humanity"; "As for ourselves, who have fought against the monstrosity of racism, we were dupes, therefore, and are now today defeated by Hitler, if our country has borrowed his ideas and means, apostasizing the human faith that we thought immanent to its essence as a nation."

15 For the world Audin had simply disappeared. A campaign was launched for information, most importantly by the Maurice Audin Committee of the League of Human Rights, which published a dossier on torture and campaigned against torture schools in France (Beigbeder, *Judging War Crimes* 109).

16 See also Sartre's "Nous sommes tous des assassins" (68–71). David Drake comments at length on Sartre's stance on the Franco-Algerian War (105–19).

17 "Today I have the feeling of at least remaining faithful to the living tradition of the Resistance."

18 *La gangrène* details torture at the rue des Saussaies between 2 and 12 December 1958.

19 "The victim and executioner merge into the same figure: a figure in our own likeness" (Calder translation, "Preface," *The Question* xxix).

20 "the man who talks becomes one with his executioner. Coupled as man and wife, these two lovers made the abject night terrible" (xxix).

21 "at El Biar, it returns every night: in France it is the ashes in our hearts" (xxix).

22 "to humiliate them, to crush their pride and drag them down to the animal level. The body may live, but the spirit must be killed" (xli).

23 "the torturer pits himself against the tortured for his 'manhood' and the duel is fought as if it were not possible for both sides to belong to the human race [...] He who gives way under questioning is not only constrained from talking again, but is given a new status, that of a sub-man" (xxxix–xl).

24 "A school of perversion for young Frenchmen" (82).

25 In letter to Jacoba Van Velde on 9 May 1960, Beckett expresses his interest in this mode of writing. He refers to Caryl Chessman, a writer on death row, who smuggled his story out of an isolation cell at San Quentin before his execution on 2 May 1960: "Pour votre travail: forcez-vous, une heure par jour pour commencer, une demi-heure. C'est le seul remède. Chessman l'avait compris" (*Letters* 334) ["For your work: force yourself, an hour a day to begin with, half an hour. It's the only remedy. Chessman understood that"]. Chessman's memoir, *Cell 2455 Death Row* (1954), was written with the encouragement of the prison warden. When the warden refused Chessman the right to write anything further, he smuggled his writing out of prison and published three more books.

26 "someone listening another noting or the same" (7).

27 "that's the speech I've been given part one before Pim question do I use it freely it's not said or I don't hear it's one or the other all I hear is that a witness I'd need a witness" (19).

28 "'You're going to talk! Everyone talks here! We fought the war in Indo-China – that was enough to know your type. This is the Gestapo here! You know the Gestapo?' Then, with irony: 'So you wrote articles about torture, did you, you bastard! Very well! It's now the tenth Paratroop Division who are doing it to you.' I heard the whole band of torturers laughing behind me" (47).

29 "But Alleg, naked, trembling with cold, tied to a plank still black and sticky from the vomit of earlier victims, reduces all these things to their pitiable true nature: they are comedies played by fools" (xxxii).

30 Beckett states that this passage and its variants are repeated "ad nauseam" throughout the novel (*Letters* 349). Dan Gunn counts twenty-nine instances in *Comment c'est* (*Letters* 349n4).

31 "To train, discipline and chastise; these are the words which obsess them. There is not enough room in Algeria for two kinds of human beings; they must choose one or the other" (xli).

8

Fictions of the Human in Postwar Japan

CLAIRE SEILER

> The people shall not be prevented from enjoying any of the fundamental human rights. These fundamental human rights guaranteed to the people by this Constitution shall be conferred upon the people of this and future generations as eternal and inviolate rights.
>
> *(Constitution of Japan, Article 11)*

What have Kazuo Ishiguro's first two novels, *A Pale View of Hills* (1982) and *An Artist of the Floating World* (1986), and Shirley Hazzard's final novel, *The Great Fire* (2003), to do with human rights and literature? Neither through genre nor through theme do these fictions of post–Second World War Japan announce their relevance to the burgeoning interdisciplinary discourse around narrative and rights. On the one hand, to the extent that they respectively approximate the conventions of the assimilation parable, the marriage plot, and the romance, *A Pale View of Hills*, *An Artist of the Floating World*, and *The Great Fire* work well outside of the genre categories on which much human rights and literature criticism has been predicated (for example, poetry of witness, *testimonio*, *Bildungsroman*).[1] On the other hand, although Ishiguro's and Hazzard's novels imagine how artists, scholars, journalists, lawyers, and scientists conceived of the human or of human beings per se in occupied Japan, they rarely speak directly to, much less advocate for, human rights. In legal terms, too, these novels would seem to lie outside of the purview of human rights and literature. The acts and events that they evoke – the United States' atomic bombings of Hiroshima on 6 August 1945 and of Nagasaki three days later, and the nominally Allied Occupation of Japan[2] – did not violate international law. The bombings were acts of war committed before the adoption of the Fourth Geneva Convention Relative to the Protection of Civilian Persons in Time of War (1949). The nearly seven-year Occupation was a condition of peace. American officials moreover justified both the bombings and the Occupation in large part by reference to humanitarianism, fundamental human rights, and democratic freedoms. Why, then, do these atmospheric fictions of occupied Japan bear on the field of human rights and literature? What might it mean for the field to turn its gaze to such unusual subjects?

A Pale View of Hills, *An Artist of the Floating World*, and *The Great Fire* participate in what scholars have described as the crucial project of denaturalizing "the human," the category on which the very idea of human rights depends. Building on Judith Butler's work on the restrictive ontology of the human, for example, Domna C. Stanton urges a "necessary vigilance in all efforts to re-articulate the universalism of human rights discourse" (68). *A Pale View of Hills*, *An Artist of the Floating World*, and *The Great Fire* participate in this project. In these novels, depictions of knowledge work and cultural production in occupied Japan challenge the putatively universal definitions of "the human" championed even – or especially – in the wake of humankind's demonstration, at Hiroshima and Nagasaki, of its capacity for self-annihilation. *A Pale View of Hills* exposes the orientalism that marks visual and textual artworks intended to memorialize the victims of the atomic bombing of Nagasaki. *An Artist of the Floating World* suspects the uneasy proximity of human rights and global capitalism. And *The Great Fire*, despite an otherwise dated portrayal of postwar Japan, offers a subtle critique of the US rhetoric of humanitarianism at Hiroshima. These novels' imaginations of how the human was artistically represented, juridically constituted, and scientifically researched invite us to think through and perhaps past the current critical horizons of human rights and literature.

In recent stocktakings of the interdiscipline, critics have sought to expand those horizons, especially on legal and stylistic terms.[3] Elizabeth Swanson Goldberg and Alexandra Schultheis Moore have argued that literary critics must seek out "spaces [that] overlap with and blur the distinction between" international humanitarian and human rights law. In their view, analysis of literary representations of legal "in between" spaces would allow rights and literature scholars to "insist upon an expanded notion of human rights law and culture" ("Meditations," 16). Welcome as it is, this effort to bring a "human rights oriented reading practice" to people, spaces, and situations neglected by international law perpetuates a tendency in the field to rely on explicitly human rights–oriented texts as the implicit grounds for its critical work and relevance (14). When Goldberg and Moore reflect on the human death and human suffering caused by the atomic bombing of Hiroshima, they cite Carolyn Forché's collection *The Angel of History* (1994). The selection is apt. *The Angel of History* epitomizes Forché's work in the "poetry of witness," that is, in a poetry that, by bearing witness to atrocity and suffering, "reclaims the social from the political and in so doing defends the individual against illegitimate forms of coercion" (Kenniston and Grey 5; Forché, "Twentieth-Century Poetry of Witness," 16).[4] In poetry of witness, the witness, as speaker, is by definition already convinced of the import of that to which she testifies.

Of course, it is an open secret that literary theories and critical methodologies elect the forms that best serve their projects. In the case of human rights and literature, however, the general selection of texts that seek to expose or redress human rights violations would seem to preclude the denaturalization of the human, of which the field admits it stands in need. Put in broad strokes, the a priori selection of texts that set out to address the violation, reparation, or protection of human rights risks creating a vertical integration of the interdiscipline: literary modes, topicality, critical methods, and political outcomes of the field of rights and literature are already understood or assumed by its artists, critical practitioners, and readers. In this model, primary texts and critical discourse will speak in the same terms and, crucially, to the same audiences.

The present essay posits that such an a priori selection of human rights texts can forestall analysis of the subtler and often more insidious means by which states, institutions, and disciplines assemble and naturalize operative definitions of the human. In fact, paradoxically for a field that is by definition interdisciplinary, literature and rights scholarship has demonstrated little interest in how various disciplines and the habits of mind inculcated by different fields contribute not only to instrumental – as opposed to universal – definitions of the human but also to formulations of the rights to which human beings are entitled. Given the capacity of literature and related arts to represent forms of knowledge and cultural production ranging from the computational to the ideational, the quantitative to the humanistic, this elision is especially strange. The art of *A Pale View of Hills*, the law of *An Artist of the Floating World*, and the science of *The Great Fire* help to correct it.

Commemorative Orientalism

Kazuo Ishiguro was born in Nagasaki in 1954, and moved with his family to England in 1960. When he was included in *Granta*'s touchstone first list of Best of Young British Novelists in 1983, Ishiguro was not yet a British subject. He took UK citizenship later that year for practical reasons. In a 2005 interview, Ishiguro remarked, "I couldn't speak Japanese very well, passport regulations were changing, I felt British and my future was in Britain. And it would also make me eligible for literary awards" (Wroe).[5] He has since won many of those awards and gongs, including an OBE. Still, publishers market, and reviewers frequently refer to, Ishiguro's "Japaneseness."[6] In the present context, the *Granta* list provides the briefest of reminders that Ishiguro came of age as a novelist in England amid the historical rise of theory writ large and of post-colonial theory in particular, the narrative self-awareness and self-referentiality characteristic of the postmodern turn in fiction, and the consolidation of multiculturalism as a Western cultural virtue (Walkowitz 109–12). *A Pale View of Hills* taps into these cultural currents of the 1980s especially in its description of artworks intended to commemorate victims of the atomic bombing of Nagasaki. Counterpointing dated public statuary of the 1950s to "poetry of witness" of the 1980s, the novel perceives the orientalist habits of mind that can compromise both reparative gestures. In this novel, old-fashioned and *au courant* works alike remake Japanese people according to the projections of white Westerners.

A Pale View of Hills initiates several of the narrative strategies that have since become Ishiguro's signatures, including the running in parallel of a past and a present narrative, the telling of both stories by an elusive first-person narrator, and the quietly subversive rewriting of a major genre category. In *A Pale View of Hills*, Ishiguro writes a ghost of the kind of interracial Occupation love story plied by postwar melodramas such as James Michener's popular 1954 novel *Sayonara*, and the 1957 film of the same name, which stars Marlon Brando as an ultimately enlightened anti-racist. In Ishiguro's first novel, a Japanese widow, Etsuko, living in England in the 1980s, recalls a summer shortly after the war when she was pregnant and living with her first husband, a Japanese man, in Nagasaki. Sometime after the Occupation, Etsuko left Japan and married her second husband, an English journalist. Her narrative discloses nothing about the series of events that led her to the journalist and out of Japan. Much about the past remains hazy. Is Etsuko's mysterious, war-traumatized friend Sachiko in fact Etsuko herself? When exactly does the past plotline take place? Her recollections float in time: "The worst days were over by then. American soldiers were as numerous as ever – for there was fighting in Korea – but in Nagasaki, after what had gone before, those were days of calm and relief" (11). Aside from such occasional references to the dwindling American presence, the most reliable evidence that the past of the novel unfolds during the late stages of the Occupation resides in the recurrence of the word "occupation" some fourteen times in the text.

In the present of *A Pale View of Hills*, too, much remains unclear. Etsuko's younger daughter, Niki, has come home following the suicide of her half-sister, Keiko. True to form, Etsuko offers no elaboration on the events that led to her older daughter's death. Instead, Etsuko emphasizes the Western stereotypes about Japan that she knows will inform, or misinform, readings of her narrative. She initiates this pattern right away. In the first paragraph of the novel, Etsuko notes that Niki is so named because her English father "wanted to give her a Japanese name" and "agreed to Niki, thinking it had some vague echo of the East about it" (9); a few paragraphs later, the first section of the novel concludes that "more than one newspaper was quick to pick up on [the] fact" that Keiko was "pure Japanese. The English are fond of their idea that our race has an instinct for suicide, as if further explications are unnecessary; for that was all they reported, that she was Japanese and that she had hung herself in her room" (10).

The observation has read itself, so to speak, and Etsuko "reports" to readers of the novel no more than the papers do. Since stereotypes are self-justifying to their propagators, the "fact" of Keiko's "race" precludes any attempt by the English papers to understand her human suffering. In other words, Etsuko voices a grasp of the self-affirming function of orientalism, a grasp that a savvy reader in 1982 would have connected to Edward Said's watershed work, *Orientalism*, first published in 1978.

As the novel progresses, artworks compound orientalist misprision of Japanese people, Etsuko included. In the past of *A Pale View of Hills*, Etsuko recalls accompanying Ogata-San, her father-in-law, on an outing to the Nagasaki Peace Park. Ogata wants to "go and look around Nagasaki 'like the tourists do'" (137). In this touristic scene, Etsuko offers an unusually extended description of the large commemorative statue that is located in the park (fig. 8.1). Since the sculptor Seibō Kitamura's statue was not dedicated until 9 August 1955, the tenth anniversary of the bombing of Nagasaki, Etsuko's visit to the park presents another instance of the uncertain dates in the novel. She conflates what would have to be, in strict historical terms, a post-Occupation memory with an Occupation narrative. This temporal slippage, however, aligns with the pointed visual imprecision of Etsuko's memory. Though Kitamura's memorial statue is a bronze, Etsuko's ekphrastic recollection of it literalizes a whiteness implied, even championed, by its aesthetic. Turning bronze to marble, Etsuko offers an unusually detailed description of "that large white statue in Nagasaki" (138). She emphasizes nothing so much as the outsize whiteness of "the memorial itself – a massive white statue in memory of those killed by the bomb – presiding over its domain":

> The statue resembled some muscular Greek god, seated with both arms outstretched. With his right hand, he pointed to the sky from where the bomb had fallen; with his other arm – stretched out to his left – the figure was supposedly holding back the forces of evil. His eyes were closed in prayer.
>
> It was always my feeling that the statue had a rather cumbersome appearance, and I was never able to associate it with what had occurred the day the bomb had fallen, and those terrible days which followed. Seen from a distance, the figure looked

8.1 | Seibo Kitamura's Peace Statue (1955), Nagasaki Peace Park.

> almost comical, resembling a policeman conducting traffic. It remained for me nothing more than a statue, and while most people in Nagasaki seemed to appreciate it as some form of gesture, I suspect the general feeling was much like mine. (137–8)

This passage at once quotes and questions the official interpretation of the statue, as well as the familiar euphemisms and passive-voice syntax that would turn the bomb into an effect of gravity – the phrase "had fallen" is repeated twice – rather than an act of war. Moreover, Etsuko uses circumlocutions to acknowledge her own and "the general feeling," while also not stating what those feelings are. She hints at the sad comedy of the unwitting resemblance of the statue to white disciplinary authority, "a policeman conducting traffic," in occupied Nagasaki. Yet over and above these subtleties of style, this passage is almost painfully obvious in its meaning: in order to memorialize the human victims of the atomic bombing of Nagasaki, the statue transforms those victims into a recognizably white ideal, into "some Greek god," rather than a Japanese person. In a humorous but

8.2 | Tourist postcard of Nagasaki Peace Park.

pointed final turn, Ogata buys a postcard of the memorial for the widow whose noodle shop he frequents back in his hometown, Fukuoka, but he struggles to think of what to write on it. He considers "send[ing] it with nothing written" (139). What he finally scribbles on the card remains untold. *A Pale View of Hills* thus registers the difficulty of finding something to say not simply about the bombing but about the Western ideals sculpted into the memorial for the victims of the bombing (fig. 8.2).

This kind of balance between incisiveness and obviousness, elision and directness is one of Ishiguro's trademarks. Lest readers take a patronizing view of the dated statuary, Ishiguro weighs the bald orientalism of the Peace Park statue against a poem in the present day of *A Pale View of Hills*. In the early 1980s sections, a friend of Niki's "is writing a poem" about Etsuko (89, 177). The motif of poet and her poem occasions some deadpan, intergenerational humour. When Niki tells her mother that the poet has "been through quite a bit herself" and therefore understands Etsuko, Etsuko responds: "I see. And how old is this friend of yours?" (89). The motif of the 1980s poet and her poem also registers a serious – and, in 1982, a seriously unfashionable – doubt about the ethical grounds for poetry of witness and related literary modes that have helped over time to open the field of human rights and literature.

"In recent years, she has taken it upon herself to admire certain aspects of my past," Etsuko remarks of Niki (10–11). The poet, too, is "impressed" by and "appreciates" Etsuko's historical experience. At one point, Niki tells her mother, "I was telling [my poet friend] about you [...]. About you and Dad and how you left Japan. She was really impressed. She appreciates what it must have been like, how it wasn't quite as easy as it sounds" (89). These young women of the 1980s want to see Etsuko as a feminist survivor of male history. Yet neither the poet nor Niki nor, for that matter, the reader of *A Pale View of Hills* ever hears anything about "what it must have been like" for Etsuko. Etsuko observes that Niki and, by extension, the poet have "built up some sort of picture" of "what actually happened during those last days in Nagasaki" from whatever version of those events Niki's late father shared with her (90). But Niki's father never quite grasped cultural difference, as witnessed by Niki's name or Etsuko's observation that "despite all the impressive articles he wrote about Japan, my husband never understood the ways of our culture" (90). Impressed and appreciative as the poet may be, her poem about Etsuko is vicarious thrice over: it is the poet's version of her friend's father's projection of her friend's mother's experience. The poet's work seems poised to line up with the erasure of Japanese bodies and experience that Etsuko sees so plainly in the Nagasaki Peace Park.

Corporate Citizens

Whereas *A Pale View of Hills* brings a critical eye to artistic representations of the Japanese, *An Artist of the Floating World* takes a critical view of the juridical reconstitution of Japan after the war. When Emperor Hirohito officially signed the surrender on 2 September 1945, the Japanese turned from subjects of a militaristic empire into citizens of a liberal democracy, with the emperor as figurehead. Citizenship was not created by a revolution from below of the kind valorized in some accounts of the emergence of human rights during the Enlightenment (such as Lynn Hunt's *Inventing Human Rights: A History*

[2008]), but by top-down legislative action of the occupying force.[7] Indeed, the first phase of the Occupation was known as "demilitarization and democratization" (1946–48). The nomenclature is telling: the alliterative pairing implies an almost causal progression from the one to the other.

The centrepiece of this first, broadly reformist phase was a new national charter for Japan. Initiated principally by General Douglas MacArthur, the Supreme Commander of the Allied Powers (SCAP), the new Constitution of Japan was drafted, in English, by February 1946, promulgated on 3 November 1946, and enacted six months later on 3 May 1947.[8] As at mid-century, the Constitution of Japan is best known today for "The Renunciation of War" (Chapter II, Article 9). Following the logic of demilitarization and democratization, the Renunciation directly precedes enumeration of "The Rights and Duties of the People" (Chapter III, Articles 10–40). The Constitution of Japan thus inscribes a paradox that has, as Hannah Arendt argues in *The Origins of Totalitarianism* (1951), always haunted the idea of basic human rights: the charter makes citizenship the condition from which rights follow (Chapter III, Article 10). With the provision of citizenship in place, the constitution outlines the privileges and protections of human rights to which the Japanese, as a people, are entitled: "The people shall not be prevented from enjoying any of the fundamental human rights. These fundamental human rights guaranteed to the people by this Constitution shall be conferred upon the people of this and future generations as eternal and inviolate rights" (Article 11). From there, the Constitution of Japan lists some twenty-eight "universal" and "fundamental human rights" that state and citizen alike are bound to respect and protect. These include rights that are American in spirit and letter, such as individuals' right to "life, liberty, and the pursuit of happiness" (Article 13), and rights that far exceed those expressly granted by the US Constitution. The Constitution of Japan bars torture (Article 36), guarantees "academic freedom" (Article 23), establishes the "equal rights of husband and wife" in marriage and the "essential equality of the sexes" (Article 24). It also grants the right of Japanese citizens to "education correspondent to their ability" (Article 26) and establishes the "right of workers to organize and to bargain and act collectively" (Article 28). More tellingly, eighteen years before the passage of the Civil Rights Act of 1964 in the US, the Constitution of Japan asserts that "all of the people are equal under the law and there shall be no discrimination in political, economic or social relations because of race, creed, sex, social status or family origin" (Article 14). The fullest utopian energies of Western power in the early Cold War are thus written into the Constitution of Japan, even as the principles and practices of SCAP presumed the racial superiority of the white American occupiers and as legal segregation in the US became a glaring liability in its Cold War project.[9]

An Artist of the Floating World charts an oblique course through a conventional English marriage plot, as the novel chronicles the disgraced imperial propaganda artist Masuji Ono's outward efforts to get his younger daughter married and his inward attempts to justify his past to himself. Inverting the precise place and indeterminate time coordinates of *A Pale View of Hills*, *An Artist of the Floating World* takes place in an unnamed Japanese city between October 1948 and June 1950. The novel thus unfolds one year after the enactment of the Constitution, and at the same time that Mao's victory in China and the Korean War, which began on 25 June 1950, pushed SCAP toward a "reverse course," as the second and much more conservative phase of the Occupation was known. Where demilitarization and democratization looked rhetorically forward with hope, the reverse course scaled back on both the rhetoric of rights and citizens' ability to exercise them. In this context, the democratic freedoms and individual rights that many of the young Japanese in the novel champion come to look more contingent than constitutional, more instrumental than fundamental.

Rights talk and juridical citizenship land squarely in *An Artist of the Floating World* in a series of conversations among three generations of the Ono family. In one representative exchange dated November 1949, Ono talks with his son-in-law, Taro, who is an employee at an electronics firm. Corporate Taro tells his artist father-in-law of the new feeling of confidence at his company: "The changes we made after the war are now beginning to bear fruit at all levels of the company. We feel very optimistic about the future. Within the next ten years, provided we all do our best, KNC should be a name recognized not just all over Japan but all over the world" (184). When Ono suggests that at least some of the old pre-war management should have been kept on, Taro has a ready answer: "We needed new leaders with a new approach appropriate to the world of today" (185). For the young man, the "optimistic" future of Japan equates to the predicted dominance of Japanese corporations in a global capitalist order. While Taro's parroting of slogans about emphatically "new" economic structures sounds patently naive, he also does foresee, if blindly, the extraordinary economic success of Japan that was very much in global news during the 1980s. Even as Ishiguro worked on this novel, Japan's economy, dubbed a "postwar economic miracle" (Morris-Suzuki 131–63), became the second largest in the world.

Ono and Taro's timely conversation about corporate restructuring turns into a conversation about "democracy and individual rights." Once more countering his son-in-law's enthusiasm for change, Ono asks whether he thinks "we might be a little too hasty in following the Americans? I would be the first to agree many of the old ways must now be erased for ever, but don't you think sometimes some good things are being thrown out with the bad?" (185). Taro is again prepared: "Father is very right. At times, I'm sure, we have been a little hasty. But by and large, the Americans have an immense amount to teach us. Just in these few years, for instance, we Japanese have already come a long way in understanding such things as democracy and individual rights. Indeed, Father, I have a feeling Japan has finally established a foundation on which to build a brilliant future. This is why firms like ours can look forward with the greatest confidence" (185–6). Like Etsuko's description of the Peace Park statue, this dialogue is at once brilliantly on the nose and deeply subtle about the conflation of democratic ideals, individual rights, and global capitalism. As Taro moves without friction between corporate "confidence" on the one hand and "democracy and rights" on the other, Ishiguro registers the complicity of rights talk in a global economic order that relies on and perpetuates inequality. The narrative records how thoroughly Taro, a low-level "office worker" rather than a titan of industry, toes the company line on the buoyant future. Taro buys rights and capitalism wholesale, and in one neat package. It is only fitting, then, that this conversation finally concludes with the young boy Ichiro, himself fascinated by American cultural products and icons, responding to the perennial question of what he would like to be when he grows up. Ichiro wants not to be "President" but "President of Nippon Electronics!" where "electronics," as much as the child Ichiro, is the sign of Japan's future (186). Through this and like conversations, *An Artist of the Floating World* doubts the quality of citizenship produced by and for a Japanese liberal democracy built in the American image. Throughout this novel, "rights" look more like a means of social control than they do "the blessings of liberty" (Preamble, Constitution of Japan).

Scientific Research, Humanist Ambivalence

Like Ishiguro's, Shirley Hazzard's citizenship trajectory has qualified her for many literary prizes. Hazzard is, to my knowledge, the only writer to have been nominated for the Booker Prize (Commonwealth), the National Book Award (US), and the Miles Franklin Award (Australia). She won the latter two for *The Great Fire*.[10] Born in Australia in 1931, Hazzard lived in Hong Kong and New Zealand as a teenager. Since moving to New York with her family in 1950, she has spent most of her adult life there and in Italy. She did not, however, take US citizenship until shortly after Richard Nixon's resignation in 1974. (The timing was not a coincidence.) In addition to her literary career, Hazzard worked for a decade at the United Nations and later became an outspoken critic of the organization. In the 1970s and 1980s, she wrote several high-profile editorials excoriating the UN record on freedom, torture, and human rights, as well as a book entitled *Defeat of an Ideal: A Study of the Self-Destruction of the United Nations* (1972). Her 1990 book *Countenance of Truth: The United Nations and the Waldheim Case* continues in this vein.[11]

Contrary, perhaps, to what this synopsis of Hazzard's life and career might suggest, and certainly in stark contrast to Ishiguro's critical vantage on orientalism and rights discourse in *A Pale View of Hills* and *An Artist of the Floating World*, *The Great Fire* proffers an unapologetically nostalgic view of the last gasp of British colonialism in East Asia. As one reviewer put it, the novel "appears to develop the theme of anti-post-colonialism" (Shulevitz). The book does have a welcome Pacific scope. In a panoramic sweep, it takes in the aftermath of the bombing of Hiroshima and the Occupation of Japan, the resumption of British colonial order and the adjudication of Japanese war crimes in Hong Kong, the civil war in China, and postwar bureaucracy in Australia and New Zealand. Nevertheless, Asian characters exist mostly in the background of *The Great Fire* and appear as flat Cold War orientalist stereotypes rather than rounded characters. When an "incalculable" young Japanese man commits suicide early in the novel, for example, his death serves mostly to ennoble the hero Aldred Leith, a humanist scholar, who alone among the white characters had grasped the young man's "pained humanity" (36, 41). The best that can be said for Hazzard's view of East Asia is that it is in painful keeping with her scrupulous, even uncanny, recreation of the 1940s British realist fictions with which she aligns *The Great Fire* (Seiler 100–5). But there is one important crack in the veneer of Hazzard's apparent recreation of 1940s style: although *The Great Fire* opens at Hiroshima in the summer of 1947, and although Leith seeks to conduct vague, ethnographic research among the survivors, the novel never countenances the official US justification for using the atomic bomb, namely, that it saved rather than cost millions of lives.

Hazzard characterizes Leith as a consummate humanist. More accurately, she idealizes him as such. Leith's American counterparts in the sciences measure, tally, and otherwise quantify the effects of the bomb. British Leith, meanwhile, learns Japanese (he already speaks Mandarin), reads Western classics, and finishes a book about China. His book is the product of two years spent walking across China with a view toward writing an account of "the last days of all [its] centuries" as "witnessed and recounted by someone who was not a spy, not a sociologist, beholden to no one" (56). Whereas Ishiguro keeps his critical distance from the principles of humanism and humanitarianism, Hazzard indulges in a vision of Leith's consummately human independence of mind and compassion for others. Within the novel, Leith has "no wish to explicate or control" the human beings he studies (34). *The Great Fire* casts Leith as a humanist who remains admirably outside the Cold War emergence of strategic area studies and who opposes the triumph of the sciences. Outside the novel, however, Leith's "identification with a few individual Japanese does not prevent him from becoming entangled in their subjectification" (Dixon 275).

As against its humanist hero, *The Great Fire* depicts scientific modes of knowledge production at Hiroshima working in lockstep with US censorship to craft and promote a compelling, future-oriented narrative of the scientific achievement represented by the atomic bomb.

This narrative would, at best, divert people from the horrors of the bomb and, at worst, preclude consideration of the bombings as war crimes. Scientific achievement provided one of the rhetorical anchors of the official announcement and initial reportage of the bombings. On 6 August 1945, US President Harry S. Truman emphasized the scientific impressiveness of the bomb in his announcement of its first use and the devastation wreaked on Hiroshima: "The greatest marvel is not the size of the enterprise, its secrecy, nor its cost, but the achievement of scientific brains in putting together infinitely complex pieces of knowledge held by many men in different fields of science into a workable plan" (Truman). After the bombings, the bomb itself underwent an "instant and seamless transposition [...] from one U.S. research project to another" (Norris 183). Organized into administrative bodies such as the Joint Commission for the Investigation of the Effects of the Atomic Bomb in Japan, the Atomic Bomb Casualty Commission, and the United States Strategic Bombing Survey, physicists, social scientists, biologists, medical doctors, and other researchers arrived in Japan to research the human and environmental effects of the bomb. At the same time as it established these investigative bodies, the Allied command created a censorship regime that "banned in the Press Code any 'destructive criticism' or publication that might 'disturb public tranquility.' This directive was interpreted to include representations of bombed Hiroshima and Nagasaki and discussion of the effects of the atomic bombs" (Sherif 75).

In its evocation of Hiroshima in the summer of 1947, *The Great Fire* links scientific research practice to Occupation censorship policy. At a few key moments, Hazzard's narrative suggests that science, writ large, contributes at least as much as censorship to creating and managing the reality of the bomb. One such passage establishes the routine of Leith's vague but humanist research. Bureaucratic structures block his access to victims of the bomb: "In order to speak with injured survivors, or with spokesmen of the community, permission was required from the American Bomb Survey, and the foreign applicant was accompanied by an appointed officer" (54). The bureaucratic passive voice undermines the reasonability of the regulations invoked here, even as Leith's status as a "foreign applicant" gives the lie to the Allied Occupation. But the ironies of the scene become only more pronounced as British Leith, his Australian driver Talbot, and their American public relations man Carroll visit the site of attack on Hiroshima: "In Talbot's jeep, they had crossed the tramline and were approaching the momentous scene – where the main force of the explosion had been received. These [...] were Carroll's words, and he never did say The Bomb. To Aldred Leith's questions, [Carroll] responded with practised and sometimes technical expressions" (54). Passive voice ("had been received"), euphemism ("main force"): Carroll speaks with the "sheer cloudy vagueness" that Orwell dismantles in his classic postwar essay "Politics and the English Language" (115). Though free indirect discourse and direct dialogue feature prominently in *The Great Fire*, Hazzard eschews them at "the momentous scene." Instead the narrator intrudes to clarify what Carroll says, to characterize how he says it ("practised and sometimes technical expressions"), and, equally important, to note what he does not say: "The Bomb."

As the passage continues, the narrator does not transcribe Leith's and Talbot's questions, but Carroll's responses indicate the substance of their inquiries. This narrative strategy registers the ease with which genuine inquiry is subsumed into a version of public relations speech whose authority (or impenetrability) derives largely from quantitative data. Straight away, Carroll's zeugmatic use of the verb "examined" inadvertently indicates that "the scientists" approach objects and persons in the same way:

> Talbot asked one question only, to which Carroll had his prompt and measured reply: Yes, the scientists examining the site and the survivors were inclined to think that there remained some danger in the atmosphere, though not for so brief a visit as our own. The girders of the dome had been examined for their unaccountable resilience. Why yes, the casualties were estimated at a quarter-million, that being a tentative figure only. Why the explosion had not been directed initially to an uninhabited zone, or why the first exercise had been followed by the raid on Nagasaki, he had no idea, those decisions having been made in the closed and no doubt wise councils of our leaders. However, he did ask Leith if he could suggest a strategic reason. He had never sought an opinion before. Aldred,

> turning to him from the front seat where he sat beside Talbot, remarked, "I doubt there was logic, other than that shaped to the predestined act. By then, neither side was interested in sparing anyone, even themselves." (54–5)

There is much to be said about this passage, which invokes some of the early concerns that shaped public debate in the US about the use of the bomb, among them the horrors of radiation sickness chronicled in John Hersey's *Hiroshima* (1946) and the choice of largely civilian targets at Hiroshima and Nagasaki. Even Carroll, confident and well-trained, tiptoes around the strategic wisdom of deploying atomic bombs. Leith, whose opinion is the only one that Carroll seeks or that the narrative quotes, sees no valid, strategic logic in the bombing.

Like the son-in-law Taro in *An Artist of the Floating World*, Carroll is all too willing to defer to the "no doubt wise councils of our leaders." What is strange is that not even Carroll voices the official American justification of the use of the atomic bomb. That justification – that the bombings ended the war and thus saved millions of other lives – had taken hold by the summer of 1947, when Leith, Carroll, and Talbot visit Hiroshima. In February 1947, former US Secretary of War Henry L. Stimson published "The Decision to Use the Atomic Bomb" in *Harper's*. This essay marked the first public articulation of what has come to be known as the "humanitarian" justification for the American use of the atomic bomb against Japan. Written in response to criticism from high-profile scientists and from citizens alike, "The Decision" describes the "events which led up to" the atomic bombings from 1941 forward (97). Stimson writes that, but for the bomb, the US and its allies would have launched an invasion that was "expected to cost over a million casualties to American forces alone. Additional large losses [would] be expected among our allies, and [...] if our campaign were successful [...] enemy casualties would be much larger than our own" (102). Stimson's justification remains contested not only among "doves" and academics, but also among military and other historians willing to take Stimson's account of strategy on its own terms.[12] Yet the belief that the atomic bombings of Hiroshima and Nagasaki saved, rather than cost, millions of lives remains broadly intact in US popular consciousness. In *The Great Fire*, Leith does not refute the nominally humanitarian justification for the nuclear attacks on

Hiroshima and Nagasaki, nor does he broach their putative morality or legality. He simply does not acknowledge it. Omission does not, unto itself, equal opposition. Despite its grossly dated vision of East Asia and its unchecked belief in the incorruptible humanity of the humanist scholar, *The Great Fire* does cast doubt on the humanitarian justification, as well as on the disciplinary structures and practices, especially scientific ones, that helped to make the bomb, then tried to make some sense of its use. To state as much is not to apologize for the pervasive orientalism of *The Great Fire* – far from it. It is rather to acknowledge the deep ambivalence of the competing constructions of the human that run through Hazzard's fiction about Hiroshima. The novel voices despair over the use of the atomic bomb, yet stops short of calling it a crime against humanity.

Is there room for such ambivalence in critical discourse on human rights and literature? If we are to expand the legal and formal scope of the field, there may have to be. For one thing, certainly in the United States, ambivalence and avoidance are built into cultural memory of the atomic bombings of Hiroshima and Nagasaki, as well as the Occupation of Japan. That ambivalence leaves both events open to manipulation, as in the Bush administration's facile likening of Iraq in the twenty-first century to Japan in 1945.[13] For another, where mimetic realism predominates in rights and literature scholarship generally, *A Pale View of Hills*, *An Artist of the Floating World*, and *The Great Fire* rank among the few American or Commonwealth realist novels that imagine the immediate psychic and material aftermath of the bombings or the conditions of the Occupation at all.[14] Their central storylines and thematic interests lie largely outside of the theoretical and practical concerns that energize the field of human rights and literature. Yet these novels do the important work of depicting how disciplinary practices and habits of mind – those of literature and literary study among them – shape the idea of "the human," whose intrinsic rights will or will not be protected from either the interference of the state or atrocity. Realist even in their ambivalence, Hazzard's and Ishiguro's fictions neither proclaim nor protest. Rather, they invite the field of human rights and literature to confront anew the extraordinary threat of human ambivalence.

NOTES

1 See Forché, "Twentieth-Century Poetry of Witness," and below; Yudice on the boom in Latin American *testimonio* in the 1970s and 1980s; and Slaughter's benchmark case for the efficacy of the *Bildungsroman* in naturalizing the human rights regime.

2 Eiji's *Inside GHQ* is the authoritative history of the American command structure of the Occupation. I have described the Occupation of Japan as "nominally Allied." For statistics on the British Commonwealth Occupied Force, see Eiji 134–5.

3 Goldberg and Moore offer the most comprehensive stocktaking of the field ("Human Rights and Literature"). On the need to vary the literary styles and modes to which human rights and literature can attend, see Anker's exemplary reading of Rushdie's *Shalimar the Clown* (2005) and Mansfield's work on non-topical human rights literature.

4 In addition to the works cited above, Forché has edited the groundbreaking anthology *Against Forgetting: Twentieth-Century Poetry of Witness* (1994) and, more recently, with Duncan Wu, the anthology *Poetry of Witness: The Tradition in English, 1500–2001* (2014).

5 In the 2005 interview with Wroe, Ishiguro said he became a British subject in 1983. Other chronologies differ. Lewis (xii) and Matthews and Groes (xv) date Ishiguro's citizenship to 1982.

6 Cheng analyzes the marketing of Ishiguro's Japaneseness; Walkowitz offers an incisive reading of the "rhetoric of presumption" that belies reviewers' claims not to be trading in stereotypes about Japan (115–16).

7 Dower describes in detail the "revolution from above" (1946–48) which "would extend to the reform of civil and criminal law, elimination of the 'feudalistic' system that had legally rendered women inferior, extension of the right to vote to women, decentralization of the police, enactment of a progressive law governing working conditions, revision of both the structure and the curriculum of the education system, renovation of the electoral system, and promotion of greater local autonomy vis-à-vis the central government" (*Embracing* 82).

8 Inoue's *MacArthur's Japanese Constitution* is the most thorough study of the origin and debates over the Constitution of Japan.

9 On racial segregation in SCAP and Occupation literature that critiques the hypocrisies of the occupying Americans' racial politics, see Molaskey 70–102; on the Cold War, the global image of the US, and the US civil rights movement, see Dudziak, Borstelmann.

10 Hazzard's novel *The Bay of Noon* was nominated for the "Lost" Man Booker Prize, awarded in 2010 to a work of fiction published in 1970. J.G. Farrell's *Troubles* won the award.

11 Olubas offers an incisive analysis of Hazzard's writing about the UN (chapter 1).

12 Bird and Lifschultz collect primary documents and critical essays pertaining to the justification of the use of atomic bombs against Japan, as well as scholarly work on the controversy surrounding American public memory of the bomb.

13 John Dower's *Cultures of War* systematically dismantles the Bush administration's practice of analogizing post-9/11 Iraq to post–Second World War Japan.

14 What Paul S. Boyer demonstrated thirty years ago remains true today: there are few "durable" fictions that are "'about' the atomic bomb in a literal sense" (252). More recently, scholars such as Adam Piette and Daniel Cordle have parsed how genre fictions (sci-fi, suspense novels) and postmodern narrative techniques bespeak the threat of the bomb and fears of nuclear war, without being precisely "about" Hiroshima or Nagasaki.

PART THREE

RIGHTS

9

Human Rights and Postwar Internationalism in *The Third Man*

MITCHELL C. BROWN

Graham Greene's postwar fiction takes as its primary subject the distressed relationship between international politics and human rights at mid-century. In these later novels, Greene portrays the extralegal spaces of rightlessness and lawlessness that persisted after the war and remained outside the boundaries of international legislature. For Greene, the problem of refugees and stateless criminals during European reconstruction and the incipient years of the Cold War resisted the collective political recognition of fundamental human rights supposed by the Universal Declaration of Human Rights (1948). His representation of international space in the late 1940s particularly engages with questions of state authority, statelessness, and interstate rule. In *The Third Man* (1949), Greene depicts international law, humanitarianism, and justice as being inevitably corrupted by the political realities of interstate spaces, which is to say zones that lie between states and therefore fall outside clear jurisdiction and governance. Greene's postwar internationalism, as represented by crime-ridden Vienna in *The Third Man*, dramatizes the parallel status shared by the refugee and the rogue: to be a truly international subject is to be at once liable to encroach upon the rights of others as well as to have one's own rights encroached upon.

Rallying behind the "Greeneland" that constitutes a backdrop to much of Greene's fiction, many critics emphasize the atmospheric consistency across his works. Misery and corruption in Greene's novels are often appropriated for the purposes of theological, namely Catholic, criticism. Catholic readings characterize these narratives of moral uncertainty as opportunities to explore the spiritual interior of Greene's characters or, in a biographical mode, of Greene himself. More recently, Stephen Land has argued for a secular or humanitarian reading of this broad terrain. Land addresses and promptly dismisses the body of Catholic criticism as "a matter for [Greene's] biographers" (4). Greene, vehemently resisting the Catholic label attached to his work, insisted that he was "a more political writer than a Catholic writer" (Donaghy 58). For Land, Greeneland's conflicts between individual moral agents and the larger geopolitical forces operative above them is more aptly and simply defined as Greene's human imperative.

Even a secular figuration of Greeneland, however, cannot be applied uniformly to Greene's canon. Neglecting to parse out the political differences between Greene's novels risks overlooking the attentive observations, reflections, and commentaries that his fiction provides on the rapidly evolving political developments that informed his writing. Each of Greene's political novels carries unique social and political markers of his first-hand experiences working as a British intelligence agent abroad: the Greeneland of Vienna differs from that of Sierra Leone, South America, and Indochina. In 1948, one political shift dramatically altered Greene's novelistic landscape. At mid-century Greene's human imperative was transformed into a necessarily political and, more specifically, international concern. Land concludes that "it is the depth of conviction of Greene's humanitarian feeling which secures his place among the major writers of the twentieth century" (272). In light of Land's observation, further examination is required of the humanitarian politics of Greeneland in the wake of international human rights law. Greene's interest in the international at mid-century centres on the evolving relationship between politics and fundamental rights. He is not interested in "who the criminal is" – a central preoccupation of the traditional spy thriller – but rather, "to what state of abandon a man hunted down for a crime can be reduced" (Donaghy 25).

In 1948, the UDHR rendered Greene's human imperative an imperative of international politics. In his written correspondence with Elizabeth Bowen and V.S. Pritchett discussing the role of the writer –

an exchange that was read on the BBC Third Program on 7 October 1948, and parts of which Greene later incorporated into his 1969 essay "The Virtue of Disloyalty" – Greene asserts that the greatest privilege and obligation of the novelist is disloyalty to the state (R. Greene 151). Although the novelist awakens sympathy, Greene specifies that this sympathy must elicit understanding "for those who lie outside the boundaries of state sympathy" (154). At the midpoint of his career Greene reconsiders his human sympathy in terms of international politics. By 1948, he could no longer avoid the political dimension of this problem, as he was able to in his earlier novels. To consider the human imperative was now necessarily to consider international rights. *The Third Man* marks a definitive departure in Greene's career, after which point his fiction remains invested in the transnational politicization of human sympathy made possible through the global attention paid to fundamental rights. If the atmosphere in Greene's fiction derives from a "sinister internationalism" that inhibits or complicates the performance of human sympathy (Land 189), then each of Greene's characters and plots can be read as offering some insight, comment, or complication on the enfolding tangle of this newly politicized humanitarianism. To consider Greeneland's "dangerous edge of things" (*A Sort of Life* 117) after mid-century requires a political reading that addresses the evolution of international human rights law.

Postwar Legislation and Mid-Century Biopolitics

The UDHR sought, first of all, to establish international law as preeminent over national juridical rule. In *The Origins of Totalitarianism*, Hannah Arendt lamented that this sphere of international law operative above nations still did not exist a decade after its legislative inception (298). At best, the UDHR performed a degree of optimism, looking rather than stepping forward in its portrayal of inalienable human rights; its constative rhetoric was in fact more aspirational than actual. Though it came as a direct response to the war crimes committed during the Second World War, this landmark consideration of the rights question examined many of the broader issues that preceded the Final Solution and, to a large degree, persisted after it. The UDHR was a response not only to Nazi atrocities, but also to the more general problem of human governance outside national authority. This era of nationalism, which found its crisis point in global conflict, came to be defined by the liminal cracks and fissures produced by military friction. With the unprecedented growth of refugee populations in Europe following the Second World War, the unlegislated international sphere began to swell, and by swelling forced its way onto the political stage. As a result, confrontations between sovereign power and the extralegal outlaws occupying this liminal space became a significant political problem in the immediate postwar period. The world of spies, spivs, refugees, and revolutionaries found representation in every media outlet in the emergent years of the Cold War.

In 1938 American journalist Dorothy Thompson spoke emphatically about the refugee "crisis" that was already overwhelming European nations. Thompson estimated that 3,650,000 refugees were moving across Europe from 1918 to 1938 – not counting the additional groups "where numbers are mere guesswork" (*Refugees* 15). She insists that "essential to any solution of the refugee problem is to divest it of the stigma of charity" (90), and that "it must be regarded now as a problem of international politics" (10). This call for state responsibility over stateless persons is one of the earliest twentieth-century iterations of universal human rights as being inherently tied to sovereign power – the authorized state application of the force of law upon those who reside outside of it. For Thompson, one viable solution to the growing problem of international governance was immigration – the emptying-out of stateless space through rapid integration. She praised the Nansen Passport, a state-orchestrated project introduced by the League of Nations in 1922, as "the greatest thing that has happened for the individual refugee. It returned to him his lost identity" (28). But this solution was both partial and temporary: it granted an acknowledgment of limited state affiliation only for the sake of interstate travel for up to one year (27). Useful as it may have been for some, this solution did not completely address the rights and protection of those who remained outside of state rule: persons without papers and individuals unwilling or unable to return to a home state. For those unable to establish themselves under a new flag within a twelve-month window, the Nansen Passport offered only a temporary suspension of their legal predicament before returning them to refugee status. Thompson's claim that a Nansen certificate restored the refugee's "lost identity" implied that the refugee had no identity without some certified instatedness. This dangerous supposition not only leaves the stateless refugee without protection while occupying international space, but it also strips him or her of any inherent human dignity. "To be stateless was to be rightless" (Stonebridge, *Judicial Imagination* 11), and, according to Thompson, it was also to be less than human.

Neither Dr Fridtjof Nansen nor Dorothy Thompson directly treated the unique legal status of the international refugee; they focused instead on the resolution of it. This legacy of integration was, rightly or wrongly, upheld in 1948. By striving to extend a nominal form of universal instatedness *outside* the boundaries of national rule, the UDHR sought to eliminate this international zone rather than try to govern it. As Joseph Slaughter observes in *Human Rights, Inc.*, the textual figurations of "human" and "rights" within this legal superstructure are constructed in the same contractual terms as a national indenture: "the 'human' cited in the title of the UDHR is not a human as such; it is a person as a member of a people or nation – a particular kind of human activated as a legal and moral unit with 'rights [...] that are formulated in society'" (58). This Society of Man was conceptual, not material. Article 28 of the UDHR states that, "Everyone is entitled to a social and international order in which the rights and freedoms set forth in this Declaration can be fully realized." Nowhere did the UDHR offer a tangible figuration or prescription of assurance to this ambiguous international order. Further, when the UDHR declared the Rights of Man inalienable, "no other authority was invoked for their establishment; Man himself was their source as well as their ultimate goal" (Arendt, *Origins* 291). This independence from all governments left human rights in isolation, "with no authority left to protect them and no institution willing to guarantee them" (292). The focus was not on how to protect stateless persons, but on how to resolve their statelessness. However aspirational the UDHR may have been, this constative declaration omitted any direct address regarding governance within the international proper and the protection of its stateless occupants.

Throughout the twentieth century, one of the most powerful weapons wielded by totalitarian politics was denaturalization

(Arendt, *Origins* 269). Neither the Nansen Passport nor the UDHR could prevent a state from stripping people of their citizenship, and thus repopulating stateless space. Stripped of their rights, refugee populations were forced to occupy what would remain largely unlegislated political geographies. Regardless of how effectively the United Nations could diminish these stateless populations through international integration policies, numberless persons were still being forced into this state of exception. For Giorgio Agamben, the politicization of the most basic human rights in the UDHR in fact facilitated this process of political expulsion. Paradoxically, the declaration that sought to protect the "bare life" of individuals ultimately dispossessed them of this very quality. Brought under the custody of the *polis*, even an encompassing international order, universal human rights were excised and thus made alienable. Taking his point of departure from Carl Schmitt's *Political Theology*, Agamben argues that the emergence of biopolitics in the twentieth century enabled an unprecedented number of executions of sovereign power over "bare life" (171), namely, crimes against humanity. To be stateless was to be vulnerable to an inhumanity quite literally beyond legal comprehension or jurisdiction.

The existence of this extrajuridical space not only facilitated the horrific, large-scale atrocities that incited the UDHR, but also rendered illicit every action made under its non-rule. The refugee's existence becomes a de facto offence when he or she resides outside the force of law. Throughout the twentieth century, the refugee found himself "on a frontier, trapped between a country that had spat him out and a country that would not let him in. In that predicament he was practically forced to disobey the orders of one government or the other" (Thompson, *Refugees* 39). To be a purely international citizen was to command an illicit mode of being. In Agamben's terms, this figurative space stood as a "threshold of indistinction," where "it [was] impossible to distinguish between transgression of the law from execution of the law, such that what violates a rule and what conforms to it coincide without any remainder" (57). To be stateless was to be rightless, but it was also to be immediately criminal. Refugees were "so completely deprived of their rights and prerogatives that no act committed against them could appear any longer as a crime" (Agamben 171).

Graham Greene's *The Third Man* examines this synonymous figuration of the international subject as stateless victim and criminal agent. Through his characterization of Vienna as a criminal *voyoucracy*, Greene explores how postwar internationalism threatens human rights and complicates all forms of state power. Jacques Derrida characterizes the stateless *voyou*, the international rogue who is always other, as "a corrupt and corrupting power of the street [...] [*V*]*oyoucracy* constitutes, even institutes, a sort of counterpower or countercitizenship" (66). An outlaw by definition, this rogue is "shady, questionable, of dubious character [*mauvais aloi*], which is to say suspicious origin [...] it is always a question of [...] *alliage* [alloy] and alliance" (68). Without a definitive state affiliation, the truly international subject is held perpetually in this questionable allegiance. In an unstable network of forced and fluctuating alliances, he is always an other, "always a second or third person" (64). Because the refugee and the rogue occupy an extralegal space within a state order from which they are excluded, their every action is covert and conspiratorial. For Arendt, "man is a social animal and life is not easy for him when social ties are cut off. Moral standards are much easier to keep in the texture of society" ("We Refugees," 271). Lacking attributable citizenship in any polity, the refugee-rogue is expelled from the shared humanity of the UDHR and is immediately seen as being equally suspect of the very same savagery to which they have been subjected (*Origins* 297). In Greene's Vienna, there is an exceedingly fine line between refugee and racketeer, victim and criminal, detective and vigilante. To straddle that line risks falling beyond the international order of man.

In *The Third Man*, postwar internationalism corrupts and dehumanizes political agents. Set in 1948 Vienna under the shared occupation of four allied states – where everyone is in on some kind of racket (324) – Greene's novella depicts postwar internationalism in terms of a problematic extralegal space beyond the reach of legislated human rights. Released in both its film and print versions in 1949, Greene's portrayal of a seedy internationalism challenges the implied relationship between the national and the supranational loosely suggested by the UDHR. Greene problematizes the inalienability of human rights through his presentation of crimes against humanity committed in a contracted, multinational space. In *The Third Man*, postwar Greeneland demonstrates the insidious underside to the development of international human rights law, "a world divided by borders, by literal frontiers the crossing of which usually entails confrontation with the consequences of some hitherto latent ambiguity" (Land 192).

The Third Man: Rights and Reconstruction

The Third Man's investment in the postwar rights movements of the late 1940s is evident first in the relationship between its two forms. As a novella, it is Greene's first sustained use of first-person narration, which Brian Thomas identifies with its journalistic techniques of presenting the narrator as survivor and witness (2). By the late 1940s, the politics of postwar reconstruction had already received several pseudo-documentary treatments. Martha Gellhorn's war correspondence, unrestricted by the "fact-finding" associated with traditional journalism, offered "literarily inclined" coverage of the everyday sentiments surrounding wartime events (Dell'Orto 303). Stephen Spender's *European Witness* (1945) narrates a search for the remnants of Germanic culture under occupation in 1945. Spender admits in his introduction that "in some cases, I have invented characters or incidents in order to convey some impression which could not be conveyed more directly. The book is simply a collection of impressions" (6). Rebecca West's *A Train of Powder* (1946) and *The Meaning of Treason* (1949) were published as book-length supplements to the unsatisfactory trial journalism covering Nuremberg and other war-crime tribunals (*Treason* vii). In *In Darkest Germany* (1947), Victor Gollancz supplemented his emphatic letters of appeal to the British government for fair wartime treatment of German civilians with his own photographs of suffering Germans. Hannah Arendt carried on this tradition in her highly personalized, reflective exposition on the trial of Adolf Eichmann. Greene's Vienna project was thus one of a series of works that sought to represent the realities of European reconstruction by blending together novelistic and journalistic forms. These texts from the immediate aftermath of the war gave aesthetic weight, even at the expense of authoritative facts, to something historical that could not be fully comprehended in documentary terms.

Graham Greene regularly incorporated journalistic observation into his fiction. Responding to the criticism that his novels were too pessimistic, Greene asked, "Where do these critics live? Do they live in Kensington and listen to traffic going past and then have a cocktail party with friends? That, I think, is a worse world than 'Greeneland,' and less true [...]. It's not that I enjoy pudding in the mess, but if there's a mess, I feel it's our duty to look at it" (Donaghy 49). In his 1971 introduction to *The Heart of the Matter*, Greene offers a rare moment of candour on the subject of his biographical influences:

> My cook who went to prison for witchcraft, my steward who was sentenced unjustly for perjury, the boy from the bush who arrived with no recommendation from anybody and took charge of me as faithfully as Ali did of Scobie, refusing bribes offered by the representative of another secret service [...] were they just inhabitants of Greeneland? As well tell a man in love with a woman that she is only a figment of his romantic imagination. (xv)

The Third Man is no different, having "issued out of Greene's contacts in the covert world of intelligence. His war work for Philby's section V in the Secret Intelligence Service (SIS), or MI6, brought him into contact with producer Alexander Korda" (Piette, *Literary Cold War* 26). The moral ambiguity that affords Greene's political fictions their aesthetic or artistic weight depends upon Greene's relationship to the political events he witnessed.

As a film, *The Third Man* preserved this stylistic alignment with pseudo-documentary postwar journalism. Greene was originally prompted to develop the story by Korda, who wanted to make a comedy about "invisible frontiers" in contemporary Vienna (Wollen, "Vienna," 17). By the late 1940s, Vienna had collapsed "from being a centre to being a frontier – at first, after World War I, a frontier with the Balkans, and then, after World War II, a frontier with the Soviet bloc" (19). During his first research trip to the occupied city in February of 1948, Greene was profoundly struck by "the dreadful circumstances of the Viennese, many of whom were collapsing in the streets from starvation" (Sherry 243–4). He saw the ruins of Allied bombing missions as well as the labyrinthine sewer networks with their white-clad police. He heard accounts of the countless rackets operating in the city, including the sale of watered-down penicillin (Sherry 251). To Greene's dismay, when he returned with Carol Reed three months later to begin filming, the city had changed. Ruins had been cleared away, decent food was being served about town, and Greene found himself insisting to Reed "over and over again [...] I assure you Vienna was like that – three months ago" (Falk 76).

In the summer of 1948 Greene and Reed were ready to shoot Korda's invisible frontiers of Vienna, only to find those frontiers rapidly hardening into Cold War political positions. *The Third Man* quickly became a historical as well as contemporary film: it is not only about postwar reconstruction, but it is also embroiled in the reconstruction process. As a result, the film required an equally journalistic approach to capture Greene's Vienna in transition. Reed had to refracture a solidifying landscape by shooting a crooked city of tilted angles and jagged cuts of light (19). Inspiration and production were driven by a documentary impulse to record Vienna as it was in the immediate postwar. Even the haunting zither music was drawn out of the disappearing rubble: Reed happened upon Mr Karas, the film's zither player, playing at a cafe (Gene Phillips 73). In *The Third Man,* Graham Greene and Carol Reed incorporated this delicate journalistic obligation in order to portray the realities of postwar internationalism and its troubled politics of rights.

In both the film and the novella, Vienna provides the landscape for the disquieting dramas of the emergent postwar internationalism. As the most easterly Western outpost in 1949, Vienna symbolized "the tough choices Britain had to make in the postwar," namely, whether or not "to act according to the corrupting, subversive and 'totalitarian' amorality of the secret Cold War" (Piette, *Literary Cold War* 28). Greene's Vienna is a distant, dark, multiply occupied city animated by kaleidoscopic divergences of identity and allegiance. On the surface, it strives for the optimistic shared governance of international democracy. It is divided into four zones – Russian, British, American, French – and at the centre of the city is an international zone, which houses the rotating authorities of the four respective states. The security forces are similarly split, with their four-man patrols containing one MP of each nationality. Even the cemetery is parsed, with the

Russian zone "marked by huge tasteless statues of armed men, the French by rows of anonymous wooden crosses and a torn tricolor flag" (Greene, *The Third Man* 312).

The city is rife with corruption bred of an endlessly contested space. The narrator reveals the dangers of navigating this inter-national landscape: "At night it is just as well to stick to the Inner Stadt [...] though even there the kidnappings occur – such senseless kidnappings they sometimes seemed to us – a Ukrainian girl without a passport, an old man beyond the age of usefulness, sometimes of course the technician or the traitor" (308). Where the central international zone is characterized by the inconsistent application of policy among its alternating powers – especially "when Russia was in the chair" (361) – the four exterior *bezirks* are caught in a deadlock between the separate forces of law competing within the city. Colonel Calloway describes how the original agreement confined each military police force to its respective zone; they needed permission to enter another's *bezirk* for an arrest or an investigation. While this agreement "worked well enough between the three Western powers," over time they began to turn down or ignore the requests of the Russians, who had started to do likewise (361). In order to pursue Allied suspects, Calloway has to catch them "outside the Russian zone" (361). In other words, citizens are treated as if they were refugees fleeing between states when they exercise their right to mobility within the boundaries of the divided city. Immobility within the police forces governing Vienna does more than hinder their operations. It provides literal avenues of escape for anyone suspected of criminal activity; it allows for an evasion of state power through the navigation of interstate spaces. The criss-crossing topography of Vienna stands as the dominant symbol for the international portrayed in *The Third Man*: a space contested by national laws and populated by a society of helpless victims and merciless rogues who slip in and out of its fabric to preserve their own interests.

The physical infrastructure of the city lends itself to *voyoucratic* mobility. Calloway's "second map" of Vienna's sewers, frequently used by deserters and burglars, traces underground passages and points of access to anywhere in the city (366). Greene depicts international space not in some idealized sphere above national space, but below it. As Adam Piette has noted, Greene identified in Vienna's sewers "the scene and trope for the political unconscious of postwar Europe" (*Literary Cold War* 30); the sewers of Vienna function as a physical reflection of the illicit, international space of the refugee and the rogue (Hepburn 128). It is a sphere that necessarily corrupts and dehumanizes those who descend into it – just as the waste and sewage are expelled from the city – but it also contains the possibility of escape. If the stateless *voyou* can learn to navigate its seedy avenues, the underworld can afford the illusion of purification. Martins describes how the sound of rushing and falling water in these passageways seemed somehow to purify the currents, a sentiment echoed by Calloway's observation of the "sweet smell" of their central arteries (377). Mitchell Breitwieser reads this figuration of a restorative underground waterway in Vienna as part of a larger pattern in Greene's later novels. He attributes archetypal significance to the Allan Quartermain allusions recollected by Calloway – found also in the dreams of Major Scobie in *The Heart of the Matter* and Maurice Castle in *The Human Factor* (1978). Invoking Greene's "The Lost Childhood" (1951), Breitwieser argues that these socially and politically unrestricted waterways afford the possibility for a mythic return to a state of childhood innocence and belonging; these aquatic worlds recall Allan Quartermain's lost city of Milosis where everyone can be accepted as citizen (463). For Breitwieser, Greene's underground rivers and sewers are transformed into "a locus of freedom rather than filth" (467).

The association between childhood and juridical freedom is essential to understanding the international mire that Greene's characters cannot extricate themselves from. Against these international spaces of corruption and illicit modes of existence, Greene depicts a persistent nostalgia for the innocence of childhood. But that "sweet smell" also represents erosion. Harry Lime can only execute his deadly penicillin racket within this fluid apolitical space; to further his international criminal plot he uses the same extralegal channels as do vagrants and refugees. This childlike state of irresponsibility, figured as the ability to navigate such pre-moral undergrounds, makes Harry Lime a public danger. He never grows up: "evil was like Peter-Pan, it carried the horrifying and horrible gift of eternal youth" (370–1). The racketeers and rogues inhabit an extrajuridical zone free from accountability. Underground, attributions of right and wrong blur. By enacting this state of exception through constant movement outside national rule, the *voyou* evades any confrontation with the force of law or any formal attributions of guilt. As a result the victim and vigilante, the refugee and racketeer, and in Harry Lime the child and the madman, become indistinguishable.

The events of *The Third Man* dramatize the conflict between this *voyoucratic* underworld and the national forces of law above it. The whole Rollo Martins affair, the "ugly story" of Harry Lime, demonstrates how this conflict does not play out in any Manichean sort of polarity, but constitutes "a landscape of seepages – of justice leaking slowly and unpredictably beyond the framework created to contain it" (Reichman 128). In this international space, the problematic status of rights is most evident in Vienna's international patrols. The patrols, "when they communicated at all" (307), hold conflicting interpretations of interstate procedures. The margin of interpretability within the inter-national rule of Vienna undercuts the principle of shared governance. All forces of law must allow for degrees of circumstantial reinterpretation, but they must also ascribe to a unified control over that process of reading – the figure of the judge, or the head of state. In upper-Vienna, the possibility of variously interpreting rules and procedures between the four occupying states, none of whom wields a definitive or declarative force over any other, unravels the force of law. Colonel Calloway, a civilian police constable from Britain, describes military police work in an occupied city as entirely unfamiliar: "the methods of one's foreign colleagues, the rules of evidence, even the procedures at inquests. I suppose I had got into the state of mind when one trusts too much one's personal judgment" (365). Rather than a force of law strengthened by its adaptability, the police activity in Vienna suffers frequent bifurcation. It is less predictable and more liable to commit abuses of power. Calloway explicitly points to this miscommunication as the cause of many unauthorized entries by the Russian police and the inevitable clashes that ensue (361). Without a singular rule of law, the occupants of upper-Vienna can never be certain of the legality of their conduct. They are forced into a state of illicit or at least suspicious *alliage*. The political thresholds of indistinction that characterize Vienna's sewers equally order the city above.

Anna Schmidt's abduction exposes not only the extent to which the execution of this shared rule of law is suspect, but also how it often incites transgressive, extralegal responses. Anna's arrest and the subsequent "clash" are plagued by suspicious conduct. This conflict begins with the Russian policeman "pulling a fast one" on his colleagues and hijacking the entire international patrol in the direction of Anna's apartment (361–2). After the comedic performance surrounding Anna's dressing and the disparate cultural valuations it betrays, the American insists, "in bad German," "they had no right to arrest an Austrian citizen," while the Russian flourishes her "bad, bad" papers that reveal her Hungarian ancestry (363). The American moves to draw his pistol but is held off by the British corporal:

> "Let it go, Pat."
>
> "If those papers ain't in order we got a right to look."
>
> "Just let it go. We'll see the papers at HQ."
>
> "If we get to HQ. You can't trust these Russian drivers. As like as not he'll drive straight through the second bezirk." (363)

While the Russian steps outside sanctioned legal conduct in order to apprehend Anna, he is right about the illegality of her papers. Given that her Hungarian origin is not unilaterally recognized as synonymous with Russian citizenship – as Calloway points out – the Russian officer remains, however, outside of his legal authority in apprehending her. This procedural farce enacts the disorder and volatility of such internal disputes within Vienna's international governance. It also dramatizes the fetishization of papers common to refugee narratives. The conflict over Anna's forged passport occurs in conjunction with the argument about her need to dress in private. The political friction of the scene is overlaid with the cultural tension surrounding her right to privacy. Because she is the genuine refugee in the novel, Anna's subjection to such mistreatments is not unexpected. Harry Lime assures Rollo that nothing *very* serious would befall her: "She'd have been sent back to Hungary. There's nothing against her really. A year in a labour camp perhaps" (372).

In response to her precarious status, the American, the Russian, and the British officers all adopt an equally precarious vigilantism. Both the American and the Russian reach for their pistols when "half incomprehensible" words cannot resolve the discrepancy; Calloway, who snatches Anna's papers from the Russian's pocket, punches him square in the face in order to bring him "to his reason" (364). Foreseeing each stage of this international farce, he knows that the Russian will bypass the international HQ and that in doing so has to pass through a particular checkpoint between Anna's apartment and the Russian zone. Calloway even notes the authorizing signature on the Russian's private orders – "useful information" for some unspoken file against his adversaries. He understands the permeable boundaries and breadth of the rule of law. His acceptance of and seemingly habitual reaction to that permeability show how extralegal procedure has been ingrained in official legal procedure. As a military policeman, Calloway keeps a criminal file on everyone, and no file, as he claims, is ever fully or finally closed (313). The city is in a state of perpetual corruption, both geographically and temporally. Just as the Russian officer steps outside of the law to execute his national impetus, so Calloway resorts to violence and entrapment to preserve law and order within his zone.

If Anna Schmidt's arrest shows the authoritarian or state abuse of this international shared governance, then the conduct of Vienna's racketeers demonstrates the rogue's criminal exploitation of it. Harry Lime's penicillin racket is emblematic of how everyday conduct, in this instance the operation of hospitals, is rendered illicit outside state authority. At the same time, it also stands as an exemplary case of the horrific potential to commit crimes against humanity within international space. Calloway describes large-scale black-market rackets as functioning "very like a totalitarian party": its individual conspirators are absolved of responsibility from the greater consequences, on the grounds that they have only played a minor role in a larger organization for which its leaders bore the guilt (354). This dissociation from the consequences of illicit conduct is repeatedly overstated in the figure of Cooler. Colonel Cooler, the exceptional humanitarian citizen implicated in a deadly medical racket, is the most vocal proponent of duty and citizenship in the novella. In his interview with Martins, Cooler dismisses Koch's belated insistence that there had been a third man at the scene of Harry's death. He then demeans Koch for not having said so in court: "you'll never teach these Europeans to be good citizens. It was his duty" (337–8). Cooler invokes this same sense of duty in his admission to helping Lime forge Anna's Austrian papers (338). When asked whether Harry was mixed up in any kind of racket, Cooler dismisses the notion as "quite impossible," because Harry Lime had "a great sense of duty" (339). Rollo's reluctance to disbelieve him reinforces this perceived compatibility between civic or humanitarian obligation and illegal activity.

Cooler has convinced himself and others that his international or humanitarian obligations are somehow unblemished by his illicit conduct: a modest tire racket, his involvement in Harbin's and Koch's deaths, and his implication in Harry's penicillin scheme. After the murder of Koch, incited by the interview with Cooler, Rollo insists that he "can't believe Cooler's concerned. I'd stake anything on his honesty. He's one of those Americans with a real sense of duty" (352). While Rollo is made to seem naive in his defence of Cooler, this dutiful American's case is in fact more complicated. His invocation of duty, specifically national or collective obligation as implicitly predominant over duties to the individual, echoes the sole use of the term in the UDHR. Article 29 states: "Everyone has duties to the community in which alone the free and full development of his personality is possible." Cooler's seemingly contradictory ethical posture reflects the ambiguous legal figuration of one's social duty. According to the UDHR, one's duty to the collective social body that will preserve international human rights comes before any direct obligation to preserve individual rights claims. In the legally ambiguous international zone demarcated by the UDHR, Cooler's statements are mutually compatible.

At the centre of the penicillin racket, Harry Lime imbues much of the narrative with its legal and moral ambiguity. As the faceless other, he manoeuvres through the shadows of Vienna. From the minute Rollo hears Koch's account of Lime's death, he is haunted by the absent presence of this "blank face without features, a grey plasticine egg, the third man" (348). In the film version, he hides in the shadows of doorways; he physically haunts Rollo. In the staging of his death, which instigates the entire plot, Lime achieves an absolute state of non-identity, a complete immersion in the extralegal realm that will enable his continued orchestration of atrocious crimes and protect him from any culpability. After his nominal funeral, he is released from all legal responsibility for the penicillin racket. The international military police forces give up their chase. Confronted by Rollo in the Ferris Wheel, Lime affirms his profound ethical remove: "Don't be melodramatic, Rollo. Look down there [...] would you really feel any pity if one of those black dots stopped moving – for ever? If I said you can have twenty thousand pounds for every dot that stops, would you really, old man, tell me to keep my money – without hesitation? Or would you calculate how many dots you could afford to spare? Free of income tax, old man. Free of income tax" (371).

Unlike Thompson's refugees, who are forced into statelessness and an illicit mode of existence, Lime deliberately takes up that mantle in the performance of his death. He steps into extralegal space of his own volition and for his own ends. As an international criminal, Lime is made all the more sinister for his charm. While he represents a threat to both universal human rights and sovereign power by manipulating the increasingly ungovernable international space, his refrain about "tax-free" profits echoes the anti-heroism of the spiv. At mid-century, spivs figured as the individualistic foils to the state-sponsored spy, exercising their freedom and agency for their own benefit in a world crippled by austerity measures, war debts, and corruption (Wollen, "Riff-Raff," 20). Harry Lime's political ambiguity and mobility cast him as a potentially alluring figure against the infinitely corrupted politics of Vienna, where "these days, old man, nobody thinks in terms of human beings. Governments don't, so why should we?" (372). The reader can almost be envious of Lime's position; "sweet it is to be not what the next man thinks one, but far more powerful [...] to put one's finger whimsically through the darkness and touch the fabric of the state, and feel the unstable structure rock, and know it was one's own doing" (West, *A Train of Powder* 21). Harry Lime's racket discloses the limitations of state power on the international stage, but it also demonstrates the extent to which international human rights go unprotected outside of national jurisdictions.

Harry Lime's factual death at the end of *The Third Man* brings the dramatic arc to a close, but it also has harrowing implications for Greene's depiction of humanitarianism and justice. Though Lime is driven in his last moments to an animalistic flight for self-preservation, he still possesses a glimmer of humanity. Calloway voices empathy for Lime's plight when Harry is wounded by a gunshot and crawls desperately up the winding sewer stair: "just as an animal creeps into the dark to die, so I suppose a man makes for the light. He wants to die at home, and the darkness is never home to us" (379). However completely Lime embraces his spectral extralegal aspect, something inalienable about his humanity remains. Calloway still recognizes him as a man. In a stark turn, however, this redemptive moment is cut short when Rollo Martins fires once more – this time to full effect. Ignoring that Rollo has just committed murder, Calloway says, "we'll forget that bit" (380). An "outlaw by definition," Lime is completely at the mercy of the police, "which itself did not worry too much about committing a few illegal acts in order to diminish the country's burden of *indésirables*" (Arendt, *Origins* 283). Although Lime possesses a sliver of humanity, he is gunned down like a vagrant animal.

Rollo Martins's direct involvement in the murder of Harry Lime demonstrates the extent to which Vienna's illicit internationalism corrupts its occupants. From the moment he enters Vienna, Martins's express intent is only to find "the real criminal" and to uncover Calloway's corruption – ultimately, to enact the plot of one of his Manichean cowboy stories (317). He is the only character afforded complete legal freedom of movement. He carries with him the *laissez-passer* papers of all four powers in Vienna. Yet throughout the novella he is wrongly implicated in the murder of Koch, unknowingly commits a fraudulent impersonation at the expense of the British Council, and finally executes a state-sanctioned *coup de grâce* against a compatriot British citizen. The trials of Rollo Martin illustrate the inevitability of corruption within an international space, regardless of whether a person has been forced into statelessness, deliberately stepped outside of the law, or strives to execute humanitarian justice. The cycle of corruption and descent finds embodiment in the dominant vertical presence on the Vienna skyline: the deteriorating carnival wheel. Invoked at the beginning, middle, and end of the novella, this solitary Great Wheel (307) allegorizes the carnivalesque nature of Greene's extralegal space. In Graham Greene's Vienna, those who pursue mobility, wealth, freedom, or justice in the extralegal underground are subjected to contamination, criminality, and death. *The Third Man* figures the international as, ultimately, a constantly revolving carnival of refugees and rogues.

International Rights in Greene's Later Fiction

For Greene, international rights in the immediate postwar period could not be dealt with apolitically. In *The Heart of the Matter*, he sought to exhaust the possibility of undertaking moral action for purely sympathetic impulses. He wanted his plot to reveal the disastrous effect of "automatic pity" on victims of suffering (241). By 1948, Greene's characteristic rhetoric of Catholic charity and benevolence, through which his earlier and more spiritual protagonists had engaged with these questions of human obligation, was no longer sufficient to address the postwar reality of international rights. In *The Heart of the Matter*, Greene relocates suffering in international human rights law. Written over a lengthy period after the war but set in the early 1940s, *The Heart of the Matter* reflects on the emergence of the problematic international spaces created by the Second World War. Sierra Leone – more particularly Freetown – embodies the threatening potential of porous political geography caused by mass migrations and the mixing of peoples, as well as the difficulty of governing such porous boundaries.

Greene's later fiction continues to explore the necessity of understanding international rights through international politics. *The Third Man*, written almost immediately following the publication of *The Heart of the Matter*, duplicates Freetown's multinational Babylonian politic in postwar Vienna and takes as its primary subject the crime and corruption running rampant therein. In *The Quiet American* (1955), Greene diagnoses the international political tensions in Indochina and their relationship to the international press. *The Comedians* (1958) presents a portrait of Papa Doc Duvalier's tyrannical Haiti, where individual rights are regularly compromised in the name of the nation's right to collective self-determination. And *The Human Factor* (1978) follows an MI6 agent during the Cold War who marries a South African refugee of apartheid. Common to all of these later novels is Greene's exploration of sinister international spaces and his postwar human imperative. By mid-century not only had human sympathy been rendered political, but this postwar internationalism had also demonstrated the extent to which that political authority could not be so uniformly administered. There remained after the war a growing network of dangerous international spaces and politically subterranean geographies – in spite of international human rights law – in which human rights seemed unassurable by either individual or state agents.

10

Loving Revolutions: Reading Mixed Race at Mid-Century

NADINE ATTEWELL

Over the past two decades, "mixed race" has become increasingly visible as a focus of identity politics, especially, though by no means only, in the multicultural metropoles of the West. In the popular press, articles such as Nicholas Hune-Brown's "Mixie Me" for *Toronto Life* (2013) celebrate the proliferation of people claiming mixed racial descent, a phenomenon, they argue, that promises an end to the mattering of race. The British cultural theorist Mica Nava likewise identifies in Londoners' growing comfort with interracial intimate relationships something she calls "visceral cosmopolitanism," that is, "an emotional economy of desire" tending toward "fusion, hybridity, mongrelisation" ("Visceral," n.p.). Unfortunately, in equating racial mixing with a politics of anti-racism and decolonization, such accounts indulge in forms of (post)racial exceptionalism that frame black and other movements of critique, resistance, and protest as problematically dependent on outmoded conceptions of identity.[1] They fail, in addition, to attend to the particular ways in which individuals of mixed racial descent affiliate in contexts where power, space, and other goods are distributed along racially differentiated lines.

Conjuring older histories of racial mixing can help to disrupt this idealization of mixed race. Certainly, as Ann Laura Stoler has demonstrated, racial mixing preoccupied nineteenth-century British, Dutch, and French policy-makers anxious to secure their hegemony against the threat of "internal contamination and [...] challenges to rule that were morally, politically, and sexually conceived" (*Carnal* 80). At the same time, the very availability of "mixed race" as a category of identity reflects the productivity of the law and other instruments of colonial governance. Although such ascriptions as "mulatto" or "Eurasian" may be "identity-forming, since they govern who may vote, who may give evidence against whom," and so on, the shifting criteria according to which they were allocated and the differing meanings with which they were imbued suggest their contingency (Salih 2). In fact, the problematization of racial mixing encouraged European thinkers to elaborate raced, classed, and gendered grammars for the distribution of citizenship and other social goods, which, if they did not entirely seal over "the fault lines of colonial authority," nevertheless worked to preserve the link between whiteness, masculinity, and power (Stoler, *Carnal* 80). Those individuals, families, and communities who, for reasons of looks, religion, social prestige, capital, or family history, were liable to find themselves interpellated as multiracial variously engaged these projects of rule, as well as the counter-projects of resistance that sprang up in response: while some sought to align themselves with local movements for decolonization, others found that the forms and processes through which they had been interpellated as racially mixed hindered their inclusion within post-colonial collectivities.[2]

In this essay, I take up the question of how colonial subjects of mixed racial descent experienced and made sense of mid-twentieth-century movements for independence and decolonization through a discussion of the work of Han Suyin, a Chinese-born writer of mixed Chinese and white European descent whose novels and autobiographical writings explore the turbulent twentieth-century history of (semi) colonial, revolutionary, and post-colonial Asia. Han's family and educational history register the complexity of China's encounter with the imperial powers of the West, whose interventions in Chinese affairs took more oblique forms than direct political control. Although Leopold II never succeeded in acquiring a Chinese colony to complement his African holdings, Belgium helped to finance several Chinese railways, becoming, in turn, a destination for young Chinese men and women seeking instruction in Western knowledges and technologies. In 1904, for example, a young Hakka man named Chou Yentung was sent to Brussels to study engineering. Here he met and married a young Belgian woman named Marguerite Denis. Thirty years later, their Beijing-raised daughter, the woman we today know as Han Suyin, returned to Brussels to pursue medical training. As a nominally if not functionally autonomous nation, a situation Tani Barlow has described as "semicolonial," China cannot be said to have undergone decolonization, at least not as this is usually defined (5).[3] Still, although China was never, because it did not need to be, formally emancipated from foreign rule, the "years of change and revolution" that Han documents in her autobiography can be thought in relation to other, more and less violent, twentieth-century movements that sought to contest European global hegemony (*Crippled Tree* 17). The works that are my focus here – Han's early autobiographical novel *A Many-Splendoured Thing* (1952) and five-volume autobiography (1965–92) – not only anatomize the racial order that structures everyday life in (semi)colonial East Asia, but grapple with the problem of how to remember and recover from the violence of its operation as part of a project of revolutionary social change, namely Communism.

In much of the scholarship on colonial histories of mixed race, belonging emerges as the arena in which mixedness takes on the greatest significance, at once troubling and helping to shape "the boundaries of European membership and the interior frontiers of the colonial state" (Stoler, *Carnal* 110). In China, the Communist victory of 1949 prompted Chinese nationals, including self-described Eurasians like Han, to reconsider their commitment to the nation. Throughout this period, as Emma Jinhua Teng observes, Chinese nationality laws followed Qing precedents that extended "Chinese citizenship to children born to Chinese fathers regardless of birthplace" (197), and to children born on Chinese soil whose foreign fathers had refused to recognize them. The growth of nationalist and revolutionary sentiments "led to backlash against Eurasians and a questioning of whether they should continue to be counted as Chinese" (199), thus contributing to what Rebecca Karl terms "a narrowed recentering of 'Chinese-ness' around ethnicity" (118). For their part, many of Han's Eurasian friends either left or did not return to China after 1949: Han explains that "a friend, a girl like myself, Chinese father, European mother," decided to "[go] away from China" because she did not "want to go back and find everything changed" (*Crippled Tree*

18). Certainly, Han's strong sense of Chinese belonging – her "feeling for China" is a throughline of the autobiography – inflects, but is also inflected by, her feelings about the Communist Revolution (*Birdless Summer* 76). It also matters that, despite her avowed "feeling for China," after 1942, Han never again lived there permanently. Between stints in Hong Kong, she settled in the British colonial outpost of Singapore. As Han navigates the affective demands of different citizenship projects, however, she also attends to the ways in which they require subjects to conceive of and even to experience such affective states as love and desire.

In this essay, I draw upon recent theoretical accounts of the politics of feeling, affect, and intimacy – politics "felt up close," as Victoria Hesford puts it (123) – to investigate Han's treatment of citizenship as a set of affective claims *and* claims about affect. Inspired by Lauren Berlant's definition of genre as "an aesthetic structure of affective expectation" (*The Female Complaint* 4), I pay particular attention to the ways in which the generic modes in which Han characteristically works, the melodramatic and the autobiographical, map the relationship between the personal and political. I begin by charting Han's dawning awareness, narrated in her writings, of the extent to which, in (semi)colonial contexts, interracial sexual relationships and configurations of mixed racial identity are conditioned by, and do not necessarily interrupt, the entailments of Euro-American hegemony. In the second half of the essay, I inquire into the reasons for which, and the consequences with which, she engages in such a project of self-reading. Han's writings register the Communist imperative, routinized in state-sponsored practices of autobiography and (self-)criticism, that subjects should "express themselves as radically social, [...] as constituted exclusively by historical forces immanent to socioeconomic structure" (Makley 55–6). At the same time, I argue, they challenge its reductive force, emphasizing the difficulty and partiality of the process of coming to know oneself in this way, as not quite autonomous.

In the twenty-first century, the political promise of racial mixing is usually taken to inhere in the mess that interracial couples and multiracial bodies ostensibly make of "people's neat conceptions of what race means" (Hune-Brown n.p.). But as Mica Nava's approving account of interracial desire makes clear, its appeal reflects, in addition, the lure of a progressivist narrative in which love and desire appear as affects that "refuse the dictates of the social skin," and the sexual and civil rights revolutions have enshrined "intimate freedom" among "the singular achievement[s] of the West" (Povinelli 176, 208). I do not intend to counter this narrative by showing how "the felicity of [the] foundational event [of intimate love] depends on an entire host of conditioning social institutions and relations" (Povinelli 194). To do so would be to repeat the very historicizing move that Han finds troubling. In *Ordinary Affects*, the American cultural theorist Kathleen Stewart describes her unease with "models of thinking that slide over the live surface of difference at work in the ordinary to bottom-line arguments about 'bigger' structures and underlying causes" (4). Han's work likewise opens up the question of how to think – or feel – about the relationship between "'bigger' structures" and the lived particularity of the ordinary as a pressing problem not just for scholars, but for all subjects who must navigate their "enfolding" within "the structures of the social world" – that is to say, all subjects (Slaughter 101). I have always liked Stuart Hall's description of identity as "formed at the unstable point where the 'unspeakable' stories of subjectivity meet the narratives of history, of a culture" (115). In what follows, I take up Han's invitation to wonder about the ways in which this encounter itself takes place, is experienced, gets narrated and read as a form of, and not only a prelude to, political work.

Melodrama and the Aesthetics of Embodiment

A Many-Splendoured Thing, the first book to appear under Han's own name,[4] was written very quickly, between September 1950 and July 1951. Under fictional cover, the novel treats Han's year-long affair with Ian Morrison, a white Australian journalist whose father, George Morrison, served as an adviser to Yuan Shikai during the latter's much-maligned tenure as China's first president. Han met Morrison in June 1949, at what was a critical juncture in her life. Eleven years earlier, she had left Belgium for China, breaking off her medical studies to contribute to China's struggle against Japan. On the trip home, she married Tang Paohuang, a Guomindang[5] army officer who proved viciously abusive. Following four tense years in central China with the Nationalist government, Pao was sent to London to serve as a military attaché for the balance of the war, during which time his wife restarted her medical training at the Royal Free Hospital. Pao did not survive the civil war. And so, after qualifying as a doctor, Han returned once more to Asia, wary of the new Communist regime, but eager to serve her compatriots. She was determined, above all, "Never, never, to love again" (63). In *A Many-Splendoured Thing*, Suyin encounters English journalist Mark Elliot a few months into her stay in Hong Kong; by August 1949, they are lovers; a year later, Mark is dead, killed while on assignment in Korea.[6]

Suyin's meeting with Mark is a historical accident, conditioned but not determined by the momentous geopolitical circumstances of its unfolding. Still, Suyin cannot help but view the affair as at once a distillation and dramatization of her relationship with Britishness, or Sino-British relations more generally. In one of the couple's earliest conversations, Suyin describes the socio-political landscape they inhabit as a divided one, in which Manichean colonial, anti-colonial, and Cold War regimes of identity and difference dovetail with and buttress one another: their affair is impossible, she insists, because "I am Chinese, and you are English; you are married, and I am a widow; you are a journalist, a front-row spectator, a looker-on not involved in the revolution of Asia; and I am a doctor, a technician, inevitably involved, with a duty towards my people" (62). Suyin worries about how their relationship will be received, not just in conservative, racist Hong Kong, but in newly Communist China, where she hopes to work. Having taken the plunge, she flirts with the idea of bringing Mark to China to meet her family. In the end, however, she dismisses this possibility as a fantasy, realizing that "with Mark, I would have to go away": "it was not Mark as a man and a lover who stood between me and China, but what he represented and what he meant. The world that he was" (300–1). Even the predicament in which she finds herself, torn between her lover and her country, she comes to see as "not mine only," "a personal choice, a settlement of fate for myself," "but that of many another Chinese, many another westernized Asian brought up between two worlds, split and two-layered" (300).

Seeking to understand "why the national novels of Latin America [...] are all love stories," literary critic Doris Sommer characterizes the relationship between the romantic and republican, or personal and political, plots of these narratives as "interlocking" (30, 35). On the one hand, sexual love requires the imprimatur of the state to acquire legitimacy. On the other hand, it functions as "*the* trope for associative behavior, unfettered market relationships, and for Nature in general," substantiating a "political legitimacy that needs to be founded on love" rather than through coercion (Sommer 35, 41). Although Sommer uses Walter Benjamin's complex definition of allegory to explain how national novels work, I am drawn, rather, to melodrama as a generic lens through which to view the interlocking personal and political plots of *A Many-Splendoured Thing*. After all, a film adaptation of the novel starring Jennifer Jones and William Holden was released during the heyday of the Hollywood melodrama (1956) and "proved a seven-handkerchief tear-jerker" (*My House* 184). To categorize *A Many-Splendoured Thing* as a melodrama is to say more than that the novel is sensationalist, its appeal essentially emotional. In melodrama, to quote Peter Brooks, "man is seen to be, *and must recognize himself to be*, playing on a theatre that is the point of juncture, and of clash, of imperatives beyond himself that are non-mediated and irreducible" (*Melodramatic* 13; emphasis added). For Brooks, melodrama is a drama of self-recognition in which players come to recognize the limits of their autonomy as selves. Even as "the spectacular enactments of melodrama seek constantly to express these forces and imperatives" in embodied form (*Melodramatic* 13), melodramatic characters experience their embodiment of these forces and imperatives as part of the trauma of selfhood. In part, the melodramatic charge in *A Many-Splendoured Thing* derives from Han's interest in the reasons for which, and consequences with which, Suyin and Mark come to see their relationship as, in Sommer's terms, allegorical.

Most people are familiar with domestic melodrama, which E. Ann Kaplan helpfully describes as "the sub-category traditionally labelled, pejoratively, in fiction the sentimental novel, and in film the 'woman's weepie'" (60). Domestic melodrama has long been derided as "heightened and hyperbolic, flat and wooden," "archaic yet without and outside history" (Gillman 4), an assessment that reflects, and has contributed to, the feminization, racialization, and depoliticization of emotion, as well as to what Sianne Ngai terms "the historically tenacious construction of racialized [and other marginalized] subjects as excessively emotional, bodily subjects" (125). However, in her account of Victorian sensation fiction, Ann Cvetkovich suggests that we see the melodramatic turn to sensation as not so much marking a shift from the political to the (ahistorical) personal as working to articulate "social problems as affective dilemmas," with complex political effects (2). Melodrama, we could say, is an "aesthetic structure" that identifies the affective realm as a key site of political experience, articulation, and action. If, as Brooks claims, melodrama is "the genre, and the speech, of revolutionary moralism," it is insofar as it elaborates "an aesthetics of embodiment, where the most important meanings have to be inscribed on and with the body" ("Melodrama, Body, Revolution," 16–17).

Building on Brooks's groundbreaking work in *The Melodramatic Imagination*, in which the "forces and imperatives" whose operations provide melodrama with its animating plots are largely moral, spiritual, and psychological, readers of sensation fiction and race melodrama have stressed the historical specificity of both the objects and modalities of the melodramatic will to revelation.[7] For example, Susan Gillman argues that late nineteenth- and early twentieth-century African American race melodramas mobilize the "readily identifiable" antinomies of Brooks's "melodramatic imagination" to make "a spectacle of what everyone knows but does not speak" about the postbellum workings of the American racial state (17, 20). Importantly, then, if melodrama turns on "an aesthetics of embodiment," if it represents "social problems as affective dilemmas," this is as a consequence of historically specifiable discourses that work to locate meaning in the entwined realms of feeling and the body. The capacity of African American race melodrama to make apprehensible, and hence contestable, the hyper(in)visibility of race in American life depends upon the very "aesthetics of embodiment" by which that racial order is secured. Returning to Han's writings with the scholarship of melodrama in mind, I want to inquire into "the histories of arrival" (Ahmed, *Queer Phenomonology* 41) that help to explain why Suyin and Mark's affair bears the weight that it does. How are "the body and the interpersonal domain" made into sites where, as Jacky Bratton, Jim Cook, and Christine Gledhill put it, "the socio-political stakes its struggles" (1)? For Han, as I show in the next section, the personal does not become political in 1949. The social import of "affective dilemmas" is, rather, a knowledge into which the everyday melodrama of life in the contact zones of semi-colonial China and imperial Europe has educated her.

Revolutionary Consciousness and the Work of Autobiography

In recent years, sexual and other kinds of intimate relationships have garnered scholarly attention as, to quote Ann Stoler, "'dense transfer points' of power," that is, as sites for, and sources of knowledge about, the operations of colonial and other projects of rule ("Tense and Tender Ties," 24). As the editors of a 2013 special journal issue on "Postcolonial Intimacies" insist, even the most intimate of interpersonal interactions manifest "entangled attachments to macro-histories of belonging, displacement and dispossession" (Antwi et al. 1). Intimate forms like the family commonly function as important institutions of social reproduction. In addition, as Stoler in particular has helped to make clear, emotional attachments, sexual practices, and domestic arrangements were targeted for management by the linked biopolitical projects of bourgeois hegemony, white supremacy, and colonial rule. With cultural competencies, including sexual habits, presumed to signal "the lines of descent that secured racial identities and partitioned individuals among them" (Stoler, *Race and the Education of Desire* 45), the imperatives of colonial governance came to require intervention in the realm of feeling, "shaping appropriate and reasoned affect [...], severing some intimate bonds and establishing others [...], establishing what constituted moral sentiments" (Stoler, "Intimidations of Empire," 2). In contexts where officials feared the "political danger" that could result from the uncertain attachments, "psychological liminality, mental instability, and economic vulnerability of culturally hybrid minorities," adherence to European norms of "sentiment and sensibility" granted some mixed-race subjects of European descent "the right to be treated as European that it did not grant others" (Stoler, *Carnal* 110, 114). Neither Han's European-style education in Beijing nor her European medical training depended upon her mixed parentage or access to European citizenship. Beginning in the nineteenth century, thousands of young Chinese men and women, including Han's own father, travelled to Europe and North America to study.[8] Still, as Han observes, at least some of this study was funded by Western governments keen to "orient" Chinese "minds, desires, emotions [...] towards the land of education rather than the land of birth" (*Crippled Tree* 145). Read alongside twenty-first-century cultural theorist Sara Ahmed's poignant meditation on her own experience of "'being-at-home' with a white mother and a brown father" in *Queer Phenomenology* (144), Han's account of her upbringing in a racially mixed household further suggests the extent to which emotions, desires, and interpersonal relations can become (contested) sites of racialization and acculturation even where white supremacy is not institutionalized at the level of the state.

"Families," Ahmed writes, "are often about taking sides": thus, for example, "the maternal and paternal are two 'sides' in the line of descent" (*Queer* 89). In her autobiography, Han invites us to reflect on the processes by which family life comes to function as an exercise in side-taking. For if the domestic world of Han's childhood is characterized by duality, a duality she usually experienced as divisive, it is as a result of the racist projects of world-making that disarticulate the world into "separate watertight compartments," turning races into sides and sides into races (*Mortal Flower* 150). If the China of Han's middle-class childhood is not quite Frantz Fanon's "world divided in two" (*The Wretched of the Earth* 3), it is nonetheless cut across by racial(ized) asymmetries of power that reflect and reproduce European economic, military, and political dominance. These are most clearly visible, to be sure, in the concession system that organized the physical and social landscape of treaty port cities like Hankou and Shanghai in unmistakably racial ways. When Marguerite first arrives in China, the couple spends time in Hankou, where, as she repeatedly tells her children, she is "so humiliated, so humiliated," "all because my husband was Chinese," unable even to enter the British, French, and Belgian concessions in the city: "I could go in and out, they always opened the barbed wire gate when they saw me, but not for your father" (*Crippled Tree* 293). Still, such divides obtain elsewhere in China as well. In Xinyang, Sea Orchid, Marguerite's second son, dies when he is denied treatment by the local doctor, a Frenchman. The doctor's wife, who is also French, prevents her husband from attending the Chous: she tells him, "I will not have you kill yourself for the sake of a halfcaste throwdown" (315).

We might assume, as Ahmed notes, that the mixed-race child will "[inherit] both lines or even both sides of its genealogy and [bring] them together" (*Queer* 144). In 1920s and 1930s Beijing, however, there is no happy middle ground between the sides. In her autobiography, Han carefully distinguishes between the experiences and feelings of her childhood self, to whom she refers in the third person as Rosalie Chou, and the narrating self, to whom I will consequently refer as Han. In *A Mortal Flower*, Han describes Rosalie's experience as a teen-aged secretary at the Peking Union Medical College. Here Rosalie learns about the "subtle well-ordered differences in status and in pay even among Eurasians, where it depended upon being more, or less, Chinese" (145): when fourteen-year-old Rosalie's salary surpasses that of the vastly more experienced and skilled clerk Mr Yeh, she observes, "I had crossed the 'Chinese' line, I was on my way towards 'Eurasian' pay, though a great deal below European pay. I would never attain the latter, unless I married a European, perhaps" (145). To inhabit "that half-world […] where the Eurasian lived," Rosalie realizes, is to cling "to the arrogant white world" (150), committing to its perpetuation at the expense of other futures. Thanks to the "straightening" project of white supremacy, which works to contain her parents' transgression as a hitch in the racial line, Rosalie must take a side, an imperative that turns the family home into a battleground in which even the most trivial of actions signifies as an expression of racial attachment.

In *Queer Phenomenology*, Ahmed recalls "walking down the street between my parents and wanting to be on the side of my mother; indeed my desire *put me on her side*," that is, the "'side' [of] whiteness," making "what was 'brown' be on the 'other side'" (144–6; emphasis in original). In Han's memory of her childhood, taking sides is something that Rosalie's parents are always requiring that she do, pulling her close, or putting her from them, in their own side-taking endeavours. Marguerite especially struggles with what she frames as her children's failure to be read as white. She warns them that "you will never have a future if you are Chinese" (*Crippled Tree* 416). Although all the children are forced, at one time or another, to confront the limited promise of their European parentage, Marguerite repeatedly casts Rosalie as a body that drags, holding her mother and siblings back from full incorporation within the community of whiteness. One day, Rosalie is late in returning to the family home, for which she is scolded by her mother. Marguerite, who is in the process of "tying big white satin ribbons sent by Grandmama [Denis] on to [Rosalie's sister's] pigtails," exclaims, "there you are at last [...] and dirty as usual. One would think you love dirt, dragging yourself in the mud" (333). In this scene, Marguerite simultaneously welcomes Rosalie back into the family home and confirms her unfitness for the domestication signified by Tiza's perfectly coiffed hair. To Marguerite, Rosalie is not simply dirty: because she is dirty, she must love dirt, a diagnosis that insists on Rosalie's predilection for getting close to things – dirt – any right-minded little girl would flee. The version of femininity that Rosalie fails – or refuses – to take up is a racialized one, as a later scene from Rosalie's childhood confirms. While walking in Beijing's Central Park with her mother and two younger sisters, Rosalie hears a European man say to his son, "Look, Peter, these are half-castes." In response, Marguerite clutches "her hand tighter as they walked, and it was the tight clasp of something fierce and gentle, like love, and suddenly Mama said: 'You look European, my children, you look like me'" (353). By demanding that they reproduce her whiteness, Marguerite works to secure herself against the accusation of her children's non-whiteness, which testifies to the inadequacy of her performance of middle-class femininity. The clutch of Marguerite's hand, which Han damningly describes as "like love," holds the children close in a gesture of protection that repeats the violence it is supposed to ward off by identifying the children's European "look" as what renders them worthy of protection. Rosalie turns murderously upon the Chinese inheritance she has learned she should wish not to possess: deciding that "half-caste" means "Papa being Chinese, and to be a Chinese in China was wrong, only being European was right," Rosalie "led troops to fight the dirty Chinese that day, since she looked European, she looked like Mama, so Mama had said" (353).

As these examples suggest, Marguerite actively tries to make Chou family life "about taking sides," yet she consistently denies that the attachments she desires for and cultivates in her children are anything but personal. Consider another incident from Rosalie's childhood, which takes place at a showing of D.W. Griffith's *The Birth of a Nation* (1915). The cinema is so packed that Rosalie is forced to sit behind her parents and younger sister Tiza. During the commotion caused by a protester, however, a boy vacates his seat, which allows Rosalie to rejoin her family. When the boy returns, he loudly reclaims his seat, which causes a second uproar. The audience "stamped, clapped, whistled, and suddenly they were all shouting, in time: 'Down with the colonialists, down with the imperialists,' and singing" (379). In the aftermath, relations between Marguerite and Yentung deteriorate. Indeed, Yentung accuses Marguerite of precipitating the affray: "you are a white woman [and] cannot insult us all the time" (379). In the cinema, Marguerite's attempt to keep her family together is interrupted by the other audience members' rage at what they perceive as another instance of the racial privilege being graphically represented onscreen. This is the perspective that Yentung tries but fails to communicate to his wife. Indeed, in their clash can be read the central conflict of their marriage, which stems not just from the uneven way in which social power is distributed between them, but from their divergent understandings of how much this means or should mean. As she navigates the segregated spaces of Beijing society, Marguerite proves unable – or unwilling – to grasp the extent to which, in this context, her whiteness is the most significant thing about her. When Han describes the agony that Yentung's critique induces in Rosalie, she frames "listening to Papa" as a taking of sides incompatible with loving Mama. If "listening to Papa was going against Mama, and one *had* to love Mama" (380), then loving Mama is incompatible with holding Mama accountable as an embodied social actor. Love, by this definition, is not just apolitical; it is a way of not seeing politically. The Central Park episode gives the lie to such assertions of love's political innocence insofar as it shows how, as Ahmed writes, "the pull of love towards another, who becomes an object of love," functions as "a way of bonding with others in relation to an ideal [here whiteness], which takes shape as an effect of such bonding" (*Cultural* 124). What the cinema episode demonstrates is that love sustains the racist architecture of Euro-American dominance to precisely the extent that its political utility is hard to apprehend, binding whiteness together with innocence in a lure Rosalie, at least, is hard pressed to resist.

Both Marguerite and Yentung lament "the unconscious hostilities, assumptions, which saw in her only a representative of the Whites" (*Crippled Tree* 288). At the same time, Yentung recognizes that Marguerite cannot transcend the history that informs this view through insisting on her particularity as a well-intentioned subject, not outside the home and possibly not inside it either. What explains this difference? To whom and why do such methodologies of reading as Yentung's, that insist on the interplay between the abstract structural and the embodied particular, come to seem appealing or necessary? After all, interpretive projects (including this one) also possess histories that condition their emergence and use. That Yentung is so much more able – or willing – than Marguerite to acknowledge the extent to which, to quote Ahmed, "encounters between embodied subjects always hesitate between the domain of the particular [...] and the general," is no accident of personality or intellectual capacity (*Strange* 8). Rather, this is a proclivity into which Yentung has been educated, the discrepancies in his and Marguerite's capacities for mobility and rights to place serving to foreground the indifference of social hierarchies to individual goodness and love. In inquiring into the particulars of this education, one of my aims is to unsettle the common scholarly assumption that critique is an essentially scholarly project, one that takes place at a remove from everyday life. As Kathleen Stewart suggests, scholars can too easily "slide over the live surface of difference at work in the ordinary to bottom-line arguments about 'bigger' structures and underlying causes" (4). And yet, the fraught, uncertain relationship of "the ordinary" to "'bigger' structures and underlying causes" is itself, I think, a part of that experience we call ordinary.

Reflecting on her decision to write a book "about China" that is also "a book about my father and mother," Han insists that "it is impossible to isolate either my father or my mother from history itself, the history of their period in China"; she concludes, "we are all products of our time, vulnerable to history" (*Crippled Tree* 17). Han's commitment to a form of storytelling that registers people's vulnerability to history derives in part, the autobiography suggests, from her upbringing in a racially mixed household. If the Central Park episode recalls the searing scene of racialization that opens the famous fifth chapter of Frantz Fanon's *Black Skin, White Masks* (1952), it matters that Rosalie's encounter with the white stranger is mediated by her white mother. In dealing with the crushing effects of racial subjectification, Han must reckon, in addition, with its intimacy, inculpating those people most close to her. If the whiteness that is received at home cannot fully be inhabited, Ahmed speculates, the structures that make this "failure" meaningful can become visible. They do not do so inevitably, of course. When Rosalie is born, shortly after Sea Orchid's death, Marguerite rejects the baby, calling her a "halfcaste brat" who is "not my child" (*Crippled Tree* 316). Mad with grief, Marguerite assigns responsibility for the turning away of the doctor and his wife to her children, rather than to the racist hierarchy of value that views her relationship with Yentung as a breach in the norms of European womanhood and construes their children as unworthy of care. In contrast, Rosalie's growing skepticism about the promise encoded in her mother's loving clasp helps attune her to the politics at work in the turn to the personal.

To recognize, in the lure of love, the demand that one take a side is to take a side, though not, perhaps, the one desired. Rosalie begins by taking her mother's side. However, realizing that Marguerite's love is not thick enough to secure her children against the depredations of racism and colonialism, of which it is itself an instrument, she grows up to identify "the Chinese people" as "the only side I am on" (*My House* 652). In other words, Han's affinity for "the dirty Chinese" at once marks and is a consequence of her commitment to a critical mode of reading that registers people's vulnerability to history. No wonder, since it is her Chinese father who most consistently models this sort of sensitivity for her. But the complex temporality of Han's autobiography – in *The Crippled Tree* (1965) and *A Mortal Flower* (1966), the volumes that most closely concern her upbringing, Han writes about events from which she is three and four decades removed – means that we must, in addition, consider the possibility that her account has been shaped by the revolutionary project of Chinese Communism. In fact, the cinema incident precipitates a break in Han's relationship with her father that is fully repaired only, or so she claims, in 1956, when the revolution "forced us to a new understanding of our passions and torments" (*Mortal Flower* 44).

Subtitled "China | Autobiography | History," Han's five-volume autobiography claims a broader scope than is usual in the genre. It is not therefore not an autobiography. Rather, just as melodrama aims to manifest subjects' vulnerability to forces and imperatives "beyond themselves," so Han's autobiographical practice theorizes the self as a product of history and place. A similar theory of self helps to explain the centrality of autobiography to Chinese Communist revolutionary practice. Traditional Chinese thought exalted writing as a key instrument of governance. Ironically perhaps, in the narrative practices of the Communist revolution, as Ann Anagnost asserts, "the project to make literature translate directly into political action" came to fruition (17). Following the establishment of the People's Republic (PRC), many Chinese citizens of "bad" class origin were made to write autobiographies, "not very long, covering about six to eight pages," which were "checked and counter-checked [...] scrutinized and possibly re-written three or four times, with requests for clarification on this or that obscure or ambiguous point" (*Crippled Tree* 55). Meanwhile, the subaltern majority were incited to produce autobiographical testimony as part of the exercise called *suku*, or "speaking bitterness." "Speaking bitterness" provided a framework for the "turn around" of *fanshen* (*My House* 124), "the reworking of consciousness in which the speaker comes to recognize himself or herself as a victim of an immoral system rather than a bearer of bad fate or personal shortcoming" (Anagnost 29). According to Anagnost, the narrative strategies that writers like Mao Dun, an important figure in early twentieth-century Chinese letters who later served as the PRC's first minister of culture, developed to represent "abstract forces operating globally" were reprised in "speaking bitterness," in which "local conflicts were made to stand metonymically for the historical collision of warring classes rendered in an idiom of known personalities" (27). In these ways, Arif Dirlik argues, the Communist Party of China (CPC) claimed "revolutionary consciousness" as a crucial arena and even form of revolutionary activity (183).

Under Communist rule, "telling one's life-story turned into a self-conscious political act with concrete, material ramifications" (Rofel 14). In his third autobiography, portions of which Han reproduces in *The Crippled Tree*, Chou Yentung acknowledges finding the CPC imperative to account for one's life annoying. This time, however, he claims actually to "*want* to write down my life, to write down everything that happened," linking the novel desire he feels to document his life to the changes worked by the revolution, as if the desire itself marked an important revolutionary change (*Crippled Tree* 59–60). It is important not to overstate the distance between PRC and other theories and practices of autobiography. In *On Not Speaking Chinese*, scholar Ien Ang reflects on the contingency of her Chineseness as an Indonesian-born, Dutch-trained, Australia-based academic of

Chinese descent in order to draw attention to the complexity of the ways in which Chineseness circulates and is inhabited in diasporic contexts. As a warrant for this autobiographical move, she cites Janet Gunn's description of autobiography as "the cultural act of self-reading," which suggests that "what is at stake in autobiographical discourse is not a question of the subject's authentic 'me,' but one of the subject's location in a world through an active interpretation of experiences that one calls one's own in particular, 'worldly' contexts, that is to say, a reflexive positioning of oneself in history and culture" (Ang 23–4). There is no reason to derive Ang's conception of autobiography from CPC traditions of thought, even if the leftist genealogies that inflect much Western literary and cultural studies scholarship mean they are not unrelated. Nevertheless, by including portions of the autobiographies that her father and third uncle produced under state compulsion, Han situates her own autobiographical impulse in relation to the demand for autobiographical testimony as a component in and evidence of revolutionary transformation.

If the attention Han pays to the process by which she came to recognize herself as a subject in history connects her writings with the narrative imperatives of the Communist state, this is not to suggest that Han's narrative practice is Communist in either origin or effect (although it is worth noting that she witnessed and participated in so-called struggle and criticism sessions beginning in 1956, around the time of the Hundred Flowers Campaign). Indeed, in Han's work, reading for structure emerges as a key methodology for survival and resistance in the semi-colonial landscape of her childhood. At the same time, Han uses the autobiographical form, just as she uses the genre of melodrama, to explore what it means to read for structure in a post-revolutionary context where reading for structure is a requirement of citizenship, a kind of compulsory performance. In fact, although Han long considered returning to live in China, she balked at submitting to the formal pedagogy of the struggle session. This demand registers her incomplete incorporation of and by the CPC's revolutionary endeavour.

In part, this was a pragmatic decision, "a certain act of calculating one's chance of survival" (*My House* 37) in the unpromising light of four interrelated factors: Han's class background as an educated woman of "big landlord origin" (*My House* 124), the worst possible;

her mixed-race identity, signalling "unchastity" for Europeans and Chinese alike (*Birdless Summer* 66); her predilection for unsuitable men, including the Guomindang official Tang Paohuang as well as Ian Morrison; and her reputation as a writer of "bad" because "near pornograph[ic]" fiction (*My House* 153, 227). In addition, she found the pedagogical rituals of the new Communist state suffocating (*My House* 124). "I need time to remould myself," she writes in *My House Has Two Doors*, "but nobody can do it for me. I have to do it myself" (179). Her recalcitrance can be read as retrogressive, stemming from a reluctance to relinquish the authority to which her status as an educated professional has accustomed her. Han acknowledges as much. But it also stems, I think, from a sense of unease about the interpretive protocols according to which her familial and intimate histories are likely to be read by a revolutionary regime in the process of normalizing itself. If, as Han herself recognizes, anticipating the claims of a later generation of post-colonial, feminist, and queer thinkers, such intimate entanglements as her parents' marriage, her relationship with her mother, or her affair with Ian Morrison, can be read as "'dense transfer points' of power," to what ends should such a reading be put?

Feel Better?

For Lauren Berlant, genres mediate "what is singular, in the details, and general about a subject" (*The Female Complaint* 4). In a way, Han's melodramatic staging of Suyin and Mark's affair in *A Many-Splendoured Thing* might be said to draw attention to the *generic-ness* that afflicts all such relationships, perhaps all relationships. In a scene dated October 1949, Mark informs Suyin that he must return to his wife in Singapore. He tells Suyin, "if I were free [...] I'd marry you tomorrow," a clichéd assurance that makes them seem "two actors on a dusty stage, among cardboard scenery, thrust into roles, mouthing words, making gestures [...]. Actions one performed with certain intentions, but the spectators did not know the intentions, neither did they care; intentions were irrelevant to the play" (*Many-Splendoured Thing* 200). The theatricality of the affair overtakes the couple, who must "act to the end" (201). At other times, Suyin vigorously resists their recruitment to familiar Orientalist melodramatic plots in which

Mark's "imperialist [...] newspaperman" cruelly dominates, tragically yearns for, or is tricked by her "cheap Hongkong Eurasian" (248, 61). Throughout the novel, Suyin and Mark strain against the "complicated[ness]" (61) of their relationship – the racism that makes it easy for white Hong Kong society to dismiss Suyin as a grasping "Eurasian [who] had acquired a married Englishman [...] and was ruining his life" (200); the exigencies of a geopolitical situation in which Mark and Suyin risk appearing either insufficiently or excessively "Red" (182) – insisting that they "just love each other" (248). Suyin in particular struggles to be permitted to choose, not (just) between different communities of belonging – East and West, China and Britain, pure and hybrid – but between love and politics, between, that is, a methodology of reading that emphasizes the embodied particular over the abstract structural, and one that prioritizes the structural.

Attending a Young Communist Group meeting on "the New Love," Suyin is made to feel "selfish, unprogressive" by the cadres' assertion that "personal emotions [are simply] a function of class consciousness and political ideologies," and therefore can and must be "reordered" (287). Worrying that she will be made to "repent, revile what I have loved" (248), she contests the implication that "we had to feel correctly" (286).[9] Even if the violence of revolutionary pedagogy took more bloody forms than this, as the ethnographers Arthur Kleinman and Joan Kleinman remind us, it is worth attending to the violence that reading for structure can end by doing to "the personally idiosyncratic and the situationally particular, to the 'blooming buzzing' confusion of the stream of living" (279–80). Gail Hershatter observes that the imperative to "speak bitterness" has not always been felt as liberatory (107). Conducting fieldwork in Tibet in the 1990s, the anthropologist Charlene Makley found her interlocutors reluctant to speak openly about their experience of state violence, in part because the repressive campaigns of the 1950s and 1960s had included mandatory struggle sessions in which Tibetan peasants were required to "produce and listen to testimonials of their participation in the Communist-led revolution, that is, life-stories attesting to their consciousness of past class-based oppression in the 'Old Society' [...] and their present 'liberation' [...] in the 'New Society'" (46–7). Even amongst Han Chinese, Anagnost suggests, the "routinization" of speaking bitterness as "an authorized structure of feeling" meant that it lost "the power to articulate with subjective experience in its failure to reflect sufficiently the 'true social present'" (33).

From the vantage point of 2016, the gossiping expatriates who congregate at Hong Kong dinner parties to condemn Mark and Suyin's relationship on moral and racial grounds appear contemptible. The cadres' critique of "personal emotions" as "a function of class consciousness and political ideologies" is less easily dismissed, however absurd or distressing the disciplinary projects they undertake as a consequence. For one thing, any binary that opposes love to politics is itself acutely political, insofar as it maps comfortably onto the dominant geopolitical divide of the post–Second World War era, between Western democratic liberalism, whose form and functioning, Elizabeth Povinelli argues, are tightly bound to the exercise of what she calls intimate sovereignty, and the emergent socialist alternatives of the East. For another, Han's later writings eloquently testify to the insidious ways in which this binary obscures the operations and effects of racialized regimes of power. Curiously, Han's parents do not figure in the plot of *A Many-Splendoured Thing*, where, indeed, they are barely mentioned. Although Han made trips to China in 1949 and 1950, staying with her father's family in Chongqing, she did not visit with Chou Yentung, then living in Beijing. Suyin's reunion with her sister Tiza (or Suchen), who was desperate to leave Chongqing in advance of the Communist takeover, is described in excruciating detail in *A Many-Splendoured Thing*. What the novel does not make clear is that Tiza was living with Marguerite at the time; when Tiza left China for the United States in 1950, she was accompanied by Marguerite. Their departure marked the final stage in the dissolution of the Chou marriage. Given this reticence, it seems significant that when Han decided, in the early 1960s, to write once again about China, she conceived of her parents as central to the project. Early in *The Crippled Tree*, she asserts that "China to me was of course my father and mother, and all I myself knew of China" (16–17). If tracing her family history allows Han to investigate the fraught career of Chinese modernity, it also takes a side in Yentung and Marguerite's battle over whether people can be "isolate[d] from history" in their relations with one another: they cannot, at least not when "history" has done so much to invest such relations with meaning. As much evidence as *A Many-Splendoured Thing* and the autobiography offer of the importance of "bottom-line arguments about 'bigger' structures and underlying causes," they also testify to the intensity of the struggle to live with, or in, the knowledge that our most intimate experiences and relationships are sites for the elaboration of "'bigger' structures and underlying causes," as well as to the force of the particularity with which these experiences and relationships assert themselves in our lives. In *On Not Speaking Chinese*, Ang engages in "the cultural act of a self-reading" in order to demonstrate that we cannot know in advance how the categories of race, gender, class, and so on, will "inscribe their salience and effectivity in the course of concrete histories" (25). In a similar way, Han's melodramatic (and) autobiographical writings draw attention to the difficulty of knowing to what extent our feelings are our own, and how this matters.

Han's writings return us to a post-revolutionary moment that seems to have little in common with our own. In fact, Wendy Brown suggests that we are "postrevolutionary" to precisely the extent that the violence of revolutionary pedagogical practices like the CPC's has made it difficult to believe in "the viability of a radical overthrow of existing social relations" ("Women's Studies," 4). But if the Chinese Revolution has not proven the positive model of radical social change that its adherents hoped it would, for that reason, as Sally Taylor Lieberman, Rey Chow, and others have argued, it remains an inheritance with which leftist intellectuals must reckon. Consider the familiar feminist slogan "the personal is political." The phrase is usually associated with Carol Hanisch, to whose 1969 essay on the feminist practice of consciousness-raising Shulamith Firestone and Kathie Sarachild gave the title "The Personal is Political." The reconceptualization of politics as "felt up close" (Hesford 123) bespeaks American feminist engagements with Chinese revolutionary theories and methodologies of social transformation, filtered through texts such as William Hinton's *Fanshen: A Documentary of Revolution in a Chinese Village* (1966). In her history of the American women's liberation movement, Victoria Hesford identifies "the personal is political" as a crucial if fraught legacy for twenty-first-century feminist and queer thinkers (120). "A powerfully enigmatic statement of and for women's liberation" (Hesford 120), "the personal is political" functions as a heuristic for analysis and names a problem to be solved. But how? Must the personal be emancipated from the political, through what Hesford describes as "a transcendent return to a presocial innocence" (145) or does their co-articulation mean, simply, that one cannot be changed without changing the other? Should we be aspiring, as Gayatri Spivak urges, to the "*uncoercive* rearrangement of desires" (526; emphasis in original)? These questions, which for Han are raised by the violence and scope of Chinese Communist practices of revolutionary transformation, remain live ones. In *Politics Out of History*, Brown invites us to consider how "past generations and events" might "inspirit our imaginations and visions for the future" (150). To revisit Han's close engagement with CPC practices of self-narration is to be reminded of the importance, yes, of consciousness raising, of apprehending the political in the personal. But we are encouraged to learn, as well, how better to inhabit the "is" that links the personal with the political, that tricky copula where "the 'unspeakable' stories of subjectivity meet the narratives of history, of a culture" (Hall 115) as not just the preliminary to a politics, but a kind of political project in itself.

NOTES

1 See the critiques of Kimberly McClain DaCosta (*Making Multiracials: State, Family, and Market in the Redrawing of the Color Line*), Jared Sexton (*Amalgamation Schemes: Antiblackness and the Critique of Multiracialism*), and Michelle Elam (*The Souls of Mixed Folk: Race, Politics, and Aesthetics in the New Millennium*) among others.

2 See, for example, *Lines of the Nation: Indian Railway Workers, Bureaucracy, and the Intimate Historical Self*, Laura Bear's ethnography of the Anglo-Indian settlement at Kharagpur, whose (self-)articulation as a distinct genealogical community during the first half of the twentieth century ultimately worked to disqualify Anglo-Indians from full belonging in the post-colonial Indian nation (152). As a consequence, Bear notes, since 1947, approximately "half the Anglo-Indian population (estimated at 200,000 at Independence) has emigrated from India looking for a new life in Australia, New Zealand, or Britain" (11). Bear is among the very few scholars who have begun to investigate mixed-race experiences of decolonization; see also Emmanuelle Saada's *Empire's Children: Race, Filiation, and Citizenship in the French Colonies*, as well as the work of Christina Firpo.

3 See Barlow's introduction to *Formations of Colonial Modernity in East Asia* for more on the intersections of Asian with post-colonial studies.

4 In 1942, *Destination Chungking*, a "fairy-tale fabulation" of Han's experiences in occupied China (*Birdless Summer* 152), was published in Britain and the United States under the name of her co-author, American obstetrician Marian Manly.

5 Throughout this essay, I follow the scholarly convention of using pinyin to render Chinese terms and place names in alphabetic script, even though Han herself usually employs the older Wade-Giles system of romanization. For clarity's sake, I also refer to the city today known as Beijing as Beijing throughout, even though it was called Beiping for much of the time that Han was resident there.

6 In this essay, I use the name "Suyin" when discussing Han's fictional avatar in *A Many-Splendoured Thing* and "Han" when referring to the writer.

7 In later essays, Brooks likewise expands his focus, foregrounding, for example, the "semiotics of the body" that, he suggests, was melodrama's signal contribution to republican projects of social differentiation in post-revolutionary France ("Melodrama, Body, Revolution," 18).

8 See Marilyn Levine's *The Found Generation: Chinese Communists in Europe during the Twenties* for more about these work-study students, some of whom went on to become leading Communist Party thinkers (including Zhou Enlai and Deng Xiaoping).

9 The cadres' dismissal of "personal emotions" as "selfish and unprogressive" should not be taken as the final word on conceptions and practices of emotional life under Communist rule. I can only gesture towards the complexity of the latter here. The Kleinmans have vigorously challenged the Orientalizing claim that "emotions in Chinese society are irrelevant to" and even suppressed in "the legitimation of the social order," pointing out that "shame, menace, loss, grief and other emotional expressions of suffering are master symbols of China's revolutionary literature" (288, 289). Elizabeth Perry refers to the CPC's 1949 victory over the Guomindang as "a textbook illustration of how emotional energy may (or may not) be harnessed to revolutionary designs" (112). Responding to a body of scholarship that treats the modern Chinese family as an essentially economic unit, anthropologist Yan Yunxiang notes that "notions of romantic love, free choice in spouse selection, conjugal independence, and individual property" have gained traction in rural China over the past fifty years (9). On the one hand, he traces this development to the effects of rural collectivization and other socialist programs of reform, which helped to carve out a private sphere of emotionality and individ-

ualism. On the other hand, he interviews a couple brought together by their work as part of an agricultural collective during the Great Leap Forward, whose "idealization of free love began in the public domain and was reinforced by the idealist political atmosphere of the 1950s, a kind of romantic and radical atmosphere" (51). It cannot then be said that there is no place for love in CPC or Communist-era Chinese theories of political action, where it emerges, rather, as a site of transformative intervention. As Mao Zedong put it in the 1942 Yan'an lectures on literature and art, "a change from one class to another" requires "a change in feelings" (462).

11

Confessional Fictions: Truth and Reconciliation in the Cold War

PETER KALLINEY

In the early stages of *Disgrace* (1999), J.M. Coetzee's novel about violence and reconciliation in post-apartheid South Africa, the narrator and central character, David Lurie, faces a disciplinary tribunal at his university. Lurie, middle-aged lecturer in English, is publicly disgraced after having an affair with a young woman who is his student. Lurie does not rape her, exactly, but even he knows that the relationship is not a meeting of equals. When brought before the disciplinary committee, he reacts defiantly. The board wants him to make an admission of guilt and to offer an apology of some sort, and then probably to go to counselling so that he understands the gravity of his offence. Lurie categorically refuses. He does not deny responsibility, but he asks for a summary sentence rather than to be compelled to avow his sins. As a result he is dismissed from his post at the university. Describing the confrontation with the disciplinary committee to his adult daughter, he says, somewhat hyperbolically, that the whole thing smacks of a Cold War show trial: "It reminds me too much of Mao's China," he explains bitterly. "Recantation, self-criticism, public apology. I'm old fashioned, I would prefer simply to be put against a wall and shot. Have done with it." When his daughter, incredulous that he would rather give up his job than make an apology, says that he is being a bit melodramatic, he continues in the same vein: "They [the disciplinary committee] wanted a spectacle: breast-beating, remorse, tears if possible. A TV show, in fact. I wouldn't oblige" (66). He knows, deep down, the whole thing sounds ridiculous. His daughter thinks a public admission of guilt and an apology would not be a terrifically unjust outcome. The fact is, he is too proud to admit his mistake in public, so he loses his job, which he has come to despise anyway.

Upon publication, *Disgrace* was immediately read by critics as an imperfect allegory of the proceedings of South Africa's Truth and Reconciliation Commission (TRC or Truth Commission hereafter), which were conducted after the implementation of parliamentary democracy, in an attempt to get the truth of the apartheid era into the public record. The commission was championed by Nelson Mandela and chaired by Archbishop Desmond Tutu. Among other things, South Africa's TRC had the power to grant or withhold amnesty from prosecution for perpetrators of political crimes who agreed to confess their deeds under oath. In *Disgrace*, when Lurie says that the university disciplinary board wanted a TV spectacle, he is making a direct comparison to the hearings of the Truth Commission, many of which were broadcast on television and radio, and covered widely by the South African and international press. The comparison of his university's tribunal to Mao's China, or to Stalinist show trials, seems a little more far-fetched. What does Lurie's situation tell us of political dissidents who were coerced into humiliating public confessions in witch hunts during the height of the Cold War? Or, if we are willing to grant the symbolic power of the allegory, in what way could South Africa's Truth Commission be likened to the infamous show trials conducted in Mao's China or in Stalin's Soviet Union, or even to the House Un-American Activities Committee hearings in the United States?

This essay will not contain an extensive discussion of South Africa's Truth Commission hearings, nor parse the long final report of the commission, nor consider any of the direct representations of the hearings as they appear in literature or journalism, such as Antjie Krog's *Country of My Skull* (1998). Instead, I will offer a more general survey of the fiction of decolonization, with a special emphasis on sub-Saharan Africa. My objective is to show that the Cold War, especially the spectacular show trials it produced, casts a long shadow over the literature of decolonization. I read the South African situation as less of a unique case, and more as the culmination of a long, uncertain process of formal decolonization across the continent. The implicit comparison of the TRC to a Cold War show trial in *Disgrace* is not, as I will argue here, as implausible or as unprecedented as the immediate context may suggest. In fact, a survey of decolonization-era African novels reveals that a great number of them are obsessed with the idea of confessions, witch hunts, public apologies, recantation, and rehabilitation. In my reading of confessional novels, then, I am offering something like a literary genealogy of the truth commission. A close examination of confessional literature shows that the idea that truth commissions might help uncover the abuses of imperialism was a recurrent trope in the late colonial and early post-colonial imagination. But the ability of a truth commission to deliver on its mandate was irreparably compromised by the history of the Cold War, in which a number of high-profile hearings and trials undermined the credibility of South Africa's TRC before it was even convened.

South Africa provides a fitting place to think about the relationship between decolonization and the Cold War. Nineteen-forty-eight was a landmark year in the Cold War and in the history of South African politics. In that year, the Soviet Union blockaded Berlin and the US responded with round-the-clock airlifts; it was also the time when apartheid as a legal code began to be formalized, and when the National Party began its long, uninterrupted rule of South Africa. Throughout the Cold War, anti-Communism was one of the principal motives behind repression of anti-apartheid groups, especially the African National Congress, which was banned for its links with international Communism. Many neutral observers believed that the National Party's rabid anti-Communism was merely a pretext for achieving other political objectives, but the pretext had real geopolitical significance, allowing the apartheid regime to gain the tacit support of the United States during much of the Cold War era. Finally, it seems that external pressure led the National Party to negotiate an end to apartheid just after the fall of the Berlin Wall. In 1990, the state removed the ban on the African National Congress, Nelson Mandela was released from detention, and the negotiations for multi-ethnic elections began. The symbolic end of European imperialism in Africa coincided with the end of the Cold War, but I will suggest in this essay that the history of decolonization and the Cold War were not merely coincident processes in South Africa and elsewhere.

Three important critics who have considered the role of confession, testimony, and public hearings guide my thinking below. Mark Sanders's *Ambiguities of Witnessing: Law and Literature in a Time of a Truth Commission* (2007) offers the most complete and erudite study of the conjunction between the TRC and South African literature. His psychoanalytically informed model suggests that witnesses, perpetrators, and victims become bound together during the process of public hearings (see also Heyns). Doris Sommer's articles on the *testimonio* genre, especially Rigoberta Menchú's controversial book, are equally germane. As Sommer argues, the *testimonio* is designed to generate feelings of complicity in the audience. The addressee is at once a sympathizer who identifies with the plight of the victim and also an implicit perpetrator with a guilty conscience – the implied reader is white and metropolitan and relatively privileged, and is encouraged to feel that he or she did nothing to stop the injustices recorded. Michel Foucault's lectures on confessional practices, *Wrong-Doing, Truth-Telling: The Function of Avowal in Justice* (1981), only recently translated into English, offer another important model. Tracing the legal and political utility of confession in different contexts, Foucault reminds us that, while avowal has a long history, the practice of confession has evolved in tandem with forms of legal subjectivity. My own thinking leans upon but modifies the work of these three critics. In my view, the political stakes of confession change markedly during the Cold War. This conflict left a deep imprint on the literature of decolonization in Africa, where truth commissions were at the same time eagerly anticipated, rarely enacted, and skeptically received.

The God That Failed, *1984*, *The Captive Mind*, and *Darkness at Noon*

Before examining some of decolonization-era fiction from Africa in more detail, I point briefly to four iconic Cold War texts: Arthur Koestler's *Darkness at Noon* (1941), George Orwell's *1984* (1949), Czeslaw Milosz's *The Captive Mind* (1951), and the anti-Communist collection *The God That Failed* (1950). These texts highlight some of the special problems associated with public hearings, testimony, and confession in a Cold War context. Although these texts alert us to chronic difficulties associated with public hearings and show trials – especially the likelihood of coerced testimony – these writers also imply that public declarations of political guilt and innocence could be deployed by individuals against the state. Confession, that is to say, is not only a tool of the state: clever subjects could use it to protect themselves against juridical institutions. It is crucial to recognize that the liberal democracies of the Cold War, in these accounts, are no more or less likely than totalitarian regimes to use public hearings and trials to score political points and to discipline citizens. By showing that confessions have the potential to be used by the state to punish individuals, but also that tactical confessions can shield the individual from state retribution, these texts point to the new kinds of ideological demands made of citizens in the wake of the Second World War. In a curious way, these texts also show that the Cold War state's obsession with public declarations and confessions binds the state to its citizens, especially to its ideologically wayward subjects, upon whom it lavishes much of its attentions.

First, confession is an ambiguous disciplinary practice, as Mark Sanders shows. This ambiguity is neatly embedded in the word "confessor." On one hand, a confessor is a person who repents, confesses, and asks for absolution or grace. On the other hand, a confessor is the person who receives the confession. This person can be someone who has the power to grant absolution, or else a figure who might intercede with a higher power on behalf of the person who has submitted an application for forgiveness. So the ambiguity of the word confessor is woven into the very fabric of the English language. Foucault neatly summarizes this ambiguity: "On the one hand he [the person confessing] accuses himself or judges himself, and on the other hand he is the one who is judged. In one sense, the examination organizes a judicial scene where the subject should play both roles at once" (*Wrong-Doing* 98).

In *1984*, some of this ambiguity folds into the character of O'Brien, the sadistic party member who encourages the protagonist, Winston Smith, to join the underground revolutionary movement, then tortures Smith to extract a full confession. O'Brien, the party official, encourages Smith and his partner in crime, Julia, to confess their heterodox thoughts to him. O'Brien gives them a revolutionary pamphlet – written partly by O'Brien himself – that sets them on their way. And of course O'Brien, in the end, tortures Smith and extracts confessions from him that implicate himself and betray Julia. In Orwell's novel, O'Brien occupies all sides of the confessional transaction: he encourages heterodoxy, he makes admissions of his own to entrap Smith, he receives Smith's voluntary confessions, he tortures Smith to extract yet more incriminating confessions, and he ultimately grants a form of limited absolution after torturing Smith.

A similar dynamic animates Koestler's *Darkness at Noon*. In this novel, the condemned main character, Rubashov, loosely based on the life of the Russian revolutionary Bukharin, has a difficult time distinguishing between the accuser and the accused, the jailer and the jailed. Shortly after being arrested and locked up, Rubashov assesses the situation:

> [Rubashov] fell once more under the familiar and fatal constraint to put himself in the position of his opponent, and to see the scene through the other's eyes. There he had sat, this man Rubashov, on the bunk – small, bearded, arrogant – and in an obviously provocative manner, had put his shoe on over the sweaty sock. Of course, this man Rubashov had his merits and a great past; but it was one thing to see him on the platform at a congress and another, on a palliasse in a cell. So that is the legendary Rubashov, thought Rubashov in the name of the officer with the expressionless eyes [his jailer]. Screams for his breakfast like a schoolboy and isn't even ashamed. Cell not cleaned up. Holes in his sock. Querulous intellectual. (22)

As with Orwell's novel, the condemned finds it difficult to differentiate his own interests and emotions from those of his captor. It is not so much that Rubashov "identifies" with his captor's viewpoint – the so-called Stockholm syndrome; rather, he believes the difference between saint and sinner is incidental, not grounded in any objective reality. All this is a game, an act, a performance of sorts: his role could be easily switched round with his captor's, and it would not alter the basic format of the proceedings. The fact that Rubashov identifies himself as an intellectual only exacerbates this ambiguity, in which he habitually assumes the role of another, who in this case is his ostensible opponent. Witness, perpetrator, victim, prosecution, defence, judge, jailer are seemingly interchangeable, even arbitrarily assigned, parts in this dramatic encounter.

Second, the dream of a truth commission is one of the great recurring fantasies of the Communist movement from the late 1930s onward. It was an equally important conceptual signpost for decolonization movements. In *The God That Failed*, Koestler describes the hope in a distant truth commission as one of the great illusions that kept so many decent people inside the party when it was apparent to all that things were not on the up and up:

> The only dialectically correct attitude was to remain inside [the party], shut your mouth tight, swallow your bile and wait for the day when, after the defeat of the enemy and the victory of the World Revolution, Russia and the Comintern were ready to become democratic institutions. Then and only then would the leaders be called to account for their actions: the avoidable defeats, the wanton sacrifices, the mud-stream of slander and denunciation, in which the pick of our comrades had perished. Until that day you had to play the game – confirm and deny, denounce and recant, eat your words and lick your vomit; it was the price you had to pay for being allowed to continue feeling useful, and thus keep your perverted self-respect. (65–6)

As Koestler points out, many Communist activists outside the USSR remained loyal to the party not because they were blind, but because they believed that a truth commission would clear the air after the dirty work of the revolution had been accomplished. In the meantime, however, there were internal truth commissions of another sort entirely: "confirm and deny, denounce and recant" are warp and woof of party life. Koestler calls this "the game," which alerts us to the duplicity involved, the theatrical nature of confessions, denunciations, and rehabilitations that masquerade as party disciplinary practices. The hope that there would be a post-Stalinist reconciliation was briefly ignited by Nikita Khrushchev's address to the 20th Communist International in early 1956, when he admitted that Stalin had purged a great many senior, loyal party activists, but those hopes were soon extinguished by events in Hungary later that year, when Soviet tanks crushed protesters in Budapest. Looking ahead to Doris

Lessing's *The Golden Notebook*, we will see that the hope of a truth commission died hard even after the great disappointments of 1956.

Third, these texts imply that the idea of truth is a literary problem, not a political or legal or even ethical question. This is to say that truth, as these great Cold War writers represent it, is allegorical or symbolic or representational, not literal or objective in any sense of those words; truth, in these texts, is part of an interpretive or hermeneutic process, and therefore best accessed as a literary construct or an imaginative exercise. Here is how Czeslaw Milosz describes Ketman, which is a game of elaborate, ritualized deception practised by all intellectuals on the wrong side of the Iron Curtain:

> A constant and universal masquerade creates an aura that is hard to bear, yet it grants the performers not inconsiderable satisfactions. To say something is white when one thinks it black, to smile inwardly when one is outwardly solemn, to hate when one manifests love, to know when one pretends not to know, and thus to play one's adversary for a fool (even as he is playing you for one) – these actions lead one to prize one's own cunning above all else. (56)

For Milosz, it would be too reductive to say simply that the kettle is black, or that 2 + 2 = 4, whatever the party fanatics may say, and leave it at that. Knowing the objective truth in a coercive environment is only a small, even inconsequential, part of the picture; what matters is how the actor – and public acting is the key concept here – secures an inner knowledge by putting on a mask for everyone else's benefit. The implications of this game are dire for the prospects of a truth commission: when everyone is acting, when performing is an integral part of being in public, the truth is the game of brinksmanship waged by all the participants, each of whom knows that everyone is lying. The objective truth is a secondary consideration at best. What matters is the skill displayed by the various actors. In *Disgrace*, Lurie likens the South African Truth Commission to a game of Ketman – a television spectacle without the possibility of getting at anything like the truth.

It would be easy to say that this kind of game playing was more or less unique to the Communist bloc, but many writers and artists of the Cold War era were equally convinced that social conformity allowed a weaker, but not less pervasive, version of Ketman to prevail in the parliamentary democracies of Western Europe and North America. This is the basic premise of *Containment Culture: American Narratives, Postmodernism, and the Atomic Age* (1995), in which Alan Nadel uses the Cold War principle of containment to describe cultural production in the United States, where social and political pressures ensured a high degree of self-censorship. It was in this context of repression that many intellectuals argued that art expresses transcendent truths. Here is Stephen Spender in *The God That Failed*:

> To my mind, although poets such as Dante and Shakespeare are certainly in a sense both men of their time and political thinkers, there is a transcendent aspect of their experience which takes them beyond human social interests altogether [...]. To me the beliefs of poets are sacred revelations, illustrations of a reality about the nature of life, which I may not share, but which I cannot and do not wish to explain away as "social phenomena." If art teaches us anything, it is that man is not entirely imprisoned within his society. From art, society may even learn to some extent to escape from its own prison. (267–8)

Spender's comments are pertinent to this discussion not only because he argues that art has a transcendent quality to it – after all, this is as conventional an argument as one might make in the mid-twentieth century – but also because he believes that society is in many senses an intellectual prison. Art expresses the things that we cannot say to one another. Representational art is the essence of dissimulation, of interpreting or representing reality, and yet Spender paradoxically describes it as the only way to access the reality of social life. For Spender, this is the only meaningful difference between the Communist bloc and the so-called free world: in the USSR, they censor the writers as well as the common people; in the US and Western Europe, the common people censor themselves, but at least the most courageous artists are allowed to express themselves fully, although they frequently suffer the abuse of their compatriots because they dare to speak truth to power. Thus for Spender and many of his fellow intellectuals in the Cold War era, the truth of art could be proven by the artwork's refusal to observe propaganda and Cold War binaries. To put this another way, for Spender, Milosz, Orwell, and other like-minded intellectuals, the main difference between the Cold War superpowers is aesthetic rather than political: both camps demand a high degree of conformity, but the liberal democracies at least perpetuate the idea that art can, or should, transcend ideological sectarianism.

Finally, these texts treat individual culpability, and therefore individual subjectivity, with a degree of skepticism. This is no doubt related to the ambiguities of confession. In *Darkness at Noon*, for instance, Rubashov speaks regularly of the "grammatical fiction," otherwise known as the first person. Within the party, the individual has no standing and is of no political consequence whatsoever. For Milosz, individuality is largely dissolved under the pressure of constant acting. The most individualistic people are also, paradoxically, the most orthodox in their behaviour, even when they believe no one is watching or listening. In *1984*, likewise, the character of O'Brien shows that it can be difficult to distinguish between the state and the individual: at precisely the moments in which O'Brien behaves as if he were a revolutionary thinker are also the moments when he is doing the disciplinary work of the state most effectively, most faithfully. O'Brien simultaneously embodies revolutionary ideals and their opposite, state orthodoxy.

The Golden Notebook

Doris Lessing's *The Golden Notebook* (1962) is a cult classic, often read, against the author's own wishes, as a clarion call for feminists. Readers familiar with the novel will recall that it is equally concerned with the fate of the British Communist Party and with revolutionary movements in Africa. It happens to be a novel about mid-century literary culture, too; the main character, Anna, is a successful novelist who is suffering from writer's block. Ironically, for a novel about writer's block, it is both dense and long. In formal terms, the novel attempts to connect these various plotlines related to feminism, global Communism, decolonization, and literature by the use of Anna's four notebooks or diaries. The frame of *The Golden Notebook* is a conventional novel, written in the third person. But this conventional narrative is broken up by fragments of four notebooks, written by Anna, the writer, who is the main character of the conventional, third-person narrative. To put this another way, *The Golden Notebook* is a highly confessional novel, since most of the notebooks are long accounts of Anna's doubts and fears, personal, political, and professional.

Anna's ruminations about the Communist Party are contained in the red notebook. The very first entry, dated 3 January 1950, recounts a discussion between Anna and Molly, who is Anna's closest friend. Molly, who is a party member, confides in Anna, who at that time is not a party member, that the party has sent Molly a questionnaire. On the questionnaire is a place to report any "doubts and confusions." Molly begins her answer, expecting to write a few perfunctory sentences, and then is overtaken with the need to confess everything, writing dozens of pages documenting her doubts and fears, her previously unvoiced criticisms of the party. "What is it I want – a confessional?" she says to Anna, then continues: "Anyway, since I've written it, I'm going to send it in." Anna – who is at this point a fellow traveller rather than a party member – advises her friend to destroy the document: "Supposing the British Communist Party ever gets into power, that document will be in the files, and if they want evidence to hang you, they've got it – thousands of times over" (153). After sleeping on it, Molly takes Anna's recommendation and destroys her responses.

From the inception of the red notebook, we can see both the urgent need to confess and the pragmatic decision to withhold confession. Part of the difficulty is that confession in this context cannot lead to absolution, but instead to excommunication or even worse. In a crucial twist, Molly turns not simply to a friend but to a conspirator of sorts – Anna is a former member of the party, and on the verge of rejoining, despite her skepticism. Anna can sympathize, but she cannot absolve Molly. When Anna asks Molly why she stays in the party, given all that she says in the ill-advised confession, the answer is revealing: there will come a day when Communism triumphs, when all the reactionaries and counter-revolutionaries will be defeated, and that will allow for rehabilitation and reconciliation. Only then will the Stalinists be ousted from party leadership. Molly's burning desire to confess is a sort of repressed or anticipatory form of the reconciliation process she hopes will happen after the final, global victory of Communism.

The second entry in Anna's red notebook is no less revealing. After Molly's midnight revelations, Anna goes the very next day to meet a party recruiter. Before the meeting, Anna resolves to keep herself free of entanglements: she might approve the official goals of the Communists, but as a novelist she is too attached to her independence to commit herself unreservedly to the party. Her recruiter, Comrade Bill, refuses to give her the hard sell when they meet: from the start of the interview his manner with Anna is "wary, his voice cool, brisk, tinged with contempt." With this show of indifference, even hostility, Comrade Bill puts Anna on the defensive, and she immediately feels "a need to apologise, almost a need to stammer" (155). Apologize for what? Comrade Bill knows that Anna is a writer, and one of the great myths within the party is that intellectuals are too aloof, too precious, too full of self-indulgent moral hesitations to devote themselves truly to the cause. In response, Anna finds herself defending herself against these charges in the only way she knows: by agreeing to join the party, and thereby demonstrating that she has the requisite loyalty to a cause greater than herself.

Not content to welcome his new comrade to the ranks with heartfelt congratulations, Comrade Bill concludes the recruitment scene by remarking acerbically, "In five years' time, I suppose you'll be writing articles in the capitalist press exposing us as monsters, just like all the rest." By "all the rest," of course, Comrade Bill means the sort of confessional essays included in *The God That Failed*. Anna, mistakenly believing her agreement to join would somehow prove her merit, is stung by the remark and retorts, "It's lucky I'm an old hand. If I were a raw recruit I might be disillusioned by your attitude." Of course, the implication is clear: Anna comes to the party already disillusioned and cynical. In a curious way, it is only this confession of cynicism that satisfies her recruiter: Comrade Bill gives Anna "a long, cool, shrewd look which said: Well, of course I wouldn't have made that remark if you hadn't been an old hand" (155). A version of Ketman, enabled by a very particular set of confessional practices, is at work. Comrade Bill is not satisfied by her willingness to join, but instead by her ability to play the game, her signal to him, in so many words and glances, that she is not for a moment taken in by the platitudes and homilies of comradeship and fraternity and social justice prevalent in the official discourse of the party.

The exchange between Anna and Bill is confession at an angle, or confession achieved paradoxically through insincerity, acting, role-playing, and interpretation or reading between the lines. Sincerity is the mark of the fool or the innocent; no one involved with the party for any length of time takes anything at face value. To use the terminology of the time, Anna is a witting participant: she confesses that the verbal jousting with her recruiter both pleases her, entitling her "to the elaborate ironies and complicities of the initiated," and makes her disconsolate, with the full knowledge that the party is built upon layers and layers of distrust and dissimulation (155). True confession is a dream deferred endlessly within party circles. In the meantime, false or convoluted confessions become a system of bonding and competition within the group, entitling the initiated to a great many delicate ironies.

A Grain of Wheat

Ngũgĩ wa Thiong'o's *A Grain of Wheat*, published shortly after Kenyan independence, is his most thorough treatment of the Kikuyu uprising known to the outside world as Mau Mau. As with many insurrectionary wars, the conflict left massive scars on the local population. The British colonial administration attempted to contain the revolt by rounding up whole communities into detention camps; they also used a variety of coercive measures to secure collaborators and turncoats. British interrogation of prisoners often focused on determining who had taken the rebel oath. Suspects who admitted to taking the oath sometimes earned special privileges, or were released altogether; prisoners who denied taking the oath were meted out harsher treatment. As in many Cold War show trials, the colonial administration put great store in the practice of extracting confessions from suspected militants. The conflict would have been an ideal candidate for a reconciliation process of some kind, but the extensive reliance on self-incrimination by the colonial authorities would have greatly undermined public confidence in testimony gathered under pressure. The forlorn hope for a reconciliation process gives Ngũgĩ the basic plot mechanism for *A Grain of Wheat*.

Ngũgĩ models the novel partly on Joseph Conrad's *Under Western Eyes* (1911), which contains a confessional plot of its own. As in that novel, a revolutionary hero, Kihika, who is on the run from the authorities, puts himself in the care of an unsuspecting civilian who betrays him. In Ngũgĩ's narrative, the Razumov character is played by Mugo, the non-partisan who betrays Kihika, the freedom fighter, to the colonial administration. The narrative present of the text is several years later, on the eve of Kenyan independence, when some of the surviving freedom fighters are on a hunt for the person who betrayed Kihika, now revered as a revolutionary legend. (The novel thus tacks between the 1950s, during the uprising, and the present, which is 1963.) Suspicion never falls on Mugo, the actual betrayer, until the very closing moments of the novel when he confesses his crime to the community, onstage, during independence day celebrations. For much of the story, Mugo is above questioning because he spent years in a British concentration camp, where he was singled out as a hard case because he refused to admit taking the oath (which, of course, was true – he was never part of the revolutionary movement). Mugo undergoes all sorts of abuse during detention, tolerating it partly because he feels guilty about betraying a man who had trusted him. In this way, the novel also resembles *Darkness at Noon.* At the end of Koestler's novel, the main character Rubashov ultimately accepts his guilt not because he is technically guilty of any of the crimes of which the Stalinists accuse him, but in penance for the many moral crimes he committed as a party activist. A guilty conscience gives Mugo the fortitude to accept punishment for a crime of which he is innocent.

In an interesting twist, the narrative in *A Grain of Wheat* pivots on two very long confessions, which precede Mugo's public declaration at the end of the novel. Both these confessions are received by Mugo, the person who feels he ought to be doing the confessing. The first comes from Gikonyo, a man whom he knows only a little. When Gikonyo approaches Mugo and unburdens himself, he does so with the expectation of finding some sympathy, some relief, some absolution, but instead he leaves frustrated by the whole experience. After telling his story to Mugo over the course of some fifty pages of the novel, Gikonyo feels himself exposed rather than consoled: "The weight had been lifted. But guilt of another kind was creeping in. He had laid himself bare, naked, before Mugo. Mugo must be judging him. Gikonyo felt the discomfort of a man standing before a puritan priest. Suddenly he wanted to go, get away from Mugo, and cry his shame in the dark" (123). Gikonyo does not know that Mugo has a bigger, more soul-engulfing secret nagging his own conscience. All the while Gikonyo is confessing, Mugo suspects that Gikonyo is only trying to gain his confidence so that Mugo will reveal his own dark secrets: "is that why he told me his own story?" Mugo thinks. "A man does not go to a stranger and tear his heart open ... I see everything ... he pretended not to look at me ... yet kept on stealing eyes at me ... see if I was frightened" (123). With this suspicion in the back of his mind, Mugo, hearing the confession impassively, offers no consolation to this person who sought out his company and confidence.

The interaction between Mugo and Gikonyo is the dialectical counterpart to the scene in *The Golden Notebook* when Anna meets the party recruiter. For Anna and the recruiter, everything is part of an act, a ritualized performance. Both Anna and her contact know the truth, and yet the way they admit to each other that they know the truth is to speak around it rather than of it. The respective parties have a tacit understanding that it is preferable to speak in code. For Gikonyo and Mugo, by contrast, a genuine confession generates immediate suspicions that the opposite party must be up to dirty tricks. Mugo thinks that Gikonyo's unprompted, agonizingly detailed confession is a set-up designed to solicit confessions from Mugo. Gikonyo, for his part, comes to the conclusion that Mugo is purer than pure; Gikonyo leaves under the mistaken belief that Mugo sits in righteous judgment. This scene in *A Grain of Wheat* provides another variation on the ambiguities of confession. It becomes almost impossible to differentiate between fact and fiction, relative guilt and relative innocence, heartfelt confession and clever dissimulation. Even when confessions are genuine, they are likely to be interpreted by others as a form of acting.

A Grain of Wheat features two other major scenes of confession, although I do not have space to discuss either of them in full detail. I will only say briefly that the novel concludes with Mugo confessing to the community that he betrayed Kihika, the revolutionary, to the British. Mugo is killed, executed by a tribunal led by a freedom fighter with the code name of General Russia, thereby directly linking Mugo's confession and execution to the Moscow show trials. The conclusion of the novel is deeply skeptical about the truth value of such public declarations of guilt. On one hand, the novel seems to recognize the need for some kind of reconciliation proceedings as part of the decolonizing process. On the other hand, the novel suggests that any reconciliation process is likely to turn into a show trial of some sort.

Life and Times of Michael K

If possible, Coetzee's *Life and Times of Michael K* is even more emphatic than *A Grain of Wheat* about the difficulty of using confession and public testimony to gather any sort of useful political knowledge in the context of decolonization. In the mid-1980s, when *Michael K* was published, Coetzee was preoccupied with confessional literature, a preoccupation that continues virtually to the present day. He published a lengthy essay on the subject, called "Confession and Double Thoughts," ranging over the writings of Augustine, Rousseau, Tolstoy, and Dostoevsky. To that list of influences, I add Herman Melville's "Bartleby the Scrivener," not mentioned in that essay, for reasons that will become apparent below.

Michael K has an allegorical, near-apocalyptic setting. There is a full-scale insurrection in the countryside and widespread disturbances in urban areas. The title character passes through the concentration and rehabilitation camps scattered across the country. Although the South Africa depicted in the novel is a more nightmarish version of the real South Africa during the 1980s, Coetzee also seems to obscure or to allegorize the primary causes of the South African crisis. There are a few oblique references to apartheid, *bantustans*, and systems of racial classification in the novel, but these are infrequent and inconclusive. More important, it is not entirely clear who the rebels are or why they are fighting against the government. To put this another way, the South African conflict tends to resemble the Cold War from the perspective of a neutral: there are two more or less nameless, faceless antagonists engaged in an ideological conflict, although it is not always clear whether the ideologies serve the combatants or the combatants their ideologies. The antagonists never say clearly what they fight for or what they fight against. Michael K emerges as a neutral, caught between these two forces. His sympathies tilt slightly toward the rebels, but when he is asked to state his loyalties, he prefers to maintain his neutrality. He tells his interrogators, "I am not in the war" (195).

When government forces discover K on a remote farm, they detain him on the suspicion that he is giving comfort to rebel forces. K ends up in a rehabilitation camp back in Cape Town, where the government sends rebel sympathizers to be re-educated, weaned from their insurrectionary tendencies. While in detention, K comes under the supervision of a medical orderly who is convinced that the authorities must have it all wrong: there is no possible way that this severely undernourished, mentally handicapped man has been running a staging post for the rebels. The man offers to help K: tell us your story, the man says to him, and we will get you out of this camp and into a more comfortable place where you belong. K refuses to concoct anything like an exculpatory narrative. Not unlike Bartleby the scrivener, he simply refuses: no reasons given, and crucially, no special treatment requested. The medical orderly tries everything: he asks nicely, begs, cajoles, demands, threatens, all to no avail. The officer even attempts a confession of his own, thinking K will relent if the prisoner knows something of his jailer's inner life. K, however, remains steadfast, resisting every request to confess or deny.

K's resistance is enigmatic, as enigmatic as the hostility between the government and the rebels. We do not know why he refuses to tell his story. But the effect of his refusal upon his interrogator, the camp's medical officer, is powerful. At first, the unnamed man, who narrates part 2 of the novel, treats K with great care and sympathy. Quickly, this excessive care turns to insatiable curiosity: if K was not assisting the rebels, how on earth did he find himself on this remote farm? Why is he starving to death? Before long, this curiosity turns into a presumption: I am shielding you from the violence of the state, and you owe me your story in return for my protection. Finally, K becomes an ethical millstone around the medical officer's neck. The officer goes so far as to write K a letter, pleading with him to cooperate:

> I am the only one who can save you. I am the only one who sees you for the original soul you are. I am the only one who cares for you. I alone see you as neither a soft case for a soft camp nor a hard case for a hard camp but a human soul above and

> beneath classification, a soul blessedly untouched by doctrine, untouched by history, a soul stirring its wings within that stiff sarcophagus, murmuring behind that clownish mask. (207)

K's refusal to cooperate, his reluctance to play the role of a confessant, forces into the open two recurring features of confessional literature. First, by balking at the demands placed before him, K calls attention to the theatricality of interrogations and confessions and partly reverses the roles. Not unlike Rubashov in *Darkness at Noon* and O'Brien in *1984*, K's questioner believes he is able to put himself in K's position, that he is uniquely qualified to understand the particularities of his counterpart's frame of reference. K's refusal is as much a refusal to play the role of supplicant or confessant demanded by his situation; he is neither hard case nor soft case, so he does not belong in the sort of camps created by this conflict. The medical officer goes so far as to give K acting lessons: just lie, make up a story for the record; it does not matter much so long as you give us something so that we can tell our superiors we did our jobs.

Second, the medical officer believes that K's real story cannot be communicated by the scripts of this ideological war. The truth, if there is a truth, cannot be explained by reference to the binary categories created by the conflict. K, the medical officer believes, is above or beyond doctrine, too fundamentally human to be reliably fitted into one side or another. At another level, however, the medical officer shows that he does not really understand K's refusal as well as he believes. In conversation with his superior officer, the medical orderly says that K does not belong in a rehabilitation camp. His superior agrees, but adds, "All I ask is that they shouldn't get the idea we are soft." For a moment, there is an uneasy silence, then K's self-appointed guardian says, "But we are soft." His boss agrees with qualifications: "Perhaps we are soft […]. Perhaps we are scheming a bit, at the back of our minds. Perhaps we think that if one day they come and put everyone on trial, someone will step forward and say, 'Let those two off, they were soft'" (181). The pair show an uncomfortable awareness that a reconciliation hearing or show trial looms in the future, nearer than either would care to admit. At some remote level, hard to quantify, the medical officer operates with an ulterior motive: if I am "soft," if I show a glimmer of understanding in the context of inhuman conditions, perhaps I may be reprieved if the war does not go the way of the state.

Finally, the novel's change in perspective means that these implications of complicity and double-dealing cut uncomfortably close to the unnamed narrator, and even to the reader. The first part of the novel is written in the third person; readers are permitted to follow K as he escapes from an embattled Cape Town and wanders through the South African veld, but we are not in a position to understand his motives fully. In short, readers are encouraged, almost forced, to put themselves in the position of an interrogator: why does he do this? What are his reasons? When the second part of the novel shifts to first-person narration, from the perspective of the unnamed medical officer, most readers have already arrived at this new narrator's position – we crave to know more but we are fundamentally blocked by the relative opacity of K's mind and a narrator who refuses to go too deeply into K's consciousness. Most readers have been asking the same sort of questions as our new narrator. In questioning K's motives, we must question our own at some level. It becomes far more difficult for the reader to detach himself or herself from the conflict in which the narrator, however unenthusiastically, finds himself participating.

Conclusion

By way of conclusion, I attempt to link the contrasting aesthetics of these decolonization-era novels with their respective portrayals of truth commissions. Although *The Golden Notebook*, *A Grain of Wheat*, and *Michael K* each feature truth commissions as a possible, even likely, outcome of decolonization movements, none of these texts is altogether satisfied that such a process would help make the transition from subjugated to democratic polity, producing citizens with full legal protections out of colonial subjects. Each novel registers its reservations, however, in a sharply divergent manner.

The Golden Notebook, for instance, is expansive, frustratingly so at times. Where the Cold War state and the Communist Party often demand, in their public hearings, fairly straightforward admissions of guilt or protestations of innocence, Lessing's novel pushes the boundaries of the confessional narrative horizontally – by making the narrative exceptionally long and complicated, and by having it move through time and space – as well as vertically – by embedding narratives within narratives, thereby adding layers of depth and instability to the characters. Lessing's novel is, above all else, an extended meditation on the emotional vicissitudes of its main character, Anna. The narrative explores fold upon fold of her inner life. It offers up protracted confession and self-revelation as a kind of defence against intrusion by the party (and against the liberal state, perhaps). Its aesthetics imply a surfeit of subjectivity, even an intricately narcissistic dwelling on the value of confession. This excess acts as a form of self-defence as well as an admission of guilt. Among the classic Cold War texts that I survey, it most resembles *The Captive Mind*, in that the political subject remains, almost by definition, an actor composed of layer upon layer; every admission both confirms and complicates what is already established. This is not to say that Anna dissimulates in her notebooks, but merely to suggest that the novel portrays political subjectivity as a game. The text's narrative trap doors reinforce the impression that the concept of individual subjectivity is both sacrosanct and not fully recognized, in all its complexity, by the liberal democratic states.

The representation of political subjectivity in *Michael K* provides a dialectical counterpoint to that of *The Golden Notebook*. Whereas Lessing's novel shows us how the coercive atmosphere of the truth commission can lead to subjects with the need to confess everything, Coetzee's novel trains its eye on how truth commissions can affect the state and its agents. K remains an enigma to us. His interrogator and presumptive patron, however, gets twisted into knots by K's intransigence, by K's refusal to explain or exculpate himself in any way. The medical officer, who narrates part 2 of the novel, becomes utterly obsessed with his patient precisely because K's actions are clear but his motives remain inscrutable: K cannot be read. K's refusal tells us very little about K himself – we never really know why he refuses to answer the medical officer's questions – but it confronts his interrogator with the limits of the liberal state, which assumes that citizens will act in their own best interests. K's fastidious abstentions and refusals of bodily appetites – his denial of his own subjectivity, in effect – do not compute in the officer's order of things. Nor do they compute in the aesthetic order of things: the narrative is nearly as abstemious as K himself. If Lessing's novel serves up a wealth of contradictory information about its main subject, Coetzee's refuses to give us much of anything at all.

On the surface, *A Grain of Wheat*'s portrayal of citizenship might seem the least complicated of the three novels. Characters both act in self-interest, unlike K, and show themselves capable of fairly uncomplicated admissions of guilt, unlike Anna. Ngũgĩ's narrative template, likewise, seems to steer a middle course. It is far more straightforward than Lessing's, in that it does not seem to double back on itself with competing, interlocked versions of events, and it is more revealing than Coetzee's, in that Ngũgĩ's third-person narrator readily supplies the reader with pertinent information about characters' thoughts and feelings.

Yet a closer examination of the narrative voice shows that *A Grain of Wheat* is no more enamoured of the confessional thrust of truth commissions – and of the form of citizenship implied by testimonial practices – than its counterparts. The narrator is not simply a disembodied third-person voice, but a communal storyteller. This voice intrudes upon the text only intermittently, but it is always there in the background, as in this passage describing how the local community waits for Mugo to make his appearance at the independence day festivities: Mugo's name "was on everybody's lips. We wove new legends around his name and imagined deeds. We hoped Mugo would come out and join us" (204). This use of the first-person plural might be glossed as an early manifestation of Ngũgĩ's experiments in communal theatre and vernacular writing, but it also affirms that debates about rights and citizenship properly belong to local communities – not to the post-colonial state, and certainly not to revolutionary parties. We might compare the relationship between narrator and implied audience to that of the chorus of a Greek play, who represent the citizens of the polis and provide commentary on the action but do not participate directly in the unfolding of the drama. It cuts across the refusal of self-assertion in *Michael K* while shying away from the bottomless subjectivity of *The Golden Notebook*. Although the early Ngũgĩ is often read as a thinker deeply influenced by both nationalism and Marxism, *A Grain of Wheat* shows him to be skeptical about the ability of the state and of revolutionary parties to assign guilt and innocence. Ngũgĩ's novel provokes an interesting debate about the function of the nascent state in post-colonial situations. The novel endorses neither a totalitarian state, in which former revolutionaries sit in judgment of their fellow citizens, nor a liberal democratic polity, in which the state guarantees the legal status of the individual – as an individual before the law – but does not possess the legal mechanisms to define collective guilt. It would be easy to read this narrative device as a kind of unthinking indigeneity, an appeal to customary practices, but I think it speaks to the particular problems of individual subjectivity created by the transition from colonial to post-colonial state. Confessional practices, *A Grain of Wheat* tells us, ought to bind citizens to their fellow citizens, not to the state, as they threaten to do in *Michael K*, and not to a revolutionary party, as they do in *The Golden Notebook*. Ngũgĩ poses an interesting narrative challenge to the principle of citizenship in a post-colonial context.

12

Writing Like a State: On Caryl Phillips's *Foreigners*

MATTHEW HART

In *Foreigners* (2007), Caryl Phillips asks us to imagine the systemic racism that causes the deaths of three black men in Britain and leaves those men unlamented, unavenged. It is a book full of outrage about the way British people and institutions treat the black men and women whose enslaved and sweated labour built the British Empire. As its title suggests, *Foreigners* recalls us to the "foreign" elements that persist within the British national story by accommodating the experiences of black historical subjects. It is not, however, only a book about national history. *Foreigners* represents the power of the British state in all its entangled but piecemeal complexity. It therefore does more than tell reparative tales about black lives that matter – lives that mattered in the past and that matter now, as black men and women continue their long struggle for full citizenship. *Foreigners* draws our attention to the hazy line between the state and civil society, and to the inadequacy of purely "political" or "social" forms of citizenship. It tells us that just because a power seems to be everywhere, it can still come from somewhere. And because it does this at the level of narrative form as much as historical subject matter, *Foreigners* models what it might mean to write like a state – and demands of us that we learn to read like one, too.

Foreigners sits somewhere between biography and fiction. All three stories concern real historical figures; two of them demonstrate the knack for the newsworthy that underwrites Phillips's many forays into the topical essay genre, as collected in *The European Tribe* (1987), *The Atlantic Sound* (2000), and *Colour Me English* (2011). Each of the stories in *Foreigners* remains, however, distinctly literary in manner, drawing deeply on Phillips's talents as the author of celebrated novels such as *Cambridge* (1992) and *Dancing in the Dark* (2005) – the latter of which is a fictionalization of the life of legendary African Caribbean vaudeville entertainer Bert Williams. Indeed, Phillips, who has asked his publisher to refrain from labelling his books fiction or non-fiction, has grudgingly admitted that *Foreigners* might be called "creative biography" (Ledent 188). This is a hybrid genre that Phillips particularly associates with the German author W.G. Sebald but which can expand to include texts as different as Truman Capote's *In Cold Blood* (1966) and Dave Eggers's *What Is the What* (2006). In a more popular vein, the term also designates Melanie McGrath's memoirs, *Silvertown* (2002) and *Hopping* (2009), in which the factual record is described as the canvas upon which the writer embroiders imaginative truths (*Hopping* xiv–xv).

The political meanings of *Foreigners* partly inhere in the formal and generic equipoise of the three stories. Such equilibrium, however, is not a function of the ambiguous relationship between fiction and the historical record. After all, such playfulness is common to much contemporary prose. Nor is Phillips's engagement with the politics of race in Britain reducible to the representation of black men's struggles as British citizens. The political wisdom of *Foreigners* is a function of the ironized and fragmented narrative form of the stories, or, better still, of the complex of meanings and intentions that are motivated when that form mediates these historical examples.

Through the exemplary nature of its stories and protagonists, *Foreigners* reveals its difference from a text such as Sebald's *The Emigrants* (1992), which also collects melancholy biographies of internal exile and institutionalized racism. Timothy Bewes argues that Sebald's prose is characterized by a systematic refusal of exemplarity, understood as a relational logic in which an instance or a case "denotes the meaningful, normative connection that accumulates around it or is attributed to it" (3). For Bewes, the notoriously enigmatic quality of Sebald's prose is partly created by its refusal to figure its characters or situations as exemplary; characters such as Max Ferber or Ambros

Adelwarth in *The Emigrants* are thus experienced by Sebald's readers "as a situation of aporia, the equal presence of the desire for connection and its impossibility" (Bewes 3). In *Foreigners*, by contrast, characters' stories accumulate normative significance even when the details of their lives remain obscure or scattered. *Foreigners* does not slough off the logic of the example in favour of an inscrutable vision of history in which, ideally, no object or person has a moral or hermeneutic significance greater than any other (Bewes 29). Differences matter in *Foreigners*. In particular, the "foreign" Briton's story needs telling more than that of the "native." Yet not all exemplarity is the same. It also matters to *Foreigners* that Phillips's stories of social violence are mediated by narrative forms that shift the burden of their exemplarity from the individual to the state. As "foreign" stories, these are not tales about men but about citizens, which is to say they are stories about ways of living and being that become most meaningful in and through their relation to authoritatively institutionalized forms of political and social power.

Foreigners is serious about the politics of multicultural representation in Britain. Its seriousness can be measured in the way it understands such representation as at once necessary and inadequate. In a recent interview, Phillips spoke of the inclusion of black British history within the UK national curriculum as "incredibly important ... we grew up with such huge absences in the type of history we were taught" (Rice 368; ellipsis in original). He expresses the hope that, if these curricular changes can be maintained, the state will have secured a "lasting legacy" that will make a material difference to British schoolchildren of all races (Rice 368). At the same time, *Foreigners* expresses skepticism about the proposition that all black Britons need are more or more brightly lit spots within the china cabinet of national history. The first tale in the volume, "Dr Johnson's Watch," concerns Francis Barber, born into slavery on Jamaica around 1735 but for many years Samuel Johnson's manservant, even helping in later years to revise his landmark 1755 *Dictionary of the English Language*. The story's role in the volume is clear: like Peter Fryer in his great social history, *Staying Power*, Phillips wants to extend the history of black Britain back before the so-called Windrush generation. In fact, the second story in *Foreigners*, "Made in Wales," appears to draw directly from *Staying Power* when it briefly narrates the often-unrecognized presence of black people in Britain from "the time of the Roman occupation" through the reign of Elizabeth I (*Foreigners* 87). These are, of course, publicly available facts, but Phillips's short history not only follows closely the chronological arrangement of Fryer's first chapter but cites signature elements of his narrative, such as the African legionaries who guarded Hadrian's Wall, the effects of Sir John Hawkins's slave-trading voyages to West Africa and the Caribbean, and Elizabeth I's proclamation expelling "blackamoores" from London (Fryer 1–11). In its allusions to Fryer's book, *Foreigners* pushes the history of black Britain back beyond the twentieth century, beyond the abolition of slavery and the slave trade, beyond even the Somersett judgment of 1772, and into the origin narrative, not just of Britain but of the English language and English literature at the point it became authorized as such. If Francis Barber counts as a "foreigner," then so too, just a little, do "Dictionary Johnson" and his works.

For all this, "Dr Johnson's Watch" is substantially torqued by narrative ironies that work against the promise of multicultural inclusion; indeed, such ironies will prove among the most important aesthetic qualities of *Foreigners*' three tales. The story is narrated by one of Johnson's acolytes, an unnamed literary man with ideas of investing in Granville Sharp's disastrous plan to resettle the "Black Poor" of London in a new "Province of Freedom" on the coast of Sierra Leone. The narrator is classically unreliable, a man of pride and prejudice. In his hands Francis Barber's life becomes less a story about the black contribution to British history than about the obstacles to that contribution: "I was now convinced," he opines, having visited Barber in his dying illness and penury, "that English air is not suitable for negro lungs and soon reduces these creatures to a state of childish helplessness" (54). *Foreigners* seems to begin by contributing towards a reparative historiography. In the end, however, Phillips uses his novelistic craft to frustrate that goal as much as foment it.

Foreigners' three stories take different generic and stylistic shape; the volume is not marked by aesthetic unity so much as by an attractive unevenness.[1] If "Dr Johnson's Watch" is a kind of historical burlesque, the next story, "Made in Wales" – the tale of Randolph Turpin, briefly middleweight boxing champion of the world in 1951 and one of the very first black British athletic stars – reads like long-form sports journalism. The shift in tone and genre between the stories is abrupt, perhaps even more abrupt than the spatio-temporal jump from Lichfield in 1801 to Leamington Spa 150 years later. For all their distinctness, the stories are joined by subject matter (especially by the fact that Turpin's life also ends badly) and by further play with lexical irony. "Made in Wales" is an extended work of ventriloquization, full of stock phrases and sporting clichés: "promising coloured fighter," "dusky English lamb" (65), "bronze tiger" (90). Some of these worn-out idioms are quoted from contemporary sources; others sound like silent verbatim borrowings; still others evoke a social scene so lazily, in such familiar phraseology, that the mind dulls even as it registers the presence of new information: "When it was announced that Sugar Ray Robinson would be visiting Britain, and that a British lad would be given the chance to enter the ring and go a few rounds with him, this was a shot in the arm to the blighted confidence of the British people" (68).

The mind dulls, but only to rebel. The complacency of the narrator's language exists in uncanny tension with the horror and sadness of Turpin's life, the cruelty and futility of which constantly overflow the boxing ring, most dramatically when he shoots himself dead after first gravely wounding his baby daughter. Furthermore, the narrator's voice is oddly stuck between historical registers: sometimes it seems hopelessly infected by the racist idioms of 1950s sporting journalism; at other times – as in the concluding section in which the narrator, now firmly located in the present, meets Turpin's adult daughters – he acts and writes as kindly and as solicitously as we would expect of Caryl Phillips himself. In fact, if anything, the narrator is at the end of the story rather too kind. "Made in Wales" concludes with one of Turpin's daughters speaking fondly about her father: "But he never hated anyone [...]. He just let people make up their own minds" (148). We can easily forgive a daughter's tenderness toward her dead father, even if he was a serial abuser of women and especially if he was abused in turn by a country that alternately hailed and ostracized him. But, as with the language of bronze tigers and blighted national confidence, the words of Turpin's daughter seem inadequate as a conclusion to the tragedy of "Made in Wales." If there is an ironic tension in this story between the somnaical comforts of journalistic cliché and the shocking reality of Turpin's violent despair, then there is an equal contradiction between the narrator's desire to tell the unvarnished truth about Turpin and his need to deliver him to us as finally ennobled by familial love and, thus, through a kind of sentimental alchemy, transformed into a fit subject for public commemoration.

Foreigners is not a book about black British heroes; if it can be said to be about heroism at all, it concerns the tragedy of a world that makes us want heroes even as its horrors make that need insatiable. A series of lexical and tonal ironies about subjects and media define the first two parts of the book. These ironies suggest the weakness of any politics of inclusion that attempt merely to add black Britons to the roll call of national history without considering how the social machinery that excluded them in the first place should be transformed. But *Foreigners* is not, so far, overtly political; at least it is not political in the sense that its settings or characters bring us into unambiguous encounter with institutions of state or citizen activism. For that shift, we need to turn to the final story, "Northern Lights," an account of the life and death of David Oluwale, who stowed away on a boat from Lagos to Hull in 1949 and was hounded to death by the Leeds police twenty years later. If there is an analytical immanence between *Foreigners*' narrative form and historical examples – and if a certain politics emerges from that relation – then "Northern Lights" provides the best test case for that argument. It is not that these claims apply only to "Northern Lights"; it is that, if they are not true about "Northern Lights," they are almost certainly not true at all.

So what sets "Northern Lights" apart? Its key thematic difference from the first two parts of *Foreigners* is that it is unambiguously a story about a young man's collision with the institutions of state. We witness Oluwale's encounters with coercive state power in the form of the police, prison service, and courts. We also bear witness to the disciplinary practices of psychiatric hospitals and government departments of health and social security. Finally, we read evidence of Oluwale's interactions with, and posthumous significance to, a wide range of civil society and para-state agents such as charity workers and community activists.

Phillips often represents these different institutions in their own words – by the reproduction of official documents, say, or by the transcription of trial testimony or what seem to be recorded interviews. As a result, "Northern Lights" is the most disjunctive and formally diverse of the three stories in *Foreigners*. It reads like a documentary collage or casebook, beginning with David's emigration and moving inexorably towards his death, but often circling back to the history of the city in which he lived and the institutions that made that city. The voice of the narrator occupies the space between documentary and testimonial evidence. Framing and arranging his materials, the narrator lets them speak but also makes them speak to one other.

The narrator is hard to pin down. He is sometimes scholarly, a historian of peoples and a place, who can lapse into third-person reportage. He is, however, also prepared to editorialize overtly. Even when he lets his informants speak, he never hides his arranging hand – the way, for instance, that the words of a National Health Doctor, speaking in 2002 about "the typical black admission" to an emergency room ("loud, paranoid, resisting strongly"), are followed by a story about Queen Victoria's 1858 visit to Leeds Town Hall: "the words around the vestibule – 'Europe – Asia – Africa – America' – reminded the people of Leeds that, only one year after the Indian Mutiny had been put down, the globe remained Britain's true sphere of influence" (188–9). The narrator is even plaintive in his occasional second-person address: "David, you wandered hungry and sick through the heart of a city [...]. You slept with the joyful brides, but once again they found you, and attempted to beat the life out of you" (230–1). In its overall effect, the narrator's voice simultaneously intrudes and decentres. He is never less than present, yet the precise nature or location of his authority and attitudes remains in doubt.

In its mess of testimony and speculation, its mix of unstable foreground and intermittent deep background, "Northern Lights" asks and answers a question, at the level of style as much as theme, which has not yet concerned many literary critics. That question is basic to social and political theory; moreover, it is fundamental to any discussion about literature and the institution of citizenship. What is a state? How do we know it or distinguish it from its others? From that follow other, more obviously literary questions, which we nevertheless cannot answer without first considering the nature of the state as such. How do we read in such a way that the state becomes visible to us? What might it mean to write like a state?

"Northern Lights" begs these questions because, by telling David Oluwale's story through such a broken and self-divided form, it gives an account of 1950s and 1960s England in which the line between social and political power, state and civil society, is constitutively uncertain. Phillips does not depict all power as the same or as originating from everywhere equally; rather, the story of state racism is told through a mix of documentary collage and uneven narration that, formally as much as thematically, lacks any final unity or coherence. At the same time, "Northern Lights" does not allow us to see state power as merely an effect of governance or culture. David Oluwale is not just routinely institutionalized, in the sense of being sometimes sent to prison or committed to mental hospitals. His life in Britain began when he was imprisoned for twenty-eight days on arrival and ended with his extra-judicial homicide. It ended when, after a prolonged campaign of police harassment and abuse, he was beaten and chased by uniformed officers. Having fallen or jumped into the River Aire in a desperate attempt to escape, he died from drowning. Sandwiched between these confrontations with the coercive apparatus of the state, David's life is described by Phillips through his encounters with the diverse institutions of power in a country still uneasily poised between its historic identities as an imperial and a welfare state. Phillips enhances this effect by omitting aspects of David's actual life that might not accord with this narrative, such as his childhood in Nigeria or his marriage and parenthood in England.[2] The result is a story framed by state power but which refuses to tell us whether the "truth" of David's life can be found in his abuse at the hands of the state or, as a local West Indian activist hopes, by the way his experience changed civil society by forcing the immigrant community in Leeds to "sit up and notice what was happening" (224). Phillips does not even help us understand whether the policeman who tried to help David, and later testified against his superior officers, was in those moments acting as the principled representative of the state – a "good cop," the epitome of what a policeman should be – or whether, as the policeman himself understands his actions, as a professional traitor, someone who, faced with a moral dilemma, chose society over the state.

If this situation says something about what it might look like to write like a state, what model of state power, if any, does writing like a state commit us to? In *Seeing Like a State*, James C. Scott writes about "high modernist" projects of state planning such as the building of Brasilia under the direction of Oscar Niemeyer. (Needless to say, these stories also end unhappily.) At the centre of Scott's argument is the conceit that states see poorly, in simplified ways that are calculated to make the complexity of the social and natural landscape "legible" for processes of bureaucratic sorting and counting. Scott returns often to the example of the cadastral map, a form of "state simplification" that was "created to designate taxable property-holders" but that, in its very brutalization of what Scott calls the "social hieroglyph," ends up describing rather more than "a system of land tenure; it *creates* such a system through its ability to give its categories the force of law" (3). Curiously, *Seeing Like a State* has lots to say about statecraft, especially as it relates to the benefit to "centralizing elites" (29–30) of standardized ways of measuring and counting, but it has almost nothing to say about the state as an institution or idea in itself. The word "state" does not appear in the index. The state is everywhere apparent as a thing that *sees* and *measures* and *moves* and *kills*. But while it is the subject of very many sentences, it is not the object of any definition. It accepts adjectives, notably "authoritarian" and "utilitarian" (5, 51). It is even defined through the traditional opposition to civil society – at least, Scott argues that the state becomes deadly when "a prostrate civil society [...] lacks the capacity to resist [its] plans" (5). While Scott assumes that we know the state by virtue of what it does and what it is not, he never proffers even the simplest theory of the state as such. The state *sees*; or rather, planners, architects, demographers, and accountants have the capacity to see *like* a state. But the state itself, conceived of as an entity distinguishable from these acts of viewing and measurement, might as well not exist. We know it only as the unspecified end of a simile.

The social-scientific literature on statehood typically concerns the problem of defining the state, especially the difficult task of describing the relation between what we might agree are state actions and what it is that gives those very different sorts of action their common "stateness." Timothy Mitchell, in a brilliant and often-republished essay on this subject, writes about how, after the Second World War, American political scientists and sociologists tended to abandon the concept of the state in favour of the analysis of political systems. The state concept seemed muddled. Where, in a world characterized by the apparently relentless growth of quasi- and para-political forces, can we locate the boundary between state and society? More importantly, the idea of the state seemed unhelpful for the analysis of political power during a Cold War era dominated by two vast imperial hegemons often competing for geopolitical influence outside their own borders.

The dilemma is, Mitchell continues, that the theoretical shift from focusing on the state to analyzing the political system solved the problem of the relation between action and authoritative actor only by extending the realm of the political into infinity. "Far from solving the problem of the uncertain boundary between state and society," Mitchell writes, "the systems approach unfolded the very space of the boundary into a limitless and undetermined terrain" (81). In the 1970s and 1980s, therefore, a new generation of researchers began to ask whether the state/society problem might be settled by conceiving of the state as a conceptual realm and society as an empirical realm of actions and actors; in this way, the state/society division was to be resolved by an appeal to "the apparently obvious distinction between [...] a subjective order and an objective order" (Mitchell 82). The social is the world in which we really act, on which we really stand; the state is the realm of political intentions, goals, agendas, and ideals. We may not be able to describe the autonomy of the state in actual fact, or so the story goes, but we can at least describe the ways in which people believe that it exists and is identifiable with specific policy goals.

This objective/subjective distinction seems to underpin Scott's approach in *Seeing Like a State*. He does not try to theorize the state because he can postulate its existence implicitly, by arguing back from effects to causes and assuming that the integrity of the state concept lies in the systematic nature of the plans made on its behalf by people who believe they are working in its interest. The problem with this approach, as Mitchell points out, is that the redefinition of the state as existing in the subjective realm depends upon its prior idealization and personification. The state is defined by analogy with a person or "policy-making actor" (88). This theory is therefore susceptible to the charge that it overestimates the unity of an idea that appears to us not as a singularity but as a congeries of symbols and goals; it is also vulnerable to anti-humanist objections that persons themselves hardly evince much ontological unity. If political actors are not autonomous, self-identical, or even rational, then little is gained by trying to define the state by analogy with them. It is as if we were to claim that "Northern Lights" is a simple enough sort of story simply because its various parts are all gathered together by one narrative presence, without remembering that its narrator is himself internally diverse and contradictory.

In a posthumously published essay, "Notes on the Difficulty of Studying the State," Philip Abrams argued that such problems are insoluble. He contended that, despite the fact that "commonsense impels us to the inference that there is a hidden reality in political life and that that reality is the state," the state, "conceived of as a substantial entity separate from society[,] has proved a remarkably elusive object of analysis" (61). This is because, he concluded, "the state is at most a message of domination – an ideological artefact attributing unity, morality and independence to the disunited, amoral and dependent workings of the practice of government [...]. The state is not the reality which stands behind the mask of political practice," he wrote. "It is itself the mask which prevents our seeing political practice as it is" (81). There is a "state-system," Abrams concedes, by which he means a set of governmental practices and institutions; there is, also, a "state idea" (82). The state itself, however, has no objective reality; it is no more than an ideological "structuration within political practice" (82). If, as Abrams says, the task of the social scientist is to demystify reality, then what better place to start than by "attending to the senses in which the state does not exist rather than to those in which it does" (82).

Mitchell ends up in a somewhat equivalent place. He argues that the state is not, as Nicos Poulantzas argued, a structure; it is, rather, the *structural effect* of many hundreds of institutional and social practices that together produce the appearance of an autonomous power. For Mitchell, the distinction between state and society does not name a real opposition. It "is not the perimeter of an intrinsic entity, which can be thought of as a free-standing object or actor," Mitchell insists. "It is a line drawn internally, within the network of institutional mechanisms through which a certain social and political order is maintained" (90). The state is not just the effect of mundane social practices such as policing or regulating or measuring or building or distributing or protecting or educating or killing. It is the "powerful metaphysical effect" that makes us believe that these very different activities have something in common. "The ability to have an internal distinction appear as though it were the external boundary between separate objects is," Mitchell writes, "the distinctive technique of the modern political order" (78). Unlike Abrams, Mitchell does not presume that the state might be analyzed away. The state is, like the cadastral map, an idealization that emerges out of concrete governmental practices and has durable material effects. Its ghostliness, rather than being the ideological mask of a power that lies elsewhere, is exactly that power.

Mitchell's theory of the state seems initially propitious for a reading of "Northern Lights," given that Phillips also seems to sense that the line between state and civil society is somehow unreal, an effect of power itself rather than of some real distinction in the social field. The problem remains, however, that Mitchell's description of the state as a structural metaphysical effect risks overstating the unity of the "subjective ideality" that is constituted in and through the distinction between state and civil society (Mitchell 95). To put it in literary terms: if the state is an "abstraction in relation to the concreteness of the social" (Mitchell 95), why does "Northern Lights" represent it, at the twin levels of style and subject matter, as so ragged and ill-defined an idea? To answer this question and to develop the kind of theoretical understanding that a political reading of *Foreigners* demands, we could follow Michael Mann in thinking of state power as "entwined" but "nonsystemic" (Mann, *Sources* 88). In the second volume of his magisterial trilogy, *The Sources of Social Power*, Mann argues that, "far from being singular and centralized, modern states are polymorphous power networks" that include what he calls "diverse crystallizations" of power (75). Most centrally, he argues that state power includes determinate military, political, ideological, and economic dimensions of social power but remains irreducible to any one source of authority and legitimacy. He uses the chemical metaphor of the "polymorph" to describe how forms of social and political power belong to different systems simultaneously: "States have multiple institutions, charged with multiple tasks, mobilizing constituencies both through their territories and geopolitically" (75). The state is usually territorially unified and, because it exists in a world of other states with which it has relations, it is typically defined from the "outside in" (56). This territorial unity gives it a kind of autonomy as an "arena" or "place" in and through which power operates

(Mann, "Autonomous," 112). And yet even this political space lacks "final unity" or consistency: "Whatever centrality, whatever private rationality, the state possesses, it is also impure, different parts of its body politic open to penetration by diverse power networks" (Mann, *Sources* 56). At the same time, the state is not merely a structural effect or abstraction: according to Mann's theory of "organizational materialism," the state is the whole variety of practices through which "dynamic social relations become authoritatively institutionalized" (53). It is the police officer and the doctor. Mann therefore teaches us not to be surprised by the difficulty of distinguishing between state and non-state actors; in fact, this blurriness is an essential aspect of the state's polymorphic nature. In addition, there is no contradiction in this theory between the proposition that the state is relatively autonomous and the idea that the governmental techniques and capacities "used by states are only a combination of [...] the means of power used in all social relationships" (Mann, "Autonomous," 123).

Although it possesses the abstraction inherent to any ideal-type model, Mann's theoretical account has many advantages. It maintains a realist attitude to the state without identifying it only with elite functions such as war making or geopolitical strategy. It is materialist but refuses to reduce the state to an ideological function of class power. It is a complex theory but, then again, that is because it describes a complicated combination of institutions and relations among institutions. Complexity makes Mann's model adequate to the figuration of social and political power in "Northern Lights." In this sense, Mann's theory does not just begin to answer the theoretical questions that I posed earlier; it also allows us to attribute political meanings to the documentary fragmentariness of "Northern Lights," which can now be described as a powerful formal allegory for authoritatively institutionalized forms of racial violence that nevertheless take no single or systemic form.

Although the three stories in *Foreigners* are generically and stylistically distinct, they share qualities of narrative irony, as well as historical subject matter. If the fragmentary narrative quality of "Northern Lights" evokes the entwined but non-systemic nature of state power, then its ironic aspect reminds us that the last of Phillips's stories of British foreignness is not just about individual or cultural strangeness but about the failure of the British state to extend the protections of citizenship to its black subjects. Phillips's title, *Foreigners*, cannot help but evoke the question of nationality – and, thus, of racial difference. The sense of national strangeness pervades the volume but is most marked in Oluwale's story, which is represented by Phillips – even at the expense of the actual documentary record – as a life of almost continual ostracism and loneliness. Ironically, none of these men is in any legal or political sense "foreign." Francis Barber, born a slave on the Bathurst family's plantation in Jamaica, was a British subject under the common-law understanding of nationality prevalent in the eighteenth century.[3] Randolph Turpin was born in Leamington Spa to an English mother and a father who, hailing from British Guyana, was a British citizen under the Nationality and Status of Aliens Act of 1914. Even Oluwale was a Citizen of the United Kingdom and Colonies under the 1948 British Nationality Act – a citizen whose imprisonment on landing in England in 1949 was not for any kind of immigration offence but for the crime of stowing away. If we must admit that Oluwale was technically an immigrant, then we must specify that he migrated from one part of the geography of British nationality to another.

Reading *Foreigners* therefore means learning to distinguish between what, channelling Raymond Williams, we might call the cultural category of *nationality* as a whole way of life and *citizenship* as the legal and political relationship between an individual and a state (Williams, *Culture* 325–7).[4] David Oluwale was as legally British as Prime Minister Harold Wilson, but in 1969 he could still suffer a police officer scratching out the word "BRIT" on the part of his arrest paperwork indicating nationality and replacing it with the racial slur "WOG" (Aspden 177).

The political aspects of citizenship are clearly not its only characteristics. For this reason, the distinction between "citizenship proper" and ethnocultural identity is always a vexed one.[5] Even a politically appointed lawyer such as Lord Goldsmith, the former attorney general of the United Kingdom, argues that citizenship today joins social, economic, and cultural bonds to the classic bargain in which "the citizen offers loyalty in return for protection" (10–12). There are aspects of citizenship that are fundamentally juridico-political, such as rights of protection or duties of allegiance or obedience. But there is also a wide range of citizenship rights that occupy an indistinct zone neither wholly inside nor entirely outside the political. Thus, in Goldsmith's report, universal suffrage is grouped among "civic rights" such as the freedom to hold public office in accordance with the 1701 Act of Settlement, even though that act is a foundation stone of constitutional law throughout the Commonwealth (5–6).[6] Perhaps most importantly, the expansive model of citizenship that now pertains within European Union states "blurs," in Goldsmith's words, the relationship between rights and obligations and what was once a "very clear" and dispositive "dividing line between citizens and non-citizens" (11). Many foreigners present in Britain are now accorded liberties and responsibilities – such as freedom of movement and suffrage rights within Britain for citizens of the Irish Republic, rights of abode and employment for EU nationals, or rights of diplomatic protection for all resident aliens – that were historically restricted to citizens of Britain or its colonies. Finally, there also exist notions of "social citizenship" in which the individual's relationship to the state is not reducible to the discourse of sovereignty, as when Desmond King and Jeremy Waldron articulate "the concept of a citizen [as] that of a person who can hold her or his head high and participate fully and with dignity in the life of her or his society" (443).

"Northern Lights" does not narrate the failure to extend citizenship rights to David Oluwale. Instead, the story recounts the way that, as a matter of institutional habit and policy rather than law, state institutions propagate a definition of Britishness that distinguishes between merely juridico-political identity and true national belonging. In other words, state institutions promulgate and enforce a vision of black British subjects as unworthy of social citizenship in the sense of full and dignified participation in society. "Northern Lights" laments a failure within the category of citizenship, which in racist Britain of the 1950s and 1960s gets cruelly subdivided into merely formal ("BRIT") and culturally substantive ("WOG") terms. This violent distinction is handled with subtle but bitter irony at the end of "Northern Lights" when the narrator visits David's grave on a hillside cemetery in Leeds. In this scene, the narrator briefly unifies the disparate perspectives of the story by describing David as a kind of unwilling *genius loci* of Leeds. From the perspective of the cemetery above the city, the narrator falls back into his second-person address: "You have achieved a summit, David. Climbed to the top of a hill, and from here you can look down" (235). David's triumph, if we are to read these lines without irony, lies in his brave refusal to give in to the police thugs who tried to chase him out of the city. The reader cannot help but feel, however, that this victory is a poor substitute for a life lived alone and on the run – a life rendered expressible only in terms of a fragmentary record in which David himself never speaks. The narrator gives voice to David by introducing, at the last minute, a discourse of land and place. In this naturalizing discourse, Leeds figures not as a social or political space but as a timeless setting: "You are in Leeds. Forever in Leeds" (235).

At this point, the unnamed narrator of "Northern Lights" becomes as unreliable as the literary gentleman whose perspective dominates Francis Barber's in "Dr Johnson's Watch"; in this context, "Forever in Leeds" reads as much like a jail sentence as a victory. The truth is that David is dead and that he lived not in the earth above Leeds, but in the city precincts, amid the people and the institutions that they built. David could never escape the brutality of the police, as Phillips emphasizes again and again, not because he "achieved" the summit of the cemetery but because he defiantly refused to leave the city centre that the graveyard overlooks. Phillips does not give us the history of David Oluwale, natural man. Despite the narrator's inclinations towards redemptive immortalization, we read instead of David's unnatural death, annotated in pathologists' reports, the notes of prison doctors, and the testimony of welfare bureaucrats. The one person we never hear from, in this story, is David Oluwale. His life is anatomized and measured: we see him "like a state," in the simplifying sense that Scott puts it – as a subject stripped of agency and initiative. But while we know that to see him that way is to see the violence done by institutions that ought to have protected him, we are not encouraged to confuse the simplifications that come from having partial and institutionalized knowledge with the idea that state and citizenship are themselves simple or singular. Indeed, we know they are not because we know how David suffers from their complex disorderliness. "Northern Lights" resists the consolations of the earth as much as it does the substitution of the cultural for the political or the delusion that a power that is everywhere must come from everywhere and nowhere. This is what it means to write – and read – like a state.

NOTES

1 Ledent discusses Phillips's deliberate deployment of different styles and registers for each story (189–90).

2 For the reasons behind Phillips's decision to omit Oluwale's family life, see Ledent (186). For the little that is known about Oluwale's wife, Gladys, see Aspden (47).

3 Barber was manumitted following the death of Colonel Richard Bathurst in 1754, although Johnson had treated him as a free man from the point Barber entered his employ in 1752. At the time of Phillips's story, which is set following Johnson's death in 1784, there is therefore no doubt that he was the formal legal equal to other Jamaican-born British adult men of small wealth. The general legal status of slaves in Great Britain was, however, ambiguous during the eighteenth century. Although the Somersett judgment of 1772 found no support for slavery in common law, Lord Mansfield's ruling in that case was arguably limited to the question of whether an enslaved person could be legally removed from England and Wales (see, e.g., Nadelhaft 194–5).

4 Strictly speaking, the idea of nationality as a whole way of life is incoherent. The distinctiveness and power of Williams's culture concept necessarily implies that nationality could never represent a lifeworld. Citizenship is itself a subset of the wider complex of institutions, practices, ideas, and feelings known as nationality. Williams's *Keywords*, for instance, contains no entry for "citizenship." Several entries in that volume nevertheless demonstrate his understanding that national identity has had distinct, if dialectically interrelated, cultural and political implications. His definition of *community*, for example, considers how that term has helped historically to distinguish between "the body of direct [i.e., socially intimate] relationships" and "the organized establishment of a realm or state" (75). The entry on *nationalist* talks about the "modern political sense" of nationality as well as its ancient and continuing racial, linguistic, and affective connotations (213–14).

5 See Janice Ho's essay in this volume regarding the racial history of citizenship in Britain.

6 Goldsmith actually refers to "the Act of Settlement 1700," the year in which the act was introduced. It should be noted that the right to hold public office is constrained by religion (Roman Catholics are excluded from succession to the monarchy) and by gender (the act legislates for male-preference primogeniture).

WORKS CITED

"2005 World Summit Outcome." UN General Assembly, 60th Session. October 2005. www.un.org/democracyfund/creation-undef-2005-world-summit-outcome. Web.

Abrams, Philip. "Notes on the Difficulty of Studying the State." *Journal of Historical Sociology* 1.1 (1988): 58–89. Print.

Agamben, Giorgio. *Homo Sacer: Sovereign Power and Bare Life.* Trans. Daniel Heller-Roazen. Stanford, CA: Stanford University Press, 1998. Print.

Ahmed, Sara. *The Cultural Politics of Emotion*. New York: Routledge, 2004. Print.

– *Queer Phenomenology: Orientations, Objects, Others*. Durham, NC: Duke University Press, 2006. Print.

– *Strange Encounters: Embodied Others in Post-Coloniality*. London: Routledge, 2000. Print.

Alleg, Henri. *La question, suivi de 'Une Victoire' par Jean-Paul Sartre*. Paris: Éditions de minuit, 1958. Print.

– *The Question*. Trans. John Calder. London: John Calder, 1958. Print.

Ambler, Eric. *The Light of Day*. 1961. New York: Vintage, 2004. Print.

Anagnost, Ann. *National Past-Times: Narrative, Representation, and Power in Modern China*. Durham, NC: Duke University Press, 1997. Print.

Ang, Ien. *On Not Speaking Chinese: Living between Asia and the West*. London: Routledge, 2001. Web.

Anker, Elizabeth. *Fictions of Dignity: Embodying Human Rights in World Literature*. Ithaca, NY: Cornell University Press, 2012. Print.

– "Narrating Human Rights and the Limits of Magic Realism in Salman Rushdie's *Shalimar the Clown*." Goldberg and Moore 149–64. Print.

Antwi, Phanuel, et al., eds. "Postcolonial Intimacies: Gatherings, Disruptions, Departures." *Interventions* 15.1 (2013): 1–9. Print.

Archibugi, Daniele. "Cosmopolitan Guidelines for Humanitarian Intervention." *Alternatives: Global, Local, Political* 29.1 (2004): 1–21. Print.

Arendt, Hannah. *The Human Condition*. 2nd ed. Chicago: University of Chicago Press, 1998. Print.

– *On Revolution*. London: Penguin, 1990. Print.

– *The Origins of Totalitarianism*. 1951. New York: Harvest, 1976. Print.

– "We Refugees." *The Jewish Writings*. Ed. Jerome Kohn and Ron H. Feldman. New York: Schocken, 2007. 264–74. Print.

Aristotle. *Politics*. Trans. and ed. Carnes Lord. Chicago: University of Chicago Press, 2013. Print.

Aspden, Kester. *The Hounding of David Oluwale*. London: Vintage, 2008. Print.

Attewell, Nadine. *Better Britons: Reproduction, National Identity, and the Afterlife of Empire*. Toronto: University of Toronto Press, 2014. Print.

Azoulay, Ariella. *The Civil Contract of Photography*. New York: Zone, 2012. Print.

– "'The Family of Man': A Visual Universal Declaration of Human Rights." *The Human Snapshot*. Ed. Thomas Keenan and Tirdad Zolghadr. LUMA Foundation, Center for Curatorial Studies, Bard College, Annandale-on-Hudson, NY: Sternberg Press, 2013. 19–48. Print.

– "Palestine as Symptom, Palestine as Hope: Revising Human Rights Discourse." *Critical Inquiry* 40.4 (2014): 332–64. Print.

Balibar, Étienne. "Propositions on Citizenship." Trans. Simon James Critchley. *Ethics* 98 (July 1988): 723–30. Print.

Barlow, Tani E. "Introduction: On 'Colonial Modernity.'" *Formations of Colonial Modernity in East Asia*. Ed. Tani E. Barlow. Durham, NC: Duke University Press, 1997. 1–20. Print.

Barthes, Roland. *Mythologies*. Trans. Annette Lavers. New York: Hill and Wang, 1972. Print.

Baucom, Ian. "Afterword: States of Time." *Contemporary Literature* 49.4 (2008): 712–18. Print.

– *Out of Place: Englishness, Empire, and the Locations of Identity*. Princeton, NJ: Princeton University Press, 1999. Print.

Bazin, Germain. "Les échanges franco-espagnols." *Revue des Beaux-Arts de France* 11 (1942–43): 3–12. Print.

Bear, Laura. *Lines of the Nation: Indian Railway Workers, Bureaucracy, and the Intimate Historical Self*. New York: Columbia University Press, 2007. Print.

Beckett, Samuel. *Comment c'est*. Paris: Éditions de minuit, 1961. Print.

– *Comment c'est et L'image: Une édition critico-génétique / How It Is and L'image: A Critical-Genetic Edition*. Ed. Edouard Magessa O'Reilly. New York: Routledge, 2001. Print.

– *How It Is*. London: John Calder, 1964. Print.

– *The Letters of Samuel Beckett, 1957–1965*. Vol. 3. Ed. George Craig, Martha Dow Fehsenfeld, Dan Gunn, and Lois More Overbeck. Cambridge: Cambridge University Press, 2014. Print.

Beigbeder, Yves. *Judging War Crimes and Torture: French Justice and International Criminal Tribunals and Commissions (1940–2005)*. Leiden: Martinus Nighoff, 2006. Print.

Bendib, Khalil. "Algerian Memories: An Interview with Henri Alleg." Arab Studies Institute. *Jadaliyya* (2007). http://www.jadaliyya.com/pages/index/13556/algerian-memories_an-interview-with-henri-alleg. Web.

Benhabib, Seyla. *The Reluctant Modernism of Hannah Arendt*. Lanham, MD: Rowman and Littlefield, 2003. Print.

Benjamin, Walter. *Charles Baudelaire: A Lyric Poet in the Era of High Capitalism*. Trans. Harry Zohn. London: Verso, 1983. Print.

Bentham, Jeremy. *Anarchical Fallacies* in *"Nonsense upon Stilts": Bentham, Burke, and Marx on the Rights of Man*. Ed. Jeremy Waldron. London: Methuen, 1987. Print.

Bergonzi, Bernard. *A Study in Greene: Graham Greene and the Art of the Novel*. Oxford: Oxford University Press, 2006. Print.

Berlant, Lauren. *The Female Complaint: The Unfinished Business of Sentimentality in American Culture*. Durham, NC: Duke University Press, 2008. Print.

Bewes, Timothy. "Against Exemplarity: W.G. Sebald and the Problem of Connection." *Contemporary Literature* 55.1 (2014): 1–31. Print.

Bezner, Lili Corbus. *Photography and Politics in America: From the New Deal into the Cold War*. Baltimore: Johns Hopkins University Press, 1999. Print.

Bhabha, Homi K. "Of Mimicry and Man." *The Location of Culture*. New York: Routledge, 1995. 121–31. Print.

Bird, Kai, and Lawrence Lifschultz. *Hiroshima's Shadow: Writings on the Denial of History and the Smithsonian Controversy*. Stony Creek, CT: Pamphleteer's Press, 1998. Print.

Borgwardt, Elizabeth. "FDR's Four Freedoms as a Human Rights Instrument." *OAH Magazine of History* 22.2 (2008): 8–13. Print.

Borstelmann, Thomas. *The Cold War and the Color Line: American Race Relations in the Global Arena*. Cambridge, MA: Harvard University Press, 2003. Print.

Bowen, Elizabeth. *The Mulberry Tree*. Ed. Hermione Lee. New York: Harcourt, 1986. Print.

Boyer, Paul S. *By the Bomb's Early Light: American Thought and Culture at the Dawn of the Nuclear Age*. Chapel Hill: University of North Carolina Press, 1994. Print.

Bratton, Jacky, Jim Cook, and Christine Gledhill. "Introduction." Bratton, Cook, and Gledhill 1–8. Print.

– eds. *Melodrama: Stage, Picture, Screen*. London: British Film Institute, 1994. Print.

Breitwieser, Mitchell. "Materializing Calloway: The Sorrows of Occupation in *The Third Man*." *Hopkins Review* 3.1 (2008): 437–68. Print.

British Nationality Act 1948. www.legislation.gov.uk/ukpga/1948/56%20/ukpga_19480056_eng. Web.

Broad, Roger. *Conscription in Britain, 1939–1964: The Militarization of a Generation*. New York: Routledge, 2006. Print.

Brooks, Peter. "Melodrama, Body, Revolution." Bratton, Cook, and Gledhill 11–24. Print.

– *The Melodramatic Imagination: Balzac, Henry James, Melodrama, and the Mode of Excess*. New York: Columbia University Press, 1985. Print.

Brown, Wendy. *Politics Out of History*. Princeton, NJ: Princeton University Press, 2001. Print.

– "Women's Studies Unbound: Mourning, Revolution, Politics." *parallax* 9.2 (2003): 3–16. Web.

Burgess, Anthony. *A Clockwork Orange*. New York: Norton, 1986. Print.

Burke, D., and N.R. Farbman. "The Bushmen: An Ancient Race Struggles to Survive in the South African Deserts." *LIFE* (3 February 1947): 40–8. Web.

Butler, Judith. *Precarious Life: The Powers of Mourning and Violence*. London: Verso, 2004. Print.

Calder, Angus. *The People's War: Britain 1939–45*. London: Cape, 1969. Print.

Carlston, Erin G. *Double Agents: Espionage, Literature, and Liminal Citizens*. New York: Columbia University Press, 2013. Print.

Chandler, James. "On the Face of the Case: Conrad, *Lord Jim*, and the Sentimental Novel." *Critical Inquiry* 33.4 (2007): 837–64. Print.

Cheng, Chu-chueh. "Making and Marketing Kazuo Ishiguro's Alterity." *Post-Identity* 4.2 (2005). Web.

Chow, Rey. *Writing Diaspora: Tactics of Intervention in Contemporary Cultural Studies*. Bloomington: Indiana University Press, 1993. Print.

Churchill, Winston S. "The General Election." *Listener* (7 June 1945): 629–32. Web.

Coetzee, J.M. "Confession and Double Thoughts: Tolstoy, Rousseau, Dostoevsky." *Doubling the Point: Essays and Interviews*. Ed. David Attwell. Cambridge, MA: Harvard University Press, 1992. 251–93. Print.

– *Disgrace*. New York: Penguin, 1999. Print.

– *Life and Times of Michael K.* New York: Penguin, 1983. Print.

Connor, Steven. "Beckett and Sartre: The Nauseous Character of All Flesh." *Beckett and Phenomenology*. Ed. Ulrika Maude and Matthew Feldman. London: Continuum, 2009. 56–76. Print.

Conrad, Joseph. *The Collected Letters of Joseph Conrad*. Vol. 3. Ed. Frederick R. Karl and Laurence Davies. Cambridge: Cambridge University Press, 1988. Print.

– *The Secret Agent: A Simple Tale*. Ed. John Lyon. 1907. Oxford: Oxford World's Classics, 2008. Print.

– *Under Western Eyes*. 1911. London: Penguin, 1985. Print.

Constitution of Ireland. archive.constitution.ie/reports/ConstitutionofIreland.pdf. Web.

Constitution of Japan. http://japan.kantei.go.jp. Web.

Constitution of UNESCO. portal.unesco.org/en/ev.php. Web.

Convention Relating to the Status of Refugees. www.unhcr.org/3b66c2aa10.html. Web.

Cordle, Daniel. *States of Suspense: The Nuclear Age, Postmodernism and United States Fiction and Prose.* Manchester: Manchester University Press, 2008. Print.

Crawford, Alice. *Paradise Pursued: The Novels of Rose Macaulay*. Madison, NJ: Fairleigh Dickinson University Press, 1995. Print.

Crossman, Richard H., ed. *The God That Failed*. 1950. New York: Columbia University Press, 2001. Print.

Cvetkovich, Ann. *Mixed Feelings: Feminism, Mass Culture, and Victorian Sensationalism*. New Brunswick, NJ: Rutgers University Press, 1992. Print.

DaCosta, Kimberly McClain. *Making Multiracials: State, Family, and Market in the Redrawing of the Color Line*. Stanford, CA: Stanford University Press, 2007. Print.

De Beauvoir, Simone, and Gisèle Halimi. *Djamila Boupacha*. Paris: Gallimard, 1962. Print.

De la pacification à la répression, le dossier Jean Müller. Cahiers de Témoignage chrétien 38. Paris: Éditions du Témoignage chrétien, 1957. Print.

Declaration of Independence. www.archives.gov/exhibits/charters/declaration_transcript.html. Web.

Declaration of the Rights of Man and of the Citizen. www.conseil-constitutionnel.fr/conseil-constitutionnel/root/bank_mm/anglais/cst2.pdf. Web.

Dell'Orto, Giovanna. "'Memory and Imagination Are the Great Deterrents': Martha Gellhorn at War as Correspondent and Literary Author." *Journal of American Culture* 27.3 (2004): 303–14. Web.

Derrida, Jacques. *Rogues: Two Essays on Reason*. Trans. Pascale-Anne Brault and Michael Naas. Stanford, CA: Stanford University Press, 2005. Print.

Dinshaw, Carolyn. *How Soon Is Now? Medieval Texts, Amateur Readers, and the Queerness of Time*. Durham, NC: Duke University Press, 2012. Print.

Dinshaw Carolyn, et al. "Theorizing Queer Temporalities: A Roundtable Discussion." *GLQ* 13.2–3 (2007): 177–95. Print.

Dirlik, Arif. "The Predicament of Marxist Revolutionary Consciousness: Mao Zedong, Antonio Gramsci, and the Reformulation of Marxist Revolutionary Theory." *Modern China* 9.2 (1983): 182–211. Web.

Dixon, Robert. "'Turning a Place into a Field': Shirley Hazzard's *The Great Fire* and Cold War Area Studies." *Reading across the Pacific: Australia – United States Intellectual Histories*. Ed. Robert Dixon and Nicholas Birns. Sydney: Sydney University Press, 2010. 265–79. Print.

Donaghy, Henry J., ed. *Conversations with Graham Greene*. Jackson: University Press of Mississippi, 1992. Print.

Dower, John. *Cultures of War: Pearl Harbor/Hiroshima/9-11/Iraq*. New York: Norton, 2010. Print.

– *Embracing Defeat: Japan in the Wake of World War II*. New York: Norton, 2000. Print.

Drake, David. "Jean-Paul Sartre and the Algerian War of Independence, 1954–1962." *Bulletin of Francophone Africa* 14 (1999–2000): 105–19. Print.

Driskill, Qwo-Li. "Map of the Americas." *Walking with Ghosts*. Cambridge: Salt, 2005. 9–11. Print.

Dudziak, Mary. *Cold War Civil Rights: Race and the Image of American Democracy*. New ed. Princeton, NJ: Princeton University Press, 2011. Print.

Eagleton, Terry. *The Ideology of the Aesthetic*. Cambridge, MA: Blackwell, 1990. Print.

Eiji, Takemae. *Inside GHQ: The Allied Occupation of Japan and Its Legacy*. Trans. Robert Ricketts and Sebastian Swann. New York: Continuum, 2002. Print.

Elam, Michelle. *The Souls of Mixed Folk: Race, Politics, and Aesthetics in the New Millennium*. Stanford, CA: Stanford University Press, 2011. Print.

Esty, Jed. *Unseasonable Youth: Modernism, Colonialism, and the Fiction of Development.* New York: Oxford University Press, 2012. Print.

European Convention on Human Rights. 1950. www.echr.coe.int/Documents/Collection_Convention_1950_ENG.pdf. Web.

Falk, Quentin. *Travels in Greeneland: The Cinema of Graham Greene*. London: Quartet, 1984. Print.

Fanon, Frantz. *The Wretched of the Earth*. Trans. Richard Philcox. New York: Grove, 2004. Print.

Fassin, Didier. "Humanitarianism as a Politics of Life." *Public Culture* 19.3 (2007): 499–520. Print.

Felski, Rita. "Critique and the Hermeneutics of Suspicion." *M/C Journal* 15.1 (2011). Web.

Firpo, Christina E. *"Abandoned" Children into "Little Frenchmen": Child Removals in Colonial Indochina, 1870–1982*. Forthcoming.

Fisher, Philip. *Hard Facts: Setting and Form in the American Novel*. New York: Oxford University Press, 1985. Print.

Forché, Carolyn, ed. *Against Forgetting: Twentieth-Century Poetry of Witness*. New York: Norton, 1993. Print.

– "Twentieth-Century Poetry of Witness." *American Poetry Review* 22.2 (1993): 9–16. Print.

– and Duncan Wu. *Poetry of Witness: The Tradition in English, 1500–2001*. New York: Norton, 2014. Print.

Foster, Hal. "The 'Primitive' Unconscious of Modern Art." *October* 34 (1985). 45–70. Print.

Foucault, Michel. *Abnormal: Lectures at the Collège de France*. Trans. Graham Burchell. New York: Picador, 2004. Print.

– *Discipline and Punish: The Birth of the Prison*. Trans. Alan Sheridan. New York: Vintage, 1995. Print.

– *The History of Sexuality. Volume 1: An Introduction*. Trans. Robert Hurley. New York: Vintage, 1980. Print.

– *Power/Knowledge: Selected Interviews and Other Writings, 1972–1977*. Ed. Colin Gordon. Trans. Colin Gordon, Leo Marshall, John Mepham, Kate Soper. New York: Pantheon, 1980. Print.

– *Power: The Essential Works of Foucault, 1954–1984, Vol 3*. Ed. James D. Faubion. Trans. Robert Hurley. New York: New Press, 2001. Print.

– *Wrong-Doing, Truth-Telling: The Function of Avowal in Justice*. 1981. Ed. Fabienne Brion and Bernard E. Harcourt. Trans. Stephen W. Sawyer. Chicago: University of Chicago Press, 2014. Print.

Freeman, Elizabeth. "Time Binds, or, Erotohistoriography." *Social Text* 23.3–4 (2005): 57–68.

Fryer, Peter. *Staying Power: The History of Black People in Britain*. London: Pluto Press, 1984. Print.

Gandhi, Leela, and Deborah L. Nelson. "Editors' Introduction." *Critical Inquiry* 40.4 (2014): 285–97. Print.

Garb, Tamar. "Rethinking Sekula from the Global South: Humanist Photography Revisited." *Grey Room* 55 (2014): 34–57. Print.

Garrity, Jane. *Step-Daughters of England: British Women Modernists and the National Imaginary*. New York: Manchester University Press, 2003. Print.

Gasiorek, Andrzej. "Rendering Justice to the Visible World: History, Politics and National Identity in the Novels of Graham Greene." *British Fiction after Modernism*. Ed. Marina MacKay and Lyndsey Stonebridge. New York: Palgrave Macmillan, 2007. 17–32. Print.

Gillman, Susan. *Blood Talk: American Race Melodrama and the Culture of the Occult*. Chicago: University of Chicago Press, 2003. Print.

Glover, David. *Literature, Immigration, and Diaspora in Fin-de-siècle England: A Cultural History of the 1905 Aliens Act*. Cambridge: Cambridge University Press, 2012. Print.

Goldberg, Elizabeth Swanson, and Alexandra Schultheis Moore. "Human Rights and Literature: The Development of an Interdiscipline." Goldberg and Moore 1–16. Print.

Goldberg, Elizabeth Swanson, and Alexandra Schultheis Moore, eds. *Theoretical Perspectives on Human Rights and Literature*. New York: Routledge, 2012. Print.

– "Meditations on a Fractured Terrain: Human Rights and Literature." *College Literature* 40.3 (2013): 15–37. Print.

Golding, William. *Lord of the Flies*. London: Faber, 1954. Print.

Green, Henry. *Caught*. 1943. London: Harvill, 1991. Print.

– *Concluding*. 1948. London: Harvill, 1997. Print.

– "Unloving." *Surviving: The Uncollected Writings of Henry Green*. Ed. Matthew Yorke. London: Chatto and Windus, 1992. 280–3. Print.

Greene, Graham. *A Sort of Life*. New York: Simon and Schuster, 1971. Print.

– *The Comedians*. London: Bodley Head, 1966. Print.

– *The End of the Affair*. 1951. London: Penguin, 1962. Print.

– *The Heart of the Matter*. 1948. London: William Heinemann, 1971. Print.

– *The Ministry of Fear*. 1943. London: Penguin, 2001. Print.

– *The Third Man*. *The Portable Graham Greene*. Ed. Philip Stratford. 1949. New York: Penguin, 2005. Print.

Greene, Richard, ed. *Graham Greene: A Life in Letters*. London: Little, Brown, 2007. Print.

Hall, Stuart. "Minimal Selves." *Black British Cultural Studies: A Reader*. Ed. Houston Baker et al. Chicago: University of Chicago Press, 1996. 114–19. Print.

Han, Suyin. *A Many-Splendoured Thing*. 1952. London: Cape, 1954. Print.

– *A Mortal Flower: China | Autobiography | History*. London: Cape, 1966. Print.

– *Birdless Summer: China | Autobiography | History*. London: Cape, 1968. Print.

– *The Crippled Tree: China | Biography, History | Autobiography*. 1965. London: Cape, 1966. Print.

– *My House Has Two Doors: China | Autobiography | History*. London: Cape, 1980. Print.

Hankins, Gabriel. "Typewriter Romances at the Secretariat: Internationalist Feminism, Paperwork, and World Governance between the Wars." Working paper, 2014.

Harman, Claire. "Introduction." Sylvia Townsend Warner, *The Corner That Held Them*, i–viii.

– *Sylvia Townsend Warner: A Biography*. London: Chatto and Windus, 1989. Print.

Hartley, Jenny. *Millions Like Us: British Fiction of the Second World War*. London: Virago, 1997. Print.

Hazzard, Shirley. *The Great Fire*. London: Virago, 2003. Print.

Henriques, Henry Straus. *Aliens Act, 1905* in *The Laws of Aliens and Naturalization*. London: Butterworth, 1906. 185–92. archive.org. https://archive.org/stream/lawofaliensnaturoohenruoft#page/184/mode/2up. Web.

Hensher, Philip. "Distant Voices, Small Lives." *Telegraph* (3 June 2006). http://www.telegraph.co.uk/culture/books/3652885/Distant-voices-small-lives.html. Web.

Hepburn, Allan. *Intrigue: Espionage and Culture*. New Haven, CT: Yale University Press, 2005. Print.

Hersey, John. *Hiroshima*. Harmondsworth and New York: Penguin, 1946. Print.

Hershatter, Gail. "The Subaltern Talks Back: Reflections on Subaltern Theory and Chinese History." *positions* 1.1 (1993): 103–30. Web.

Hesford, Victoria. *Feeling Women's Liberation*. Durham, NC: Duke University Press, 2013. Print.

Heyns, Michiel. "The Whole Country's Truth: Confession and Narrative in Recent White South African Writing." *Modern Fiction Studies* 46.1 (2000): 42–66. Print.

Houen, Alex. *Terrorism and Modern Literature, from Joseph Conrad to Ciaran Carson*. Oxford: Oxford University Press, 2002. Print.

Howard, Anthony. "'We Are the Masters Now.'" *Age of Austerity*. Ed. Michael Sissons and Philip French. Oxford: Oxford University Press, 1986. 1–20. Print.

Hugo, Victor. *L'homme qui rit. Oeuvres complètes*. Vol. 8. 1868. Paris. Éditions Rencontre, 1967. Print.

Hune-Brown, Nicholas. "Mixie Me." *Toronto Life* (March 2013). Web.

Hunt, Lynn. *Inventing Human Rights: A History*. New York: Norton, 2007. Print.

Ignatieff, Michael. "State Failure and Nation-Building." *Humanitarian Intervention: Ethical, Legal and Political Dilemmas*. Ed. J.L. Holzgrefe, Robert O. Keohane. Cambridge: Cambridge University Press, 2003. 299–321. Print.

Inoue, Kyoko. *MacArthur's Japanese Constitution: A Linguistic and Cultural Study of Its Making*. Chicago: University of Chicago Press, 1991. Print.

Ishiguro, Kazuo. *A Pale View of Hills*. London: Faber, 1982. Print.

– *An Artist of the Floating World*. New York: Vintage, 1989. Print.

Jameson, Fredric. *The Antinomies of Realism*. London and New York: Verso, 2013. Print.

Johnson, M. Glen. "The Contribution of Eleanor and Franklin Roosevelt to the Development of International Protection for Human Rights." *Human Rights Quarterly* 9 (1987): 19–48. Print.

Judt, Tony. *Postwar: A History of Europe since 1945*. New York: Penguin, 2005. Print.

Kaplan, E. Ann. *Motherhood and Representation: The Mother in Popular Culture and Melodrama*. London: Routledge, 1992. Print.

Karl, Rebecca. *Staging the World: Chinese Nationalism at the Turn of the Century*. Durham, NC: Duke University Press, 2002. Print.

Kenniston, Ann, and Jeffrey Gray. Introduction. "Saying What Happened in the 21st Century." *The New American Poetry of Engagement: A 21st-Century Anthology*. Ed. Ann Kenniston and Jeffrey Gray. Jefferson, NC: MacFarland, 2012. 1–15. Print.

Kerson, D.L.A. "The European Convention for the Protection of Human Rights and Fundamental Freedoms." *California Law Review* 49.1 (1961): 172–86. Print.

King, Desmond J., and Jeremy Waldron. "Citizenship, Social Citizenship and the Defence of Welfare Provision." *British Journal of Political Science* 18.4 (1988): 415–43. Print.

Kleinman, Arthur, and Joan Kleinman. "Suffering and Its Professional Transformation: Toward an Ethnography of Interpersonal Experience." *Culture, Medicine, and Psychiatry* 15.3 (1991): 275–301. Web.

Knox, Ronald. *God and the Atom*. London: Sheed and Ward, 1945. Print.

Koestler, Arthur. *Darkness at Noon*. Trans. Daphne Hardy. 1941. New York: Scribner, 1968. Print.

Krog, Antjie. *Country of My Skull: Guilt, Sorrow, and the Limits of Forgiveness in the New South Africa*. New York: Random House, 1998. Print.

Kynaston, David. *Austerity Britain, 1945–51*. London: Bloomsbury, 2007. Print.

Land, Stephen K. *The Human Imperative: A Study of the Novels of Graham Greene*. New York: AMS, 2008. Print.

Ledent, Bénédict. "Only Connect: An Interview with Caryl Phillips on *Foreigners*." *Conversations with Caryl Phillips*. Ed. Rénee Schatteman. Jackson: University Press of Mississippi, 2009. 184–91. Print.

Leen, Nina. "An American Family in Trouble." *LIFE* (26 July 1948): 83–91. Print.

LeFanu, Sarah. *Rose Macaulay*. London: Virago, 2003. Print.

Lehmann, Rosamond. "An Absolute Gift." *Times Literary Supplement* (6 August 1954): 508. Print.

Lepenies, Wolf. *Between Literature and Science: The Rise of Sociology*. Trans. R.J. Hollingdale. Cambridge: Cambridge University Press, 1988. Print.

Lesser, Wendy. "From Dickens to Conrad: A Sentimental Journey." *ELH* 52.1 (1985): 185–208. Print.

Lessing, Doris. *The Golden Notebook*. New York: Bantam, 1962. Print.

Levine, Marilyn A. *The Found Generation: Chinese Communists in Europe during the Twenties*. Seattle: University of Washington Press, 1993. Print.

Lewis, Barry. *Kazuo Ishiguro*. Manchester: Manchester University Press, 2000.

Lewis, C.S. *That Hideous Strength*. New York: Scribner, 2003. Print.

Lieberman, Sally Taylor. "Visions and Lessons: 'China' in Feminist Theory-Making, 1966–1977." *Michigan Feminist Studies* 6 (1991): 91–107. Web.

Liu, Lydia H. "Shadows of Universalism: The Untold Story of Human Rights around 1948." *Critical Inquiry* 40.4 (2014): 385–417. Print.

Lombroso, Cesare. *Criminal Man*. Ed. Mary Gibson and Nicole Hahn Rafter. Durham, NC: Duke University Press, 2006. Print.

Lord Goldsmith, QC. "Citizenship: Our Common Bond." United Kingdom Ministry of Justice. (2008): 10–12. http://image.guardian.co.uk/sys-files/Politics/documents/2008/03/11/citizenship-report-full.pdf. Web.

Lu, Catherine. "Humanitarian Intervention: Moral Ambition and Political Constraints." *International Journal* 62.4 (2007): 942–51. Print.

– *Just and Unjust Interventions in World Politics: Public and Private*. 2006. London: Palgrave Macmillan, 2011. Print.

Lukács, Georg. *The Historical Novel*. Trans. Hannah and Stanley Mitchell. Lincoln and London: University of Nebraska Press, 1962, 1983. Print.

Macardle, Dorothy. *Children of Europe: A Study of the Children of Liberated Countries: Their War-time Experiences, Their Reactions, and Their Needs, with a Note on Germany*. Boston: Beacon, 1951. Print.

Macaulay, Rose. *Crewe Train*. 1926. London: Virago, 1998. Print.

– "The Fifth Freedom: Getting About." Undated Manuscript (ca. 1945), ERM8(22), Trinity College Archives, Cambridge, UK.

– *Letters to a Friend, 1950–1952*. Ed. Constance Babbington Smith. London: Collins, 1961. Print.

– *Letters to a Sister*. Ed. Constance Babbington Smith. New York: Atheneum, 1964. Print.

– *The World My Wilderness*. London: Collins, 1950. Print.

Madsen, Mikael Rask. "From Cold War Instrument to Supreme European Court: The European Court of Human Rights at the Crossroads of International and National Law and Politics." *Law and Social Inquiry* 32.1 (2007): 137–59. Print.

Makley, Charlene. "'Speaking Bitterness': Autobiography, History, and Mnemonic Politics on the Sino-Tibetan Frontier." *Comparative Studies in Society and History* 47.1 (2005): 40–78. Web.

Mann, Michael. "The Autonomous Power of the State: Its Origins, Mechanisms and Results." *States in History*. Ed. John A. Hall. Oxford: Blackwell, 1986. 109–36. Print.

– *The Sources of Social Power, Vol. II: The Rise of Classes and Nation–States, 1760–1914*. Cambridge: Cambridge University Press, 1993. Print.

Mansfield, Nick. "Human Rights as Violence and Enigma: Can Literature Really Be of Any Help with the Politics of Human Rights?" Goldberg and Moore 201–14. Print.

Mao, Zedong. "Talks at the Yan'an Forum on Literature and Art." *Modern Chinese Literary Thought: Writings on Literature 1893–1945*. Ed. Kirk A. Denton. Stanford, CA: Stanford University Press, 1996. 458–84. Print.

"Maquis." *Oxford English Dictionary*. 3rd ed. www.oed.com. Web.

Marrou, Henri. "France ma patrie." *Le Monde* (5 April 1956). http://ldh-toulon.net/Henri-Marrou-France-ma-patrie.html. Web.

Matthews, Sean, and Sebastian Groes, eds. *Kazuo Ishiguro: New Critical Perspectives*. London: Continuum, 2009. Print.

Mauriac, François. "La question." *L'Express* (15 January 1955). www.lexpress.fr/actualite/monde/afrique/algerie-des-1955-francois-mauriac-denoncait-la-torture-dans-l-express_1201581.html. Web.

Mbembe, Achille. "Necropolitics." Trans. Libby Meintjes. *Public Culture* 15.1 (2003): 11–40. Print.

McGrath, Melanie. *Hopping: An East End Family at Work and Play*. London: Fourth Estate, 2010. Print.

Mellor, Leo. *Reading the Ruins: Modernism, Bombsites and British Culture*. Cambridge: Cambridge University Press, 2011. Print.

Miller, Tyrus. "Beckett's Political Technology: Expression, Confession, and Torture in the Later Drama." *Samuel Beckett Today / Aujourd'hui* 9 (2000): 255–78. Print.

Milosz, Czeslaw. *The Captive Mind*. 1953. Trans. Jane Zielonko. New York: Vintage, 1981. Print.

Mission to Haiti: Report of the United Nations Mission of Technical Assistance to the Republic of Haiti. Lake Success, NY: United Nations Publications, 1949. Print.

Mitchell, Timothy. "The Limits of the State: Beyond Statist Approaches and Their Critics." *American Political Science Review* 85.1 (1991): 77–96. Print.

Moffitt, John F. *Art Forgery: The Case of the Lady of Elche*. Gainesville: University Press of Florida, 1995. Print.

Molaskey, Michael S. *The American Occupation of Japan and Okinawa: Literature and Memory*. New York: Routledge, 1999. Print.

Montefiore, Janet. "Englands Ancient and Modern: Sylvia Townsend Warner, T.H. White and the Fictions of Medieval Englishness." *Intermodernism: Literary Culture in Mid-Twentieth-Century Britain*. Ed. Kristen Bluemel. Edinburgh: Edinburgh University Press, 2009. 38–55. Print.

Moretti, Franco. *The Way of the World: The Bildungsroman in European Culture*. 2nd ed. New York: Verso, 2000. Print.

Morris-Suzuki, Tessa. *A History of Japanese Economic Thought*. New York: Routledge, 1989. Print.

Morton, Stephen. *States of Emergency: Colonialism, Literature and Law*. Liverpool: Liverpool University Press, 2013. Print.

Mulford, Wendy. *This Narrow Place: Sylvia Townsend Warner and Valentine Ackland: Life, Letters, and Politics, 1930–1951*. London: Pandora, 1988. Print.

Nadel, Alan. *Containment Culture: American Narratives, Postmodernism, and the Atomic Age*. Durham, NC: Duke University Press, 1995. Print.

Nadelhaft, Jerome. "The Somersett Case and Slavery: Myth, Reality, and Repercussions." *Journal of Negro History* 51.3 (July 1966): 193–208. Print.

Naipaul, V.S. *The Mimic Men*. New York: Knopf, 2001. Print.

Nava, Mica. *Visceral Cosmopolitanism: Gender, Culture, and the Normalisation of Difference*. Oxford: Berg, 2007. Print.

– "Visceral Cosmopolitanism: The Specificity of Race and Miscegenation in UK." *Politics and Culture* 3 (2003). Web.

Newby, P.H. *The Novel 1945–1950*. London: Longmans Green, 1951. Print.

Ngai, Sianne. *Ugly Feelings*. Cambridge, MA: Harvard University Press, 2005. Print.

Ngũgĩ wa Thiong'o. *A Grain of Wheat*. London: Heinemann, 1967. Print.

Nohrnberg, Peter. "'I Wish He'd Never Been to School': Stevie, Newspapers, and the Reader in *The Secret Agent*." *Conradiana* 35 (2003): 49–61. Print.

Norris, Margot. *Writing War in the Twentieth Century*. Charlottesville: University of Virginia Press, 2000. Print.

Nussbaum, Martha C. *Poetic Justice: The Literary Imagination and Public Life*. Boston: Beacon, 1995. Print.

O'Reilly, Edouard Magessa. "Introduction française." *Comment c'est et L'image: Une édition critico-génétique / How It Is and L'image: A Critical-Genetic Edition*. xxxvii–lxiv. Print.

Olubas, Brigitta. *Shirley Hazzard: Literary Expatriate and Cosmopolitan Humanist*. Amherst, NY: Cambria, 2012. Print.

Orwell, George. *1984*. 1949. New York: Penguin, 1977. Print.

– "To Michael Meyer." *George Orwell: A Life in Letters*. Ed. Peter Davison. London: Harvill Secker, 2010. 450–51. Print.

– "The Politics of the English Language." *Why I Write*. New York: Penguin, 2005. 102–20. Print.

Parekh, Bhikhi. "Rethinking Humanitarian Intervention." *International Political Science Review* 18.1 (1997): 49–69. Print.

Péju, Marcel. *Le procès du réseau Jeanson*. Paris: Éditions Français Maspero, 1961. Print.

Perry, Elizabeth J. "Moving the Masses: Emotion Work in the Chinese Revolution." *Mobilization* 7.2 (2002): 111–28. Web.

Phillips, Caryl. *Foreigners*. New York: Vintage, 2007. Print.

Phillips, Christopher. "The Judgment Seat of Photography." *October* 22 (1982): 27–63. Print.

Phillips, Gene. *Graham Greene: The Films of His Fiction*. New York: Columbia University Press, 1974. Print.

Piette, Adam. "The Fictions of Nuclear War, from Hiroshima to Vietnam." *The Edinburgh Companion to Twentieth-Century British and American War Literature*. Ed. Piette and Mark Rowlandson. Edinburgh: Edinburgh University Press, 2012. 160–71. Print.

– *The Literary Cold War: 1945 to Vietnam*. Edinburgh: Edinburgh University Press, 2009. Print.

– "Muriel Spark and the Politics of the Contemporary." *The Edinburgh Companion to Muriel Spark*. Ed. Michael Gardiner and Willy Maley. Edinburgh: Edinburgh University Press, 2010. 52–62. Print.

Pong, Beryl. "The Archaeology of Postwar Childhood in Rose Macaulay's *The World My Wilderness*." *Journal of Modern Literature* 37.3 (2014): 92–110. Print.

Potter, Rachel, and Lyndsey Stonebridge. "Writing and Rights." *Critical Quarterly* 56.4 (2014): 1–16. Print.

Povinelli, Elizabeth A. *The Empire of Love: Toward a Theory of Intimacy, Genealogy, and Carnality*. Durham, NC: Duke University Press, 2006. Print.

Power, Eileen. *Medieval English Nunneries, c. 1275–1535*. Cambridge: Cambridge University Press, 1922. Print.

"Preparatory Work on Article 3 of the European Convention of Human Rights" (22 May 196). http://www.echr.coe.int/LibraryDocs/Travaux/ECHRTravaux-ART3-DH(56)5-EN1674940.pdf. Web.

Raven, Simon. "Heavens Below." Rev. of *The Girls of Slender Means*. *Spectator* (20 September 1963): 354. Print.

Reichman, Ravit. *The Affective Life of Law: Legal Modernism and the Literary Imagination*. Stanford, CA: Stanford University Press, 2009. Print.

Reiss, Tom. "The True Classic of Terrorism." *New York Times* (11 September 2005). http://www.nytimes.com/2005/09/11/books/review/11reiss.html?pagewanted=all&_r=0. Web.

"Report to the National Security Council by the Executive Secretary (Lay)." Foreign Relations of the United States, 1952–1954, Volume 11, Part 2. Ed. Lisle A. Rose and Neal H. Peterson. Washington: Government Printing Office, 1983. Document 355. Print.

Rice, Alan. "A Home for Ourselves in the World: Caryl Phillips on Slave Forts and Manillas as African Atlantic Sites of Memory." *Atlantic Studies: Global Currents* 9.3 (2012): 363–72. Print.

Richardot, Jean B. "Technical Assistance Board Activities in Haiti (January to September 1962)." New York: United Nations, 1962. Print.

Richards, J.M., ed. *The Bombed Buildings of Britain*. Notes by John Summerson. Rev. ed. London: Architectural Press, 1947. Print.

Roberts, John. *The Art of Interruption: Realism, Photography, and the Everyday*. Manchester: Manchester University Press, 1998. Print.

Rockefeller, Nelson A. "ADDRESS BY THE HONORABLE NELSON A. ROCKEFELLER Special Assistant to the President of the United States at the Preview of THE FAMILY OF MAN." New York: Museum of Modern Art, 24 January 1955. Web.

Rofel, Lisa. *Other Modernities: Gendered Yearnings in China after Socialism*. Berkeley: University of California Press, 1999. Print.

Rose, Nikolas. *The Politics of Life Itself: Biomedicine, Power, and Subjectivity in the Twenty-First Century*. Princeton, NJ: Princeton University Press, 2007. Print.

– *The Psychological Complex: Psychology, Politics and Society in England, 1869–1939*. London: Routledge, 1985. Print.

Rose, Sonya O. *Which People's War? National Identity and Citizenship in Britain 1939–1945*. Oxford: Oxford University Press, 2003. Print.

Saada, Emmanuelle. *Empire's Children: Race, Filiation, and Citizenship in the French Colonies*. Trans. Arthur Goldhammer. Chicago: University of Chicago Press, 2012. Print.

Salih, Sara. *Representing Mixed Race in Jamaica and England from the Abolition Era to the Present*. New York: Routledge, 2011. Print.

Sandeen, Eric. "The Family of Man on the Road to Moscow." *The Cold War: Cold War Culture and Society*. Ed. Lori Lyn Bogle. New York: Routledge, 2001. 57–71. Print.

– *Picturing an Exhibition: The Family of Man and 1950s America*. Albuquerque: University of New Mexico Press, 1995. Print.

– "'The Show You See with Your Heart': The Family of Man on Tour in the Cold War World." *"The Family of Man," 1955–2001: Humanismus und Postmoderne; eine Revision von Edward Steichens Fotoausstellung ("The Family of Man," 1955–2001: Humanism and Postmodernism: A Reappraisal of the Photo Exhibition by Edward Steichen)*. Ed. Jean Back and Viktoria Schmidt-Linsenhoff. Marburg, Germany: Jonas, 2004. 101–19. Print.

Sanders, Mark. *Ambiguities of Witnessing: Law and Literature in a Time of a Truth Commission*. Stanford, CA: Stanford University Press, 2007. Print.

Sartre, Jean-Paul. "Colonialisme et néo-colonialisme." *Situations V*: 23–48. Print.

– "Nous sommes tous des assassins." *Situations V*: 68–71. Print.

– Rev. of Albert Memmi, *Portrait du colonisé* and *Portrait du colonisateur*. *Situations V*: 49–56. Print.

– *Situations V*. Paris: Gallimard, 1964. Print.

– "Une victoire.'" *La question*: 99–122. Trans. John Calder. Preface Jean-Paul Sartre. In Alleg xxvii–xliv. Print.

– "Vous êtes formidables." *Situations V*: 57–67. Print.

Sauerber, Lars Ole. *Secret Agents in Fiction: Ian Fleming, John le Carré and Len Deighton*. London: Macmillan, 1984. Print.

Scarry, Elaine. *The Body in Pain: The Making and Unmaking of the World*. Oxford: Oxford University Press, 1985. Print.

Schama, Simon. *Citizens: A Chronicle of the French Revolution*. Toronto: Vintage, 1989. Print.

Schindler, Dietrich. "European Convention on Human Rights in Practice." *Washington University Law Review* 2 (1962): 152–65. Print.

Scott, James C. *Seeing Like a State: How Certain Conditions to Improve the Human Condition Have Failed*. New Haven, CT: Yale University Press, 1998. Print.

Seed, David. "Spy Fiction." *The Cambridge Companion to Crime Fiction*. Ed. Martin Priestman. Cambridge: Cambridge University Press, 2003. 115–34. Print.

Seiler, Claire. "The Mid-Century Method of *The Great Fire*." *Shirley Hazzard: New Critical Essays*. Ed. Brigitta Olubas. Sydney: Sydney University Press, 2014. 97–110. Print.

Sekula, Allan. "Between the Net and the Deep Blue Sea (Rethinking the Traffic in Photographs)." *October* 102 (2002): 3–34. Print.

– "The Traffic in Photographs." *Art Journal* 41.1 (1981): 15–25. Print.

Sen, Amryta. "Elements of a Theory of Human Rights." *Philosophy and Public Affairs* 32.4 (2004): 315–56. Print.

Sexton, Jared. *Amalgamation Schemes: Antiblackness and the Critique of Multiracialism*. Minneapolis: University of Minnesota Press, 2008. Print.

Sheehan, Paul. "A World without Monsters: Beckett and the Ethics of Cruelty." *Beckett and Ethics*. Ed. Russell Smith. London: Continuum, 2009. 86–101. Print.

Sherif, Ann. "Hiroshima, or Peace in a 'City of Cruelty and Bad Faith': Japanese Poetry in the Cold War." *Global Cold War Literature: Western, Eastern, and Postcolonial Perspectives*. Ed. Andrew Hammond. New York: Routledge, 2010. 72–86. Print.

Sherry, Norman. *The Life of Graham Greene*. Vol. 2. London: Cape, 1994. Print.

Shulevitz, Judith. "Old-World Style: Shirley Hazzard's Long-Awaited Novel." *Slate* (30 October 2003). Web.

Sillitoe, Alan. *Saturday Night and Sunday Morning*. 1958. London: Harper, 2008. Print.

Simmel, Georg. "The Metropolis and Mental Life." *The Blackwell City Reader*. Ed. Gary Bridge and Sophia Watson. Malden, MA: Blackwell, 2010. 103–10. Print.

Simon, Pierre-Henri. *Contre la torture*. Paris: Éditions de Minuit, 1957. Print.

Simonin, Anne. *Le droit de désobéissance: Les Éditions de Minuit en guerre d'Algérie*. Paris: Éditions de Minuit, 2012. Print.

Slaughter, Joseph R. *Human Rights, Inc.: The World Novel, Narrative Form, and International Law*. New York: Fordham University Press, 2007. Print.

Smith, James. *British Writers and MI5 Surveillance: 1930–1960*. Cambridge: Cambridge University Press, 2013. Print.

Smith, Myron J., and Terry White. *Cloak and Dagger Fiction: An Annotated Guide to Spy Thrillers*. 3rd ed. London: Greenwood, 1995. Print.

Smith, W. Eugene. "My Daughter Juanita." *LIFE* (21 September 1953): 165–71. Print.

Solomon-Godeau, Abigail. *"The Family of Man": Den Humanismus für ein postmodernes Zeitalter aufpolieren* (*"The Family of Man": Refurbishing Humanism for a Postmodern Age*). *"The Family of Man," 1955–2001: Humanismus und Postmoderne; eine Revision von Edward Steichens Fotoausstellung* (*"The Family of Man," 1955–2001: Humanism and Postmodernism: a Reappraisal of the Photo Exhibition by Edward Steichen*). Ed. Jean Back and Viktoria Schmidt-Linsenhoff. Marburg, Germany: Jonas, 2004. 28–55. Print.

Sommer, Doris. "No Secrets." *The Real Thing: Testimonial Discourse in Latin America*. Ed. Georg M. Gugelberger. Durham, NC: Duke University Press, 1996. 130–57. Print.

Sontag, Susan. *On Photography*. New York: Macmillan, 1977. Print.

Spark, Muriel. "African Handouts." *New English Weekly* (28 April 1949): 32–3. Print.

– "Awkward Saint." Rev. of Joseph-Marie Perrin and Gustave Thibon, *Simone Weil as We Knew Her*. *Observer* (20 September 1953): 10. Print.

– *The Girls of Slender Means*. 1963. New York: New Directions, 1998. Print.

– *The Golden Fleece: Essays*. Ed. with preface by Penelope Jardine. London: Carcanet, 2014. Print.

– *The Hothouse by the East River*. New York: Viking, 1973. Print.

– *Robinson*. 1958. New York: New Directions, 2003. Print.

– Muriel Spark Papers. McFarlin Library, University of Tulsa. 86 boxes. Print.

Spender, Stephen. *Citizens in War – and After*. Photographs by John Hinde. Foreword by Herbert Morrison. London: Harrap, 1945. Print.

– *European Witness*. London: Hamish Hamilton, 1946. Print.

Spivak, Gayatri Chakravorty. "Righting Wrongs." *South Atlantic Quarterly* 103.2/3 (2004): 523–81. Web.

Stannard, Martin. *Muriel Spark: The Biography*. London: Weidenfeld and Nicolson, 2009. Print.

Stanton, Domna C. "Top Down, Bottom Up, Horizontally: Resignifying the Universal in Human Rights Discourse." Goldberg and Moore 65–86. Print.

Steichen, Edward, and Carl Sandburg. *The Family of Man*. New York: Museum of Modern Art New York, 1955. Print.

Steigman, Karen. "The Literal American: Rereading Graham Greene in an Age of Security." *College Literature* 39.1 (2012): 1–26. Web.

Stern, G.B. *Trumpet Voluntary*. London: Cassell, 1944. Print.

Stewart, Kathleen. *Ordinary Affects*. Durham, NC: Duke University Press, 2007. Print.

Stimson, Blake. *The Pivot of the World: Photography and Its Nation*. Cambridge, MA: MIT Press, 2006. Print.

Stimson, Henry L. "The Decision to Use the Atomic Bomb." *Harper's* (February 1947): 97–107. Print.

Stoler, Ann Laura. *Carnal Knowledge and Imperial Power: Race and the Intimate in Colonial Rule*. Berkeley: University of California Press, 2002. Print.

– "Intimidations of Empire: Predicaments of the Tactile and Unseen." *Haunted by Empire: Geographies of Intimacy in North American History*. Ed. Ann Laura Stoler. Durham, NC: Duke University Press, 2006. 1–22. Print.

– *Race and the Education of Desire: Foucault's* The History of Sexuality *and the Colonial Order of Things*. Durham, NC: Duke University Press, 1995. Print.

– "Tense and Tender Ties: The Politics of Comparison in North American History and (Post) Colonial Studies." *Haunted by Empire: Geographies of Intimacy in North American History*. Ed. Ann Laura Stoler. Durham: Duke University Press, 2006. 23–67. Print.

Stonebridge, Lyndsey. *The Judicial Imagination: Writing after Nuremberg*. Edinburgh: Edinburgh University Press, 2011. Print.

– *The Writing of Anxiety: Imagining Wartime in Mid-Century British Culture*. London: Palgrave, 2007. Print.

Stowell, Ellory C. "Humanitarian Intervention." *American Journal of International Law* 33.4 (1939): 733–6. Print.

– *Intervention in International Law*. Washington, DC: John Byrne, 1921. Print.

Sutherland, John. *Stephen Spender: A Literary Life*. New York: Oxford University Press, 2004.

Teitgen Report. http://assembly.coe.int/Conferences/2009Anniversaire49/DocRef/Teitgen6.pdf. Web.

Teng, Emma Jinhua. *Eurasian: Mixed Identities in the United States, China, and Hong Kong, 1842–1943*. Berkeley: University of California Press, 2013. Print.

Tétart, Philippe. *Histoire politique et culturelle de France: Observateur 1950–1964: Aux origines du Nouvel Observateur, vol. 1 (1950–1957)*. Paris: Éditions L'Harmattan, 2001. Print.

Thirkell, Angela. *Love among the Ruins*. Wakefield, RI: Moyer Bell, 1997. Print.

– *Miss Bunting*. Wakefield, RI: Moyer Bell, 1996. Print.

Thomas, Brian. *An Underground Fate: The Idiom of Romance in the Later Novels of Graham Greene*. Athens: University of Georgia Press, 1988.

Thompson, Dorothy. *Refugees: Anarchy or Organization?* New York: Random House, 1938. Print.

– "Refugees: A World Problem." *Foreign Affairs* 16.3 (1938): 375–87. Print.

Thomson, Matthew. *The Problem of Mental Deficiency: Eugenics, Democracy, and Social Policy in Britain, ca. 1870–1959*. Oxford: Clarendon Press, 1998. Print.

Truman, Harry S. *Statement by the President Announcing the Use of the A-Bomb at Hiroshima*. 6 August 1945. Harry S. Truman Library and Museum. http://www.trumanlibrary.org/publicpapers/index.php?pid=100&st=&st1=. Web.

Turner, Fred. "The Family of Man and the Politics of Attention in Cold War America." *Public Culture* 24.1 (2012): 55–84. Print.

Ulloa, Marie. "Memory and Continuity: The Resistance, the Algerian War and the Jeanson Network." *Memory, Empire, and Postcolonialism: Legacies of French Colonialism*. Ed. Alec G. Hargreaves. Lanham, MD: Lexington, 2005. 112–24. Print.

Universal Declaration of Human Rights. www.un.org/en/documents/udhr/. Web.

Vasak, Karel. "The European Convention of Human Rights beyond the Frontiers of Europe." *International and Comparative Law Quarterly* 12.4 (1963): 1206–31. Print.

Walkowitz, Rebecca L. *Cosmopolitan Style: Modernism beyond the Nation*. New York: Columbia University Press, 2006. Print.

Wallace, Diana. *The Woman's Historical Novel: British Women Writers, 1900–2000*. London and New York: 2005. Print.

Wallerstein, Immanuel. "The Construction of Peoplehood: Racism, Nationalism, Ethnicity." Ed. Étienne Balibar and Immanuel Wallerstein. *Race, Nation, Class: Ambiguous Identities*. London and New York: Verso, 1991. 71–85. Print.

Warner, Sylvia Townsend. *The Corner That Held Them*. 1948. London: Virago, 2000. Print.

– *The Diaries of Sylvia Townsend Warner*. Ed. Claire Harman. London: Chatto and Windus, 1994. Print.

– *Letters*. Ed. William Maxwell. New York: Viking, 1982. Print.

– "The Historical Novel." 1940. Rpt. *Journal of the Sylvia Townsend Warner Society* (2007): 53–55. Print.

Warner, Sylvia Townsend, and William Maxwell. *The Element of Lavishness: Letters of Sylvia Townsend Warner and William Maxwell, 1938–1978*. Ed. Michael Steinman. Washington, DC: Counterpoint, 2001. Print.

Warner, Val, and Michael Schmidt. "Sylvia Townsend Warner in Conversation." 1975. *PN Review* 23: "Sylvia Townsend Warner 1893–1978: A Celebration." Ed. Claire Harman. 8.3 (1981): 35–37. Print.

Watt, D. Cameron. "Critical Afterthoughts and Alternative Historico-Literary Theories." *Spy Fiction, Spy Films, and Real Intelligence*. Ed. Wesley K. Wark. London: Frank Cass, 1991. Print.

Waugh, Evelyn. "Aspirations of a Mugwump." *The Essays, Articles and Reviews of Evelyn Waugh* 537. Print.

– "Basil Seal Rides Again, or The Rake's Regress." *The Complete Stories of Evelyn Waugh* 502–34. Print.

– *Brideshead Revisited*. 1945. Boston: Back Bay, 1999. Print.

– *The Complete Stories of Evelyn Waugh*. New York: Little, Brown, 2000. Print.

– *Decline and Fall*. 1928. Boston: Back Bay, 1999. Print.

– *The Essays, Articles and Reviews of Evelyn Waugh*. Ed. Donat Gallagher. London: Methuen, 1983. Print.

– *Love among the Ruins*. *The Complete Stories of Evelyn Waugh* 469–501. Print.

– "Manners and Morals – I." *The Essays, Articles and Reviews of Evelyn Waugh* 587–90. Print.

– *Put Out More Flags*. 1942. Boston: Back Bay, 2002. Print.

– "The Scandinavian Capitals: Contrasted Post-War Moods." *The Essays, Articles and Reviews of Evelyn Waugh* 339–41. Print.

– "Scott-King's Modern Europe." *The Complete Stories of Evelyn Waugh* 374–429. Print.

– "What to Do with the Upper Classes: A Modest Proposal." *The Essays, Articles and Reviews of Evelyn Waugh* 312–16. Print.

Weil, Simone. *Gravity and Grace*. Trans. Emma Craufurd. Intro. Gustave Thibon. London: Routledge, 1952. Print.

– *Lectures on Philosophy*. Trans. Hugh Price. Intro. Peter Winch. Cambridge: Cambridge University Press, 1978. Print.

– "The Power of Words." *The Simone Weil Reader*. Ed. George A. Panichas. New York: David McKay, 1977. Print.

West, Rebecca. *The New Meaning of Treason*. New York: Viking Press, 1964. Print.

– *A Train of Powder*. London: Macmillan, 1955. Print.

"Why Not War Writers: A Manifesto." *Horizon* 4 (July–December 1941): 236–9. Print.

Whyte, Jessica. "Human Rights: Confronting Governments? Michel Foucault and the Right to Intervene." *New Critical Legal Thinking: Law and the Political*. Ed. Matthew Stone, Illan Rua Wall, and Costas Douzinas. New York: Routledge, 2012. 11–31. Print.

Williams, Raymond. *Culture and Society: 1780–1950*. New York: Columbia University Press, 1983. Print.

– *Keywords: A Vocabulary of Culture and Society*. Rev. ed. New York: Oxford University Press, 1983. Print.

Wollen, Peter. "Riff-Raff Realism." *Sight and Sound* 8.4 (April 1998): 18–22. Web.

– "The Vienna Project." *Sight and Sound* 9.7 (1999): 16–19. Web.

Wood, Nancy. *Germaine Tillion, une femme-mémoire*. Paris: Autrement "Mémoires/Histoire," 2003. Print.

Woolf, Virginia. *Flush: A Biography*. 1933. London: Hogarth; Toronto: Oxford University Press, 1947. Print.

Wroe, Nicholas. "Living Memories." *Guardian* (18 February 2005). http://www.theguardian.com/books/2005/feb/19/fiction.kazuoishiguro. Web.

Wyman, Mark. *DP: Europe's Displaced Persons, 1945–1951*. Philadelphia: Balch Institute, 1989. Print.

Yan, Yunxiang. *Private Life under Socialism: Love, Intimacy, and Family Change in a Chinese Village, 1949–1999*. Stanford, CA: Stanford University Press, 2003. Print.

Yudice, George. "'Testimonio' and Postmodernism: Whom Does Testimonial Writing Represent?" *Latin American Perspectives* 18.3 (1991): 15–31. Print.

Zahra, Tara. *The Lost Children: Reconstructing Europe's Families after World War II*. Cambridge, MA: Harvard University Press, 2011. Print.

Ziarek, Ewa. "Bare Life." *Impasses of the Post-Global: Theory in the Era of Climate Change Vol. 2*. Ed. Henry Sussman. Ann Arbor, MI: Open Humanities Press, 2012. http://quod.lib.umich.edu/o/ohp/10803281.0001.001/1:11/--impasses-of-the-post-global-theory-in-the-era-of-climate?rgn=div1;view=fulltext. Web.

CONTRIBUTORS

NADINE ATTEWELL is associate professor in the Department of English and Cultural Studies at McMaster University. She has published articles on H.D., Virginia Woolf, Dorothy Richardson, Kim Scott's *Benang*, *Gravity's Rainbow*, and other topics. Her book, *Better Britons: Reproduction, National Identity, and the Afterlife of Empire*, was published by University of Toronto Press (2014).

MITCHELL C. BROWN holds a BA from Western University and an MA in English from McGill University. He is currently pursuing a JD at Dalhousie University.

MATTHEW HART is an assistant professor in the Department of English and Comparative Literature at Columbia University. He is the author of *Nations of Nothing but Poetry: Modernism, Transnationalism, and Synthetic Vernacular Writing* (2010) and founding co-editor of the "Literature Now" series at Columbia University Press. His current projects include a special issue of *ASAP/Journal*, "Site Specificity without Borders" (co-edited with David J. Alworth), and a new book manuscript, "Extraterritorial: A Political Geography of Contemporary Fiction."

ALLAN HEPBURN is James McGill Professor of Twentieth-Century Literature at McGill University. He is the author of *Intrigue: Espionage and Culture* (2005) and *Enchanted Objects: Visual Art in Contemporary Fiction* (2010). He has edited three volumes of materials by Elizabeth Bowen – short stories, essays, broadcasts – and a fourth volume devoted to book reviews is forthcoming. He is writing a book about faith and mid-century British culture.

JANICE HO is associate professor of English at University of Colorado Boulder. Her book, *Nation and Citizenship in the Twentieth-Century British Novel*, was published by Cambridge University Press (2015). She has published essays on Leonard Woolf, Salman Rushdie, Joseph Conrad, and liberalism.

EMILY HYDE is assistant professor of English at Rowan University. She has published articles on Chinua Achebe, W.H. Auden, and ekphrasis. She previously taught at the University of Pennsylvania.

PETER KALLINEY holds the William J. Tuggle Chair in English at the University of Kentucky, where he is also associate chair of the Department of English. His books include *Cities of Affluence and Anger: A Literary Geography of Modern Englishness* (2007), *Commonwealth of Letters: British Literary Culture and the Emergence of Postcolonial Aesthetics* (2013), and *Modernism in a Global Context* (2016). He is working on a book about decolonization and the Cold War. In addition to receiving an NEH fellowship, he has been a visiting fellow at the John W. Kluge Center at the Library of Congress.

MARINA MACKAY is the author of *Modernism and World War II* (2007) and *The Cambridge Introduction to the Novel* (2011). Her essays have appeared in *ELH*, *PMLA*, *Modern Fiction Studies*, *Representations*, and numerous other journals and essay collections. She has recently been working on a book about Ian Watt and the wartime rise of the novel. She teaches at St Peter's College, University of Oxford.

MELANIE MICIR received her PhD from the University of Pennsylvania in 2012. She is currently an assistant professor in the English Department at Washington University in St Louis. She has published essays on Virginia Woolf and Sylvia Townsend Warner. She is writing a book about biographies and the intimate archives of late-modernist female writers.

ADAM PIETTE is professor of English in the School of English at the University of Sheffield. He previously taught at Paris XIII, Lausanne, Geneva, and Glasgow. He is the author of *Imagination at War: British Fiction and Poetry 1939–1945* (1995), *Remembering and the Sound of Words: Mallarmé, Proust, Joyce, Beckett* (1996), and *The Literary Cold War, 1945 to Vietnam* (2009). He co-edited *The Edinburgh Companion to Twentieth-Century British and American War Literature* (2012), and he co-edits the international poetry journal *Blackbox Manifold.*

CLAIRE SEILER is assistant professor of English at Dickinson College. She has published essays on W.H. Auden, Elizabeth Bishop, Elizabeth Bowen, Frank O'Hara, and other writers. She is currently completing a book that develops suspension as a heuristic for transatlantic literature of the mid-century.

IAN WHITTINGTON is assistant professor of English at the University of Mississippi in Oxford. He is completing a monograph about the cultural function of radio in the Second World War. He has published articles on Zoe Wicomb and Louis MacNeice's wartime broadcasts.

INDEX